SCIENCE, SOCIETY AND THE ENVIRONMENT

In an era when pressing environmental problems make collaboration across the divide between sciences and arts and humanities essential, this book presents the results of a collaborative analysis by an anthropologist and a physicist of four key junctures between science, society, and environment. The first focuses on the systemic bias in science in favour of studying esoteric subjects as distinct from the mundane subjects of everyday life; the second is a study of the complex political-economic dynamics of "vernacular" landscapes, focusing on the fire-climax grasslands of Southeast Asia; the third reworks the idea of "moral economy", applying it to the way that the costs versus benefits of natural resource management are recognized versus obscured; and the fourth focuses on the evolution of the global discourse of the culpability and responsibility of climate change. The volume concludes with the insights of an interdisciplinary perspective for the natural and social science of sustainability. It argues that failures of conservation and development must be viewed systemically, and that mundane topics are no less complex than the more esoteric subjects of science. The book addresses a current blind spot within the academic research community by focusing attention on the seemingly common and mundane beliefs and practices that ultimately play such a central role in human interaction with the environment.

This book will benefit students and scholars from a number of different academic disciplines, including conservation and environmental studies, development studies, studies of global environmental change, anthropology, geography, sociology, politics, and science and technology studies.

Michael R. Dove is the Margaret K. Musser Professor of Social Ecology in the School of Forestry and Environmental Studies, Professor of Anthropology, and Curator of the Peabody Museum of Natural History, Yale University, New Haven, USA.

Daniel M. Kammen is Professor at the Goldman School of Public Policy and Energy and Resources Group at the University of California, Berkeley, USA. He is also Vice President of Renewable Energy at the World Bank.

"This book combines the best of natural and social scientific thinking to address the sustainability of human-environmental interaction in new ways. Dove and Kammen have produced a magisterial work that is a must read for all who wish to understand how interdisciplinary collaboration can prompt fresh thinking on the social and environmental challenges of our times."

–Raymond Bryant, King's College London, UK

"This book is the fruit of a decades-long collaboration between two prominent scholars from two very different disciplines. Recognizing that both sets of theories and methods are necessary to tackle current global dilemmas, they provide fresh, powerful accounts of key issues such as agriculture, biodiversity and climate change, and reshape the entire terms of debate over sustainable development."

–Ben Orlove, Columbia University, USA

"Michael Dove and Daniel Kammen succeed in redefining sustainability as a thoroughly interdisciplinary and systemic study of human-environmental relations – one which we must get right if we are in fact to sustain ourselves on this planet."

–Thomas Thornton, University of Oxford, UK

SCIENCE, SOCIETY AND THE ENVIRONMENT

Applying anthropology and physics to sustainability

Michael R. Dove and Daniel M. Kammen

LONDON AND NEW YORK

First published 2015
by Routledge
2 Park Square, Milton Park, Abingdon, Oxon OX14 4RN

and by Routledge
711 Third Avenue, New York, NY 10017

Routledge is an imprint of the Taylor & Francis Group, an informa business

© 2015 Michael R. Dove and Daniel M. Kammen

The right of Michael R. Dove and Daniel M. Kammen to be identified as author of this work has been asserted by him/her in accordance with sections 77 and 78 of the Copyright, Designs and Patents Act 1988.

All rights reserved. No part of this book may be reprinted or reproduced or utilised in any form or by any electronic, mechanical, or other means, now known or hereafter invented, including photocopying and recording, or in any information storage or retrieval system, without permission in writing from the publishers.

Trademark notice: Product or corporate names may be trademarks or registered trademarks, and are used only for identification and explanation without intent to infringe.

British Library Cataloguing-in-Publication Data
A catalogue record for this book is available from the British Library

Library of Congress Cataloging in Publication Data
Dove, Michael, 1949–
Science, society and the environment : applying anthropology and physics to sustainability / Michael R. Dove and Daniel M. Kammen.
    pages cm
  Includes bibliographical references and index.
  1. Environmental sociology. 2. Sustainability – Social aspects.
  3. Environmental sustainability. 4. Human ecology.
  5. Applied anthropology. 6. Science and the humanities.
  I. Kammen, Daniel M., 1962– II. Title.
  GE195.D68 2015
  304.2–dc23   2014037787

ISBN: 978-0-415-71598-0 (hbk)
ISBN: 978-0-415-71599-7 (pbk)
ISBN: 978-1-315-88039-6 (ebk)

Typeset in Bembo
by HWA Text and Data Management, London

CONTENTS

List of figures	vi
List of tables	viii
Preface	ix
Acknowledgments	xii

1 Introduction: the anthropology and physics of sustainable environmental systems   1

2 The virtues of mundane science: studying the everyday   21

3 Nature, society, and science in anthropogenic grasslands: studying declensionist discourses   43

4 High modern vs local folk views of dearth and abundance: studying failure vs success in resource management systems   68

5 Differences in perceptions of climate change between and within nations: studying science, scientists, and folk   94

6 Conclusion: reflections on the interdisciplinary project   118

References   134
Index   156

FIGURES

1.1	Google Ngram frequency of the use of the terms "disciplinary" and "interdisciplinary" in book titles, 1800–2000	5
2.1	Studying the rich variety of biomass fuels exploited by a farm household in Pakistan's semi-arid *barani* districts	24
2.2	An array of different cookstoves for sale in Kibera, the largest shanty town in Nairobi	28
2.3	A Pokot woman in Laikipia District, Kenya, examining improved efficiency cookstoves	29
2.4	Solar torches all sold under the banner of "Lighting Africa" products	31
2.5	An expanded range of off-grid lighting products, all certified by the Lighting Africa program	31
2.6	The theory of destructive (vicious) or constructive (virtuous) feedback	33
2.7	A mini-grid deployed in the Crocker Highlands of Sabah, Malaysian Borneo	34
2.8	Liter of Light – a plastic bottle with bleach provides an excellent lighting source	34
3.1	Linnaeus' drawing of *Imperata cylindrica*	44
3.2	Central Javanese wedding paraphernalia, including *Imperata cylindrica*	48
3.3	Banjarese oxen and plough for cultivating grasslands	53
3.4	Banjarese livestock grazing on *Imperata cylindrica*	53
3.5	Javanese transmigrant grazing cattle on *Imperata cylindrica* in South Sumatra	60
3.6	Braving volcanic hazards on the slopes of Mt. Merapi in Central Java to cut *Imperata cylindrica* for stall-fed cattle	61

3.7	Banjarese hunting wild cattle on grasslands near the last Banjarese *kraton* 'palace'	62
4.1	A Kantu' man carrying a basket of jackfruit and durian home from the forest during the mast season	74
4.2	A bountiful swidden rice harvest gathered at a Kantu' longhouse	75
4.3	A flooded river in front of a Kantu' longhouse	78
4.4	A Kantu' man sacrifices a pig to the spirits as thanks for a good swidden harvest	80
4.5	Natural afforestation of the previous year's swidden in front of a newly burned swidden	81
4.6	A Kantu' hunter with a wild pig (*Sus barbatus*) shot in a rubber grove near the longhouse	85
4.7	The use of surplus in swidden cultivation versus green revolution agriculture	87
5.1	Countries with the highest net greenhouse gas emissions	97
5.2	Yo! Amigo!! We need that tree to protect us from the greenhouse effect!	99

TABLES

2.1	Breakdown of causes of death from indoor air pollution in less-developed countries	27
2.2	Analysis of development prospects for solar ovens and solar bottle lights	35
3.1	Spatial patterning of Banjarese land use in South Kalimantan	51
4.1	The conception of abundance in mast-fruiting, swidden cultivation, and HYV agriculture	76
4.2	The conception of exchange in mast-fruiting, swidden cultivation, and HYV agriculture	82
4.3	Alternative names for high-yielding varieties	84
5.1	The early lines of the global warming debate	98
5.2	Major events in the development of the international climate policy regime, 1979–2010	104
5.3	The North–South dimension during the evolution of the international climate policy regime	105

PREFACE

Our collaboration was initiated by a chance conversation at a 1993 conference on "Polluted or Pristine?: Scientific, Cultural, and Policy Impacts of Pre-Industrial Anthropogenic Impact on the Global Carbon Cycle" at the East-West Center in Honolulu.[1] One of us, Dove, was talking about native beliefs of reciprocity between nature and culture; and the other, Kammen, was talking about the principles of thermodynamics – and suddenly we both saw a parallel or analogy between the two fields of study.[2] This moment initiated a lengthy period of collaboration, which ultimately led to this volume.

There was clearly an element of serendipity in this moment; and the substantive interests that we brought to this initial meeting were quite dissimilar – Kammen was interested in energy dynamics, whereas Dove was interested in indigenous knowledge and native cosmology – but we were thinking about our respective subjects in some similar ways. We shared an interest in ideas of balance, reciprocity, and the linkage of costs and benefits; we were both interested in the dynamics of resource flows; and we both recognized the existence of scientific norms and were willing to objectify and problematize them, including their global politics. These were our "boundary objects", discussed in Chapter 1 and then at greater depth in Chapter 6, meaning ideas that "are both adaptable to different viewpoints and robust enough to maintain identity across them" (Star and Griesemer 1989).

Moreover, it was not by chance that we could both seize on the vision of a cross-disciplinary analogy. We were both primed for this moment by our respective intellectual and professional histories. Kammen at the time was working at the Woodrow Wilson School of Public Policy at Princeton, had previously worked at the California Institute of Technology, and has since been based at the Energy and Resource Group at University of California, Berkeley; whereas Dove was then based at the East-West Center on the University of

Hawaii campus, had previously worked in South and Southeast Asia for the Ford, Rockefeller, and Winrock Foundations, and has since been based at the School of Forestry and Environmental Studies at Yale University. All of these institutions are interdisciplinary; they are all practice-oriented; and they all placed us at the fringes of our individual disciplines. As a result, we both brought to the 1993 conference habits developed over many years of talking and listening across disciplinary boundaries.

We first published early versions of all of the chapters in this volume as journal articles. In each case, we began with an idea, which we would brainstorm together over a period of months or in some cases years. If this process brought us to the point where we felt we had something worth putting to paper, one of us would then take the initiative to outline our argument. The other would then edit, revise, and expand this outline; and then the first writer would take another turn; and so on. Progressively detailed outlines would eventually be expanded, and continue to be passed back and forth until we deemed the text ready for circulation among students, colleagues, public presentation, and then eventual submission for review by a journal. Individual chapters were presented in professional meetings, and complete drafts of our manuscript were taught in graduate seminars at our respective institutions. Our practice of collaboration consisted, therefore, of reciprocal discussion, reading, writing, editing, and revision.

Our search for an academic audience for our work was illuminating. The world of academic publishing is far from hostile to interdisciplinary ventures, as attested to by the proliferation over the past generation of edited collections bringing together the work of both natural and social scientists writing about conservation and development. But the vast majority of these collections only bring the respective works of social and natural scientists into *proximity* with one another; any actual interdisciplinary work or insight is left up to the readers. The challenges are reflected in our own experiences publishing in journals earlier drafts of the chapters in this book. Once published, the papers have been reasonably well-cited, which suggests that they are successful in having something to say and in reaching an interested audience; but getting published in the first place was often challenging. There was not always an easy publishing niche for these papers. Not only do most journals still have a single-discipline bias, but even some of the interdisciplinary ones had trouble identifying what we have been trying to do.

The challenge is illustrated by our experience with Chapter 5 – "Differences in Perceptions of Climate Change Between and Within Nations: Studying Science, Scientists, and Folk". Our initial draft focused on the 1990–1991 exchange between the World Resources Institute (WRI) in the U.S. and India's Center for Science and Environment (CSE), regarding the relative responsibility for climate change of the northern and more developed versus the southern and less-developed countries. Our objective was not to determine who was right and who was wrong in the dispute, but to ask what the dispute itself told us about the problem. One of the peer reviewers for this article, a prominent natural resource scientist, wrote of our paper: "[It] argues that there are crude and sophisticated interpretations of the global warming debate, and illustrates the difference with examples. It provides no argument, however, as to why one interpretation is better than the other; the [paper] therefore reads more like an idle opinion than reasoned analysis." The object of our paper was to study the difference between the global North and South in views of climate change, however, it was not to find fault with this difference; it was not determine which view was "best". This does not mean that certain views are not in fact more empirically valid than others; it does mean that the views of the northern scientific establishment, which we might have expected to be more empirically based, were clearly guilty of some implicit – if unconscious – self-privileging of the geopolitical position of the more developed Northern nations.

Beliefs about nature, natural resources, and their use, certainly have a factual dimension: they may be more or less empirically accurate, more or less factual. But any belief about nature, regardless of its empirical content, is an also a social fact. If it is believed, then it is a social fact. Bridging these two dimensions – the facts of nature and the facts of our social experience of nature – lies at the core of our collaborative project. Indeed, this may lie at the core of any collaborative study of the environment by natural and social scientists. Bridging these two often antithetical perspectives is not always easy, but it is always necessary; for the environment that we live in is comprised of both sorts of facts; and only by studying and comprehending both can we have any hope of bringing both halves of science to bear on the achievement of sustainable environmental relations.

Michael R. Dove
Killingworth, CT

Daniel Kammen
Oakland, CA

July 2014

Notes

1 This conference led to the first publication (Dove 1994) of one of the papers that form the bases for the chapters in this volume.
2 Cohen (1994: 35) writes that "Analogy has always functioned as a tool of discovery, reducing a problem to another that has already been solved or introducing some element or elements that have proved their worth in a quite different area of knowledge." Cohen (1994: 64–65) goes on to suggest that the utility of analogies does not always depend on their exactness; distortion or transformation are common and misinterpretation may even be fruitful. He cites Claude Ménard as saying that the creative use of analogies always "highlights a difference" (Cohen 1994: 62–63). But see also the economist Alfred Marshall (1898, cited in Cohen 1994:48), "[It is] well to know when to introduce them [analogies], it is even better to know when to stop them off."

ACKNOWLEDGMENTS

Michael R. Dove wishes to thank students in the following graduate seminars at Yale who read and very insightfully commented on earlier versions of this manuscript: "Disaster, Degradation, Dystopia: Social Science Approaches to Environmental Perturbation and Change" Spring 2014, Spring 2011, Spring 2010, Fall 2008. He also wishes to thank several research interns for assistance with library research: Katie Hawkes, Julia Fogerite, and Sarah Casson. For administrative and financial matters, he has relied upon the attentiveness of his administrative assistants, Laurie Bozzuto and Julie Cohen.

For work on graphics, the authors are indebted to Heather G. Salome of Metaglyfix.

Earlier versions of the chapters (in whole or in part) in this volume were published in the following places:

Chapter 2:

Kammen, Daniel M. and Michael R. Dove. 1996. *"Mundane Science": The Missing Link in Sustainable Development Research.* Princeton University Center for Energy and Environmental Studies, Report No. 298.

Kammen, Daniel M. and Michael R. Dove. 1997. The Virtues of Mundane Science. *Environment* 39(6):10–15,38–41.

Chapter 3:

Dove, Michael R. 2004. Anthropogenic Grasslands in Southeast Asia: Sociology of Knowledge and Implications for Agroforestry. *Agroforestry Systems* 61:423–435.

Chapter 4:

Dove, Michael R. and Daniel M. Kammen. 1997. The Epistemology of Sustainable Resource Use: Managing Forest Products, Swiddens, and High-Yielding Variety Crops. *Human Organization* 56(1): 91–101.

Chapter 5:

Dove, Michael R. 1994. North–South Relations, Global Warming, and the Global System. Special issue on "Human Impacts on the Pre-Industrial Environment", Daniel M. Kammen, Kirk R. Smith, A. Terry Rambo, and M.A.K. Khalil eds. *Chemosphere* 29(5):1063–1077.

1
INTRODUCTION

The anthropology and physics of sustainable environmental systems

> All the facts in natural history taken by themselves, have no value, but are barren, like a single sex. But marry it to human history, and it is full of life. Whole Floras, all Linnaeus' and Buffon's volumes, are dry catalogues of facts; but the most trivial of these facts, the habit of a plant, the organs, or work, or noise of an insect, applied to the illustration of a fact in intellectual philosophy, or, in any way associated to human nature, affects us in the most lively and agreeable manner.
> Ralph Waldo Emerson (1849)

I. The quandary of disciplines

In his landmark study of the interaction between the natural sciences and the social sciences, Cohen (1994) argued that one of the greatest weaknesses in understanding this subject is a lack of historical perspective.

1. The two cultures

The classic study of this historical relationship is C. P. Snow's *The Two Cultures* (1959/1998), which was a contribution to a debate between Snow and his fellow Cambridge scholar and literary critic, F. R. Leavis.[1] In his introduction to the latest edition of this work, Snow argues that a divide between science on the one hand and the arts and humanities on the other hand is not ancient – dating in fact just from the seventeenth or eighteenth centuries. Prior to this time, from the early Middle Ages through the end of the Renaissance, many of the most prominent scholars of the western world – for example, Agassiz, Audubon, Boyle, da Vinci, Galileo, Jefferson, Pasteur – freely combined study of the natural/physical sciences with explorations in philosophy, economics, and the human condition in general. Whereas their combining of what today are perceived to be disparate, even antagonistic fields of study was then taken to be a mark of their intellectual energy and prowess, this value judgment was reversed by the end of the nineteenth century, when such *dis*-allegiance to a particular discipline came to be seen as the mark of an amateur scholar.

Snow claims that the term "science" did not come to apply narrowly to just the biological and physical sciences until the mid-nineteenth century, and it did not then enjoy the high social status accorded it today. Until late in the nineteenth century, science was stigmatized as a grubby and vocational activity compared with classical, literary education.[2] This is reflected in the parallel divide within the European scientific community between fieldworkers and theoreticians. In the 1850s, the Ethnological Society of London published a manual propounding a two-tiered division of labor: fact-gatherers in field versus thinkers back home (Vetter 2006: 94). As this language suggests, the armchair theoretician had the higher status (Vetter 2006: 97); they needed but also scorned collectors (Endersby 2003: 387).[3] Darwin, for example, suggested that Wallace, whose personal finances obliged him to merge the roles of theoretician and field observer (Vetter 2006: 90), was a collector of facts not a genuine theorist; and he (Darwin) opined that ordinary entomologists "cannot be considered scientific men but must be ranked with collectors of postage stamps and crockery" (Endersby 2003: 398).[4]

Since the time of Wallace and Darwin, a hierarchical divide between field observer and theoretician has disappeared in most disciplines, but the broader division between social science (and the humanities) on the one hand, and the natural sciences on the other hand, has only become more institutionally embedded. What Leopold wrote 75 years ago, for the most part still holds true today (in Meine and Knight 1999/1935: 272):

> One of the anomalies of modern ecology is that it is the creation of two groups, each of which seems barely aware of the existence of the other. The one studies the human community almost as if it were a separate entity, and calls its findings sociology, economics and history. The other studies the plant and animal community and comfortably relegates the hodge-podge of politics to the liberal arts.

The anomaly referred to by Leopold reflects the discipline-based structure of academia, which is even more pronounced today, with ever greater specialization the norm. The U.S. scientific community recognizes both the continued strengths of disciplinary boundaries, and the impediment that this presents to addressing at least some matters of theory and policy, by the funding of mechanisms like the Integrative Graduate Education and Research Traineeship Program (IGERT) of the National Science Foundation, which is specifically designed to use federal funds as leverage to overcome academic constraints on interdisciplinary doctoral study. Interdisciplinary academic bodies abound, but true interdisciplinary institutions, whose faculty do not have their "homes" in discipline-based departments, are still quite rare.[5] And even in these rare institutions, the typical ethos is that the faculty should first demonstrate mastery of their own discipline before pursuing interdisciplinary work, and that it is really the students, not the faculty, who do the most crossing of disciplinary lines.

A number of developments at the turn of the twentieth century have led to increased interest in engagement between the social and natural sciences, and to routinized calls for more interdisciplinary collaboration (e.g., Newell et al. 2005; Kotchen and Young 2007; Liu 2007; and Clark et al. 2011). One such development was the emergence of post-structural perspectives toward the end of the twentieth century, which led to self-reflective examination in the arts, humanities, social sciences, and to some extent the biological and physical sciences. Interest in the way that scientists work and communicate led to the emergence of Science and Technology Studies as a robust field of study, encompassing for example studies of engineering philosophy (Florman 1976), scientific knowledge (Jasanoff, 2004b), institutional ethnographies (e.g., Rhee, 2006; Star and Griesemer, 1989; Traweek, 1988), actor-centered analyses of science (Latour, 1988, 1990), post-structural analyses of nature and culture (Haraway, 1991), and studies of the production and practice of scientific knowledge (Pickering, 1992, 1995).[6] Science studies particularly flourished in fields where delivery of successful results seemed to be problematic, as in the inter-related fields of natural resource management and environmental conservation. The manifest degradation of the global environment and the widely-publicized failures of many conservation efforts in the latter half of the twentieth century led to challenges to the tradition of strictly natural science approaches to conservation and to calls for greater collaboration between the natural and social sciences. This was manifested by the proliferation of interdisciplinary journals, professional societies, academic programs, and field projects, notably the efforts to combine nature-oriented and people-oriented approaches in Integrated Conservation and Development Projects (ICDPs) (Agrawal and Redford 2006; Brandon, Redford, and Sanderson 1998; Brechin et al. 2003).

This rapprochement between the social and natural sciences has not been unproblematic, however. The troubled history of many ICDPs led to an ideological backlash against them and a revival of the "fortress nature" model of conservation (Peres and Terborgh 1995; Brandon, Redford and Sanderson 1998; Soulé and Lease 1995; Terborgh 1999). This was but a small skirmish in a much larger academic contest termed the "science wars", in which natural and social scientists debated the wisdom and validity of science studies (Gross and Levitt 1994; Sokal and Bricmont 1998; Ross 1996). One of the most revealing events of this era was the publication of an intentionally error-ridden paper in the journal *Social Text* by a New York University physicist, Alan Sokal (1996). Quite unexpectedly, given the rancor of the time, the "science wars" have practically disappeared in the dozen-odd years since, with no winners or losers declared, for two reasons. First, a hostile attitude toward science has developed in a significant part of the U.S. political establishment, which sees scientists as simply another set of political actors, with no fine distinctions being made between scientists with or without post-structural sympathies. Second, climate change has emerged as the foremost global environmental challenge of the twenty-first century, and efforts to address it have been vastly complicated by this same anti-science stance among politicians. This convergence of potentially destructive environmental and political change is seen as so worrying, indeed, that it has driven the leading global contributor to science studies, Bruno Latour (2004), to re-think the political implications of his objectifying of science.[7] Environmental, political, and academic trends all point, therefore, to an opportune moment today for a collaborative effort by a social scientist (Dove, an anthropologist) and a natural scientist (Kammen, a physicist) to examine the premises, methods, promises and challenges of interdisciplinary research.

The term "interdisciplinary research" has been succeeded in some quarters by the term "multi-disciplinary research" and then most recently "trans-disciplinary research", each iteration being presented as more enlightened than the last. We read the calculation of such fine distinctions, and the purported evolution of the field, as the modern academic equivalent of counting angels on the head of a pin, having more to do with the politics of academic reproduction than with actual differences. Accordingly, we use the term "interdisciplinary" throughout this volume, while considering all three terms as effectively synonymous.

2. Disciplinarity and interdisciplinarity

In addition to asking what promotes collaboration across the natural and social sciences, we believe that it is necessary to ask what promotes their continuing differentiation. Both questions are critical ones, and indeed, there are attractions to both disciplinary and interdisciplinary work. The dynamics of academic reproduction – the norms, the premises, the problems, the costs and benefits, even the politics – are different within disciplines as opposed to between disciplines. Both sets of dynamics have their strengths as well as their challenges. It is obvious that it can be productive to honor disciplinary boundaries as well as productive to cross or violate them, as we do in this volume. If this were not so, there would be fewer disciplines and fewer interdisciplinary efforts. There is an ongoing push–pull dynamic to both honor and transgress disciplinary boundaries, which we see not as a historical stage but an ongoing condition of the modern era. Accordingly, we see calls to end disciplinarity (or interdisciplinarity, for that matter) as fruitless.

There is another reason that neither disciplinarity or interdisciplinarity are going away: disciplinarity and interdisciplinarity both need one another, in the sense that each helps to define the other. Put otherwise, there is no interdisciplinarity without disciplinarity, the project of disciplinarity makes

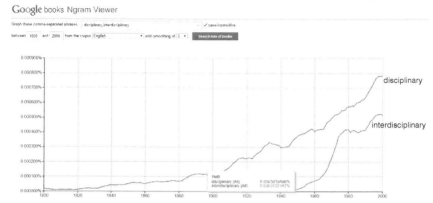

FIGURE 1.1 Google Ngram frequency of the use of the terms "disciplinary" and "interdisciplinary" in book titles, 1800–2000

Source: Google Books Ngram Viewer, http://books.google.com/ngrams

the project of interdisciplinarity possible, and the reverse also is true. The continued, vigorous tradition of disciplinarity is what gives value and meaning to interdisciplinary initiatives like ours. A century ago, perhaps one-half century ago, when disciplinarity was less rigorous, our effort would have made less sense – it would have been less needed. As disciplinarity waxes, so too does interdisciplinarity, albeit lagging behind. Google's Ngram viewer shows a gradual rise in the term "disciplinary" in book titles over the past two centuries (1800–2000), whereas "interdisciplinary" shows a sharp rise beginning in 1940 and continuing to the present (Figure 1.1).[8]

Post-structural scholars would push this analysis one step further and ask how different the terms of this apparent dichotomy really are. Nearly one-half century ago, the late, great French anthropologist Claude Lévi-Strauss (1966) characterized the difference between the mind of the modern western scientist and the mind of "savage" peoples as the difference between the "engineer" and the *"bricoleur"* (cf. Agrawal 1995:414, 424). The thinking of the engineer is single-minded and deterministic, whereas the thinking of the *bricoleur* incorporates multitudinous perspectives and possibilities. This distinction maps nicely onto our distinction between discipline- and interdiscipline-based thinking. Derrida (1978:285), however, commenting on Lévi-Strauss' work, argues that the distinction between savage and civilized minds, or *bricoleurs* and engineers, is a "myth". Derrida sees such myths as the product of a fundamental and universal epistemological problem, which he characterizes as "the problem of the status of a discourse which borrows from a heritage the resources necessary for the deconstruction of the heritage itself" (Derrida 1978:282). That is, we must use the concept of the engineer to talk about the concept of the *bricoleur*. By analogy, interdisciplinarity must draw upon disciplinarity to differentiate itself, and the reverse also is true. Indeed, there often appears to be a Derridean logic at work in efforts to be interdisciplinary, meaning a reliance *upon* disciplinarity in efforts to get *away* from disciplinarity. Through the very critique of disciplinarity in interdisciplinary work, we may say that the two are linked.

We suggest that it may be productive, therefore, to see disciplinarity and interdisciplinarity as a single system. In Chapter 5, where we discuss the debate over climate change, we suggest that the relation between science and non-science, or folk belief, may be seen in the same light. Certain scientific and non-scientific communities are highly critical of one another – far more so than in the case of disciplinarity and interdisciplinarity, although this certainly generates its own politics – but each also draws on the other for self-definition. To give an ethnographic analogy, we may liken the relations between science and non-science, and also between disciplinarity and interdisciplinarity, to the historic relationship between the lowland civilizations of Southeast Asia and the upland barbarian, tribal peoples (Scott 2009). In this ethnographic example, each half of this divide disparaged and often fought with the other, but they also engaged in an ongoing relationship, which served as a continuous source of both material and ideological resources for their construction of self-identity. In a similar way, those engaged in disciplinary and interdisciplinary projects, and scientific and non-scientific projects, provide an ongoing source of resources for the definition of both self and "other".

II. Interdisciplinary collaboration

Although disciplinarity and interdisciplinarity are linked, one or the other often dominates specific fields – more often than not the former, as the older of the two – not always the more appropriate of the two. On the one hand, it is impossible not to see the value of discipline-based research and knowledge in the advancement of modern science; but on the other hand, it is equally impossible to deny that this disciplinarity bears a cost. Our goals in the interdisciplinary collaboration represented by this volume are to illustrate the continued dominance of disciplinary approaches in conservation and development and illuminate their shortcomings; to illustrate how interdisciplinary work can be done and what can be expected of it; and to show how such work can contribute to solving tenacious problems of conservation and development planning and the search for sustainable environmental relations.[9]

1. An anthropologist and a physicist

Contemporary, real-world problems of conservation, development, and environmental change are complex, clearly span the natural and social sciences, demand both theoretical and practical perspectives, and challenge disciplinary boundaries. In addressing such challenges, interdisciplinary approaches often have proven to be more tractable, successful, and more theoretically robust as well. Snow (1998/1959) saw interdisciplinary collaboration as a locus of advancement in science, saying "The clashing point of two subjects, two disciplines, two cultures – of two galaxies, so far as that goes – ought to produce creative chances. In the history of mental activity that has been where some of the break-throughs came." Using even more dramatic language, Leopold (in Meine and Knight 1999/1935: 272) wrote that "The inevitable fusion of the two lines of thought [viz., studies of human versus plant and animal communities] will, perhaps, constitute the outstanding advance of the present century." Interdisciplinary efforts continue to be seen as creative crucibles. Strathern (2006: 201) writes that "Interdisciplinary collaborations seem to promise innovation and creativity by means other than criticism. Instead of generating disagreement and multiplying future possibilities by informed comment from within, interdisciplinary conversations hold out the hope of new sources of synergy. Hope is still there." The sense that bridging the divide can be rewarding, whereas not bridging it can be problematic, has drawn the attention of many scholars.

There are numerous models for collaborative and interdisciplinary work, beginning with the likes of Gregory Bateson, whose own career path led him across different disciplines, which is reflected in the breadth and creativity of his work (e.g., Bateson 1972; cf. C. M. Bateson 1984). Sometimes, even the melding of two different views within a single discipline can be powerful (e.g., Gudeman and Rivera's [1990] *Conversations in Columbia* in Anthropology or Levins and Lewontin's [1985] *Dialectical Biologist* in Biology).[10] There are stellar examples of collaborations across the divides between social science, journalism, and photography, for example James Agee and Walker Evans' (1939) *Let Us Now Praise Famous Men* and Hecht and Cockburn's (1989) *The Fate of the Forest*. An early effort to write across the social and natural sciences, within the field of conservation, was Daly and Umana's (1982) *Energy, Economics, and the Environment*. The years since have produced a number of similar multi-disciplinary edited works, many stimulated by combined conservation and development projects (see the citations on p. 3 of this Introduction) and studies of adaptive management (Berkes and Folke 2000; Berkes, Colding, and Folke, 2003). Others have come out of the somewhat less heated but still contentious work on indigenous knowledge and environmental conservation (e.g., Brush and Stabinsky 1996; Nazarea 1999; Posey 1999; Ellen et al. 2000; Selin 2003; Ellen 2007; Sillitoe 2007). More recently, similar works have come out of the ongoing surge of interest in human society, climate (Grove and Chappell 2000) and climate change, both historical (Bawden and Reycraft 2000; McIntosh et al. 2000; Hass and O'Dillon 2003; Sandweiss and Quilter 2008) and contemporary (Ribot et al. 1995; Strauss and Orlove 2003; Pettenger 2007; Roberts and Parks 2007; Orlove et al. 2008; Crate and Nuttall 2009). The vast majority of these works are not co-authored volumes but edited ones, however, in which, even if they have multiple editors who hail from different fields, the character and process of any interdisciplinarity is not addressed and the actual interdisciplinary work is left up to the readers.

2. Borrowing

Scholars have taken interest in different aspects of interdisciplinarity. A handful, such as the aforementioned works by Snow (1998/1959) and Cohen (1994), have produced seminal studies seeking to place interdisciplinary divides and crossings in wider context (cf. Marks 2009). Others have examined the dynamics of collaboration of specific disciplines, for example biology and anthropology, ranging from Sahlins (1976b) spirited critique of "sociobiology", to more recent efforts that recognize the inevitability of some joint work by these two fields (Peterson et al. 2008; Hardin and Remis 2006; Ingold 1990). Still others have examined the very important, most manifest dimension of interdisciplinary relations, namely the "borrowing" of ideas and concepts from one discipline by another. Kellert (2008) provides a useful survey of this subject, focusing on the recent example of chaos theory. Examples of borrowing have a considerable lineage in modern science. Looking at seminal figures within the history of anthropology, for example, Durkheim (1964/1933) drew from natural science organic metaphors for his analysis of the division of labor in human society;[11] Radcliffe-Brown (1952:12) borrowed from biology the metaphor of organic structure (of the human body or even a single cell) to illustrate his concept of "social function"; and Leslie White (1959, 1969/1949) borrowed a focus on energy from thermodynamics to analyze the evolution of society. Conklin (1954), Berlin et al. (1974) and others borrowed the tools of linguistics and systematic botany to develop the sub-discipline of ethnoscience; and most recently, anthropologists have borrowed methods for textual deconstruction from the humanities, in particular literary criticism. One of the most ardent and successful borrowers from the natural and physical sciences was the late Roy A. Rappaport. He drew from authors such as Bateson (1958/1936), Goldman (1960), Margalef (1968), and Wynne-Edwards (1965) concepts of cybernetics, feedback loops, and circuits, which he used to explain cognitive models, adaptation, and ritual functions (Rappaport 1984).[12] Perhaps most important was Rappaport's borrowing from ecology; his announced intention in going to the field was "to study a local group of tribal horticulturalists in the same terms that animal ecologists study populations in ecosystems" (Rappaport 1994:167). Rappaport's initial work in the 1960s was followed by wide interest in adapting the ecosystem concept within anthropology (e.g., Bennett 1977; Moran 1984; cf. Machlis, Force, and Burch 1997; Pickett and Cadenasso 2002). In recent years a small but influential literature has developed that looks at the dynamics of such borrowing. Particularly interesting have been studies of what makes environmental and other concepts in one field "borrow-worthy" to another (Dove 2001, 2006).[13] Scholars have variously glossed concepts that have this capacity as "immutable mobiles" (Latour 1990) or "boundary objects" (Fujimura 1992; Star and Griesemer 1989). Given the attractions of interdisciplinary borrowing, conspicuous cases of resistance to borrowing also have attracted attention (Cosgel 2009).

To simply call this "borrowing" elides a great deal of complexity, however. Is one discipline straight-forwardly taking and applying a concept from another discipline, or is it first translating or adapting the concept? Is the borrowed concept being used in such a way that the two disciplines involved – the borrower and the donor – can be said to "share" use? Or is the concept at issue being used, rather, to identify an analogue or homologue in the recipient discipline? Is the concept at issue serving in a metaphorical role, to try to illuminate a comparison between the two disciplines? For stimulating examples of the drawing of analogies between the social sciences on the one hand and the arts and humanities on the other hand, see Diamond (1990) and Holling, Taylor, and Thompson (1991). Adger (2000) provides an excellent illustration of the intellectual promise of asking these sorts of questions in his application of the ecological concept of "resilience" to human society. He critiques the simple application of this concept to social systems, as though there were no differences in behavior and structure between the two (Adger 2000: 350). He usefully distinguishes between the comparative use and the translation of the concept between the two cases. That is, he distinguishes between the use of the concept as analogy, on the one hand, and on the other hand the use of the same concept to refer to a shared and linked characteristic in society and environment.[14] This is similar to Bennett's (1977:177) distinction between applying biological concepts to social data "(1) *analogically*, where the biological concepts and mathematical techniques are used to describe or simulate nonbiological phenomena; and (2) *literally*, in which case the actual biological or physical dimensions of the human phenomena would be identified and the same measurements performed on them." Adger's key question is whether resilience in nature leads to or is associated with resilience in society, for example whether resilient ecosystems lead to resilient social ideologies or cosmologies.[15] He concludes that it is not clear whether ecological resilience leads to resilient social communities but that the ecological concept of resilience is useful for describing the capacity for innovation in social communities. A small number of social scientists have attempted studies of literal (not merely analogous) nature–culture relationships. For example, Adas (1979: 97–98) suggests that the cultural sensitivity of the Javanese to cosmic perturbation arises from their living on a geologically very active island; and global concern over biodiversity loss has led to study of the functional correlation between biological diversity and cultural diversity (e.g., Maffi 2001; Roué 2006).

Another source of complication in interdisciplinarity involves its directionality. At given times and places, some disciplines tend to be consistently borrowers whereas others are consistently donors. Sometimes this is due to the characters of the disciplines involved. Some established disciplines, like economics, seem to thrive best when they draw their boundaries most tightly – which allows them to be borrowed from but not borrowers themselves. On the other hand, it may strategically benefit other disciplines, at critical stages in their development, to borrow heavily from more influential disciplines. Lenoir (1997) has insightfully interpreted such borrowing in terms of Bourdieu's (1977) concept of "symbolic capital" (social prestige and reknown that can be accumulated and is convertible into economic capital). He suggests that the symbolic capital that can be deployed by a given field at a given time can often be significantly augmented through strategic borrowing from other disciplines (Lenoir 1997:9).[16] Dove (2001, 2006) has argued that early work in ecological anthropology in the 1960s borrowed heavily from then more ascendant fields such as systems theory, ecology, and nutritional biology to augment its authority.[17] In more recent years, the political capital of anthropology has risen, as evidenced, for example, by the borrowing of the discipline's signature methodology of "ethnography" by a variety of other disciplines. As for the other discipline represented in this volume, physics, its political capital has been high since the nuclear weapons programs of World War II, as reflected in the familiar caricature of the view of physics from other disciplines as "physics envy" (Lenoir 1997).

3. Theorizing collaboration

Theorization of collaboration is often conspicuous by its absence from interdisciplinary projects, as it was also largely absent in our own case. For example, Levins and Lewontin (1985: ix) write in the preface to their book, on a quarter-century of collaborative work on "dialectical biology", that their writings illustrated but did not explain their dialectical method, leading them to "discover that in twenty-five years of collaboration we had never discussed our views systematically!" Reaching across disciplinary boundaries, often as not, is not consciously strategic. Dove (2006) has interpreted the interdisciplinary borrowing of Rappaport's pioneering research in New Guinea in the 1960s in terms of enhancing the authority of his message. But when Dove presented this interpretation to the senior scholar who was Rappaport's doctoral advisor, he (the advisor) averred that they had not been guided by such considerations – which is a typical response. In fact, few scholars, in any discipline, can readily objectivize the socio-political context of and influences on their own scholarship. Barbour (1996: 45) carried out a path-breaking analysis of the shift in the 1950s within the field of ecology from Clements' model of "predictability, uniformity, cooperation, stability, and certainty", to Gleason's model of "individualism, competition, a blur of continuous change, and probability". Examining this unexpected and complete alteration of paradigms within the short space of a dozen years, Barbour (1996: 48) clearly links it to wider transformations in society:

> I propose that there were links between ecology and technological, social, and cultural actions that celebrated individualism, rebellion from previous norms, and a profound acceptance of uncertainty. It could be that ecologists consciously or unconsciously swam with the currents of their surroundings culture to change some fundamental opinions, to take

new research directions, and to view nature in a reductionist, rather than a holistic way.

When Barbour interviewed 34 senior ecologists who were at the center of this shift, however, these "links" were firmly denied:

> The great majority of those interviewed agreed with Peter Greig-Smith, who wrote back to me, "There may be parallels between ecology and politics but if so I suspect they are coincidental. I... see no parallels between my political or social attitudes and my ecological views." Only a dozen respondents admitted to seeing even the smallest connection between society – or their own personality – and their ecological research.

Even if the societal politics of interdisciplinary borrowing are denied, the academic politics of such work are often starkly apparent. To return to the case of Rappaport, for example, critics saw him as borrowing "whole cloth" concepts from the natural sciences and applying them directly – and erroneously in their view – to human society. These critics characterized his work as "an attempt to dress up ethnography as hard science" (Rappaport 1984:370); they accused him of "a kind of 'ecology fetishism'" (Sahlins 1976a:298); and he was advised to "quit whoring after the strange gods of physics", as Rappaport (1979:82) himself put it. Bennett (1976:181) attacked Rappaport's work as "fundamentally an analogic operation, in which ecosystemic complexities and a generalized impression of ecological causation are plausibly suggested but never worked out in detail". Bennett (1977:177) also more generally critiqued the application of feedback models from the natural sciences to studies of human society, saying "[W]hile such concepts have their uses in social analysis, their emphasis on stability and reversion of the system to previous states tends to obscure the dynamism and adaptive change so characteristic of human societies."

Rappaport seemed at times to accept this view of his work at face value and seek to defend himself on these grounds, and at other times to argue that his use of equilibrium theory and cybernetic models were "illustrative" and of "heuristic value" only (1984: viii, 359), which is closer to Bennett's view and also to Strathern's (2006:200) observation: "It is probably fair to suggest that interdisciplinary collaborations work best not as tools (means) in research, but as representations (signs) of desired ends in knowledge management." The continued volatility of interdisciplinary borrowing was dramatically illustrated by the physicist Sokal's (1996) aforementioned publication of an intentionally mock application of physics to post-modern literature, which he then exposed as an example of the inanity of efforts by the humanities to borrow from the physical sciences. The consistent message in all of these cases is that reaching across disciplines is rarely politically neutral: it may reflect differences in political capital; it may privilege the borrower; it may threaten the donor.

III. Four case studies

There are four foci to our collaboration: first, the relative neglect in studies of sustainable resource use of "mundane" subjects of everyday importance – like village household economics, cooking, and lighting – in favor of the pursuit of more esoteric subjects of study, and the implications of this for understanding and supporting sustainable systems of natural resource management; second, a case study of the "vernacular" Southeast Asian landscape of fire-climax grasslands, the logic of their local management, and the way that history, culture, and politics inhibit recognition of this logic; third, the contrast between indigenous systems of natural resource management that link costs and benefits and high-modern systems that deny this linkage, and the implications for sustainability of this difference, based on a comparison of forest gathering, swidden cultivation, and Green Revolution agriculture in Indonesia; and fourth, the differing perceptions of the problem of global climate change, as revealed in a twenty-year history of the development of the global climate change policy regime, and the policy as well as scientific implications of denying versus recognizing these differences. In each case, new insights into theoretical and policy impasses are provided by bringing the premises and methods of each of our respective disciplines into conversation with each other.

1. Chapter 2: The virtues of mundane science: studying the everyday

In Chapter 2 we focus on the factors that influence the way that science selects its subjects, especially esoteric subjects as distinct from the mundane subjects of everyday life. As noted earlier in Snow's analysis of the rise of the culture of science in the nineteenth and twentieth centuries, science initially labored under the conceptual baggage of being seen as a vocational versus scholarly activity. Given this perception, in order for science to elevate itself and increase its political capital, it behooved science to distance itself from the domain of everyday life, to become a "high art". Whatever the cause, a bias against the mundane created a conceptual *cordon sanitaire* in science, which distinguishes the pure and purportedly theoretically more "robust" field from the less robust, "impure" one. The importance of this *cordon sanitaire* is reflected in the fact that the greatest professional awards are generally reserved for those working within "pure" science,[18] even though it is by avoiding complex mundane realities and applying "technically sweet" methods to more delimited fields of study that the chances for more successful solutions are heightened. But we argue in this chapter that the pure/applied divide in science is artificial, that it leads to both bad science and bad policy, and that grappling with messier, more complex, real-world topics produces more robust theory and more successful policy.

Avoidance of the mundane sphere has been a continuing characteristic of modern science, without prejudice to particular disciplines. Anthropologists and sociologists long tended not to study the culture of hunger in the developing societies in which they work (Sen 1981); agricultural scientists valorized the high-tech green revolution agriculture and ignored low-tech, native systems of managing forests and fields; health experts pursued "exotic" diseases (like Severe Acute Respiratory Syndrome [SARS]) while ignoring ubiquitous problems like infant diarrhea and indoor air pollution from cookstoves; political scientists wrote off bribery and corruption as problems for but not of development; research on exotic bio-fuels trumped the study of everyday measures of efficiency and conservation; energy experts regarded community-level energy sources like photovoltaics as "small potatoes"; and development and resource economics focused on products that entered formal markets as opposed to those that did not (like the biomass fuels and non-timber forest products discussed in Chapters 2 and 4). This disdain for the common obtains in both the natural (biological and physical) sciences and social sciences. Disdained topics are called "small science" in the physical sciences, whereas they are given labels such as the "science of suffering" (Scheper-Hughes 1995) in the social sciences.[19] This bias against the mundane plays out anew in each generation of global natural resource and environmental science, the latest example being seen in the field of global climate change. Disproportionate amounts of attention by scientists, policymakers, and the public, as well as research and development dollars, are being devoted to the emergence of exotic threats and esoteric technologies. The loss of habitat for polar bears, the development of floating houses in the Netherlands, or the threat of climate change refugees from small island states, all capture attention and resources (Moore 2010). But they are irrelevant to the much greater populations who face far more common, "mundane" challenges such as groundwater salinization or the impact of heat stress on crops.

In Chapter 2, therefore, we challenge the premises and implications of this mundane/exotic divide in science. We begin by discussing the importance of mundane topics and the history of their scientific study or lack therefore, then we present three case studies: the Grameen Bank's 30-year-old program of micro-credit in Bangladesh, which shows some success and some problems; efforts over the same period to improve traditional cookstoves, focusing on the African case, which again show mixed results; and more recent and seemingly promising efforts to electrify rural Africa through development of mini-grid and off-grid, decentralized technologies. Based on our analysis of these three cases, we then enumerate six "fallacies" of mundane science, which we follow with a discussion of implications for theory and practice in this field.

Since we first started working on this topic, the academic and policy worlds have increasingly recognized the relevance of mundane topics. The everyday scourge of malaria has been taken up by the Gates Foundation, the food security of the global poor has become a hot topic, and scholars and policymakers alike are applauding the de-centralized, bottom-up development in Africa of household-level communication (cellular telephones) and power (photovoltaics) infrastructures. Not all experiments with mundane topics have been triumphs, however, as demonstrated by emergent problems with microcredit and continuing resistance to dissemination of improved cookstoves, which may indicate that older, failed paradigms are simply being applied to new topics in some cases.

Our aim is not simply to encourage scientists to tackle mundane research topics. Influenced by the debates about indigenous knowledge, which is also a movement toward mundane science, we hope to encourage the wider rethinking of orthodox domains of knowledge and science. Our elevation of the mundane, our argument that the answers to great and enduring questions lie in mundane topics is consistent with its complex etymology in the English language, which includes meanings of both "belonging to this world" and "pertaining to the cosmos or universe" (*Oxford English Dictionary* 1999).

2. Chapter 3: Nature, society, and science in anthropogenic grasslands: studying declensionist discourses

In the next chapter we carry out an in-depth study of a specific mundane topic, the fire-climax grasslands of Southeast Asia. Tropical grasslands and savannas are one of the most important ecosystems on the planet, in both human and ecological terms, and one of their most important characteristics is that they are often characterized by contention – locals and external observers often see them very differently. This revealing dimension is curiously missing from grassland studies, however. We explore the reasons for this lacuna in Chapter 3, focusing on the grasslands of Southeast Asia, especially those dominated by the famous or infamous grass, *Imperata cylindrica* beauv. L.

We begin the chapter with a discussion of the role of grassland versus forest in Western and non-Western culture history and symbolism. Modern science has focused on the perceived "natural" forest as opposed to the "cultural" grassland – which we term "forest fundamentalism". The difference on which this focus is based is more problematic than once thought, however, and as Cronon (1995) writes, it shifts our attention away from the sorts of landscapes, like grasslands, on which most humans actually live and depend. The modern bias in favor of forest biotypes leads to the popular interpretation of grasslands as examples of resource-use failure, as moral lessons about what can happen to forests if not properly managed and conserved. This interpretation is based on a perception of grasslands as terminal climax communities, but current research suggests that fire-climax grasslands are unstable and dependent upon continued human management for their existence.

The fact that such grasslands are seen as unmanaged is the most important aspect of their social reality, and it is more often than not incorrect. A prime reason for the ubiquity and tenacity of this perception of lack of management is the constant presence of fires in grasslands; but the association of humans, fire, and grasslands is ancient, purposeful, and functional. Following Williams (1980), we interpret the deprecation by outside observers of fire and the grasslands they maintain as deprecation of local peasant communities and their culture and agriculture.

Since colonial times, governments in Southeast Asia have viewed grasslands – especially those dominated by *Imperata cylindrica* – as "wastelands" eligible for "reclamation" and alternate, state-approved uses. But the history of grassland reclamation efforts is hugely problematic, however, which raises the question: given that reclamation of grasslands is not technically difficult and is successfully accomplished by local communities using nothing more sophisticated than a hoe or a digging stick, what drives such efforts? We suggest that one purpose of official depictions of grasslands as a problem that only officialdom can solve is to create an argument for the extension of state governance, even through the medium of failed state programs (Ferguson 1990).

Finally, we argue that it is important to treat the misunderstanding of grasslands in science and policy circles as a systemic phenomenon, something that is not accidental but produced. The research and development emphasis, not on how locals manage grasslands but on how outside actors can eliminate them, is not a random bias; it directly supports intervention and appropriation by state elites. In this chapter we argue for the need to think about the political and economic implications of subjective perceptions of the absence of purpose and reason from the production of everyday landscapes.

3. Chapter 4: High-modern versus local folk views of dearth and abundance: studying failure versus success in resource management systems

The next chapter also deals with subjective and contested representations of natural resource management. Our analysis in Chapter 4 is based on a reworking of the idea of "moral economy" from Scott (1976) and before him Thompson (1963, 1971). Scott applied this concept to socio-economic relations in rural Malaysia. The moral economy is essentially a mutual social guarantee of preservation of subsistence; and when this is violated, it predictably leads to political unrest. We apply this concept not to relations among people, between rich and poor, but to relations between nature and culture, between environment and society.

In this chapter, we compare three systems of production: forest fruit gathering in Borneo, swidden agriculture in Borneo, and the green revolution cultivation of high-yielding varieties throughout Indonesia and elsewhere in the tropics. We unpack the production cultures of each of these systems to reveal their underlying logics of natural resource management. We argue that the ecological realities underlying all three production systems are similar, but the perceptions of these realities are not. We especially look at the way each production system draws its boundaries, specifically with respect to how it measures and evaluates its success.

One indicator that we examine is whether or not resource flows into and out of the production system are recognized, reflecting a real versus unreal view of the permeability of its boundaries. Another indicator is an emphasis on production alone, which reflects a narrower drawing of boundaries, versus an equal emphasis on production and distribution, which reflects a wider view of system boundaries.

The way that the boundaries of the production system are perceived greatly affects assessments of the system's sustainability. For example, a narrow drawing of boundaries, one that excludes social and natural externalities, can make a system appear to be more sustainable than it really is.[20] The manipulation of system boundaries, their widening or narrowing, is not simply a question of rhetoric; it can affect the sustainability of the system. That is, normative misstatements of system boundaries can undermine the production system's actual capacity for sustainability. Acknowledging the reality of costs, losses, and failures, paradoxically, leads to fewer costs, losses, and failures in the long run than an ideological refusal to grant their reality and inevitability.

4. Chapter 5. Differences in perceptions of climate change between and within nations: studying science, scientists, and folk

Chapter 5 also deals with the way that system boundaries are drawn and the resulting implications for questions of morality and responsibility. The subject of this chapter is the evolution of the global discourse of the causes and consequences, culpability and responsibility, of climate change. We begin with an anecdote of climate change as "the gorilla in the room", which illustrates interdisciplinary differences in the view of climate change as an isolated, geophysical problem as opposed to a problem embedded in a cluster of natural and social changes and challenges.

We then analyze an iconic exchange, carried out in 1990–1991 between the World Resource Institute (WRI) and India's Center for Science and Environment (CSE), which launched the global debate over climate change. In what was to establish some long-lived fault lines of this debate, WRI assigned some of the responsibility for global warming to less-developed countries, such as India; whereas CSE heatedly refuted this charge, claiming that the real culprits were the industrialized countries like the U.S. The two parties to this exchange arrived at different conclusions because they emphasized different aspects of the problem, used different time-scales in their analyses, and so on – each engaged in partisan "boundary definition" that privileged the self-interests of the global North versus South.

The two positions were the product, in part, of different histories, an asynchronous world history. Such differences are obscured by the compelling "one-world" perspective so common to environmental discourse. The elision of difference in this perspective is useful in mobilizing disparate parties to collective action; but it is inherently subjective and this subjectivity may ultimately undermine global cooperation on pressing environmental issues like climate change.

Next in this chapter, we examine the post-1990/1991 evolution of the global climate change policy regime, assessing the extent to which it continued to be characterized by a North–South schism. We find that although North–South tensions did not disappear, they were eventually eclipsed in importance by differences within the North, with different Northern nations fighting one another over recognition and discharge of responsibility for bearing the costs of this regime.

Next we look at different stances with respect to climate change that have arisen within individual nations in the South as well as the North. In particular, we examine the rise of the critique of climate science by climate change deniers in the U.S., which falls within an age-old tradition of folk belief regarding the climate. Although these denialist beliefs are ignored by natural and social scientists alike – seen at best as an impediment to "doing what needs to be done" – we suggest that they constitute not merely an obstacle on the path to addressing the problem of climate change, but are an intrinsic part of this problem, which demands as much study and intervention as any other part of the problem.

Since humanity began to keep written records, ideas about climate have been imbricated in ideas about the self and the "other". This suggests to us that one explanation for the "inexplicable" rage against climate science (Krugman 2014) may be that the idea of a change in climate – which has too often been articulated by illustration to distant, alien people, places and things – threatens deeply-held ideas about self-identity. We ask if the global discourse of climate science is co-producing a folk discourse of climate change denial.

5. Chapter 6. Conclusions: reflections on interdisciplinarity, sustainability, and thermodynamics

In our final chapter, we attempt to synthesize some of the lessons of our collaboration on the four case studies. In the first section, we examine what we can learn about the nature of the collaborative project itself. Our collaboration was based not on the simple application of anthropology to physics or physics to anthropology, but on our shared use of a number of key conceptual constructs, which we earlier referred to as "boundary objects". The most important of these are as follows: the value of studying conservation and development discourses; the insights to be gained from the subaltern view; the power of historical and comparative analysis; skepticism toward development "miracles"; the value of studying conservation and development failures; the robustness of science when engaged with the real world; the need for reflexivity; and faith that the same reality underlies all disciplines and thus validates interdisciplinary work.

In the next section of the chapter, we draw out the lessons of our collaborative studies for sustainable environmental relations. First, we argue for the need to view chronic failures of conservation and development systemically, not as accidents but as inherent, purposeful, and revealing characteristics of the field. Second, we argue that mundane, everyday topics like those analyzed in our case studies are no less complex than the more esoteric subjects of science; consequently the view of them as "simple" is de-privileging and thus political. Third, we consistently found in our studies that knowledge is not the politically neutral terrain that we generally think it to be. There are often multiple, conflicting knowledges pertaining to any given topic; the recognition of one and ignoring of another is thus often a political act; and as much energy and resources may be devoted to the production and dissemination of ignorance as actual knowledge. Fourth, there is a systematic aversion within science to accepting as a subject for serious study – as opposed to a venue for intervention and improvement – the everyday knowledge and practices of peoples less economically and politically privileged. In this and other respects, the objectivity and privilege of science is coming under unprecedented attack today, especially with respect to climate change, which argues for development of a scientific hermeneutics, a self-reflexive and critical awareness of how, and why, and for whom science does what it does.

In the final section of the chapter, we discuss those theories of physics most often related to human society, the laws of thermodynamics. We suggest that the first law, concerning the conservation of energy – namely, the total amount of energy in an isolated system remains constant; and thus energy cannot be created nor destroyed – illuminates our critique of the most infamous myths of conservation and development policy: "miracle" programs, benefits without costs, winners without losers. All such claims would appear to violate the principles of the first law. The second law of thermodynamics states that the entropy of an isolated system which is not in equilibrium will tend to increase over time, approaching a maximum value at equilibrium. Over the past century and a half there has been extensive application of this law to the workings of human society, especially in the field of economics. Of most relevance to our own work is the way that this second law illuminates the forces promoting the dispersal versus concentration of wealth, representing entropy versus enthalpy. We give examples of the two forces at work in contemporary Indonesian society and in the historic "biographies" of some of Indonesia's famous gemstones. The inevitable triumph of entropy over enthalpy is reflected in folk sayings around the world regarding the limits on inter-generational wealth transfer.

From the analytic distance and perspective afforded by the laws of thermodynamics, we suggest that the goal of sustainable resource management should be not to attempt to counter the forces of either entropy or enthalpy but rather to accept the existence and power of both, and to moderate the violence and thus the social and ecological costs of the swings between them.

Notes

1 Snow's formulation of the terms of this debate continues to draw attention. Most recently, Ortolano (2009) interprets the Snow–Leavis debate in terms of wider

issues including Britain's past, present, future, and cultural politics of the 1960s; and Kagan (2009) updates this debate with his analysis of "The Three Cultures".
2 Science was also seen as relatively easy. There is a (perhaps apochryphal, but still telling) quote attributed to the wife on an Oxford don in the 1920s, who assured a dinner companion that any student with a first-class degree in the classics "could get up science in a fortnight" (Gottlieb 2014).
3 "Simply" being paid as a professional cast doubt on one's standing as a scientist who could attend meetings of scientific societies and publish in their journals" (Endersby 2003: 397).
4 Darwin's comment is the intellectual antecedent of the famous statement by the early twentieth-century British scientist Lord Rutherford, that "All science is either physics or stamp collecting" (quoted in Birks 1962). The shift in valorization from biology to physics, between Darwin and Rutherford, reflects the relative ascendance of the latter's field from the mid-nineteenth century through the first quarter of the twentieth century and, indeed, long after.
5 The authors' home institutions, the School of Forestry and Environmental Studies at Yale and the Energy and Resources Group at the University of California, Berkeley, are examples of exceptions to this rule.
6 See Franklin (1995) for a review of science studies from the perspective of anthropology.
7 The explosion of political concern over and academic interest in climate change, a quintessential anthropogenic environmental problem, is pushing interdisciplinary collaboration between the social and natural sciences to the fore (e.g., Orlove et al. 2002).
8 Google Ngrams show a sharp rise in use of the term "multidisciplinary" beginning around 1950, with about one-half the frequency of "interdisciplinary"; and it shows a sharp rise in the use of the term "transdisciplinary" beginning around 1970, with about one-tenth the frequency of "multidisciplinary". Google Ngrams for "disciplinary", "interdisciplinary", "multidisciplinary", and "transdisciplinary", 1800–2000: https://books.google.com/ngrams/graph?content=disciplinary&year_start=1800&year_end=2000&corpus=15&smoothing=3&share=&direct_url=t1%3B%2Cdisciplinary%3B%2Cc0; https://books.google.com/ngrams/graph?content=interdisciplinary&year_start=1800&year_end=2000&corpus=15&smoothing=3&share=&direct_url=t1%3B%2Cinterdisciplinary%3B%2Cc0; https://books.google.com/ngrams/graph?content=multidisciplinary&year_start=1800&year_end=2000&corpus=15&smoothing=3&share=&direct_url=t1%3B%2Cmultidisciplinary%3B%2Cc0; https://books.google.com/ngrams/graph?content=transdisciplinary&year_start=1800&year_end=2000&corpus=15&smoothing=3&share=&direct_url=t1%3B%2Ctransdisciplinary%3B%2Cc0.
9 See Blewitt (2013) for a comprehensive four-volume survey of the field of sustainable development.
10 See Clark and York (2005) for a twenty-year retrospective on Levin's and Lewontin's work.
11 Marx (1887) had earlier applied the concept of biological metabolism to socio-ecological processes (Swyngedouw 2006).
12 Contemporaneous with Rappaport and equally if not more influential was the ecologist Howard Odum's (1971) application of systems analysis to human society. More recently, the anthropologist Stephen Lansing (1991, 2006) has applied computer modeling to the analysis of temple irrigation systems in Bali.
13 Cf. Brosius (1997), Li (2000), and Tsing (1999) on what makes environmental concepts sufficiently attractive for the public to "pick them up" from scholars, or not.
14 Cf. Cohen's (1994:16) distinctions among analogy (similarity in function), homology (similarity in form), and metaphor in interdisciplinary interaction.

15 If we reverse the causal arrow, this relationship seems more self-evident. That is, it seems self-evident that non-resilient ideologies lead to non-resilient ecosystems.
16 The seeming asymmetries in interdisciplinary borrowing notwithstanding, Lenoir (1997:16,17) argues that interdisciplinary borrowing is so ubiquitous that no field is autonomous; each is a transformed version of all others, each is "homologous" with all others.
17 Cf. Rosaldo's (1993) interpretation of the work of the anthropologist Harold C. Conklin, who was exemplary in drawing on the bio-physical sciences (botany, agronomy, cartography) in his research and writing in the mid-twentieth century (1954, 1955, 1980). Rosaldo (1993:186) suggests that by adopting the language and concepts of the physical sciences, Conklin could assume the "authoritative high ground" and adopt a guise of "self-effacing detachment and scientific authority" in what was essentially a political defense of his subjects (see also Dove 2007a). Cf. what Ménard (cited in Cohen 1994:72) called the "polemical function of an analogy".
18 Those scientists who work full-time (as opposed to as occasional consultants) in development or applied work, as opposed to pure academic work, are rarely recognized as the leaders of their respective disciplines.
19 Schumacher (1973), in his landmark book *Small is Beautiful*, presented an influential critique of the orthodox position that "small science" is irrelevant science.
20 This is a central point of Rich's (1994) critique of World Bank environmental policy, namely that the conceptual boundaries of its projects are drawn so narrowly that they artificially exclude most of their real impacts on the environment.

2
THE VIRTUES OF MUNDANE SCIENCE

Studying the everyday

> I had when a youth read and smiled at Pliny's account of a practice... to still the waves by pouring oil into the sea.... The learned, too, are apt to slight too much the knowledge of the vulgar.
> Benjamin Franklin (1773 letter to William Brownrigg, cited in Herschbach 1995:44)[1]

In 2009 the *New Yorker* published a story entitled "Hearth Surgery: The Quest for a Stove that Can Save the World" (Bilger 2009). It focused on activities at two different sites then prominent in the world of cookstove research: one was a village in the mountains of Guatemala, where a professor from the University of California at Berkeley was carrying out the world's longest running study of traditional cookstove use and its impact on health, with funding from the N.I.H.; and the other was "Stove Camp" in the Oregon woods, where an American NGO (the Aprovecho Research Center) annually brought together "engineers, anthropologists, investors, foreign-aid workers, and rogue academics" to spend a week "designing stoves and testing wood-burning stoves" and "cooking under the stars and debating thermodynamics". The fact that two such disparate places, and projects, could be addressing the same subject, reveals some of the complexities, contradictions, and paradoxes of the science of mundane matters in the modern era.

I. Introduction

Many if not most scientists hold the reasonable – for them – belief that the solutions to life's problems are scientific in nature. The truth is often more complicated. For example, while new and emerging "high profile" diseases attract some of the greatest attention in medical science and public health, very different illnesses take the greatest overall toll on poor communities in less-developed nations. Globally, acute respiratory infections, malnutrition, diarrhea, malaria, and measles account for over 70 percent of the 12.2 million deaths of children less than five years old (WHO 2014). In central Kenya, for example, the overwhelming majority of medical cases reported – respiratory infections; skin, eye, and ear ailments; diarrhea; and urinary tract infections – stem largely from such commonplace factors as indoor air pollution from cooking fires and a lack of potable water and adequate food (see Barnes et al., 1994; Kammen, 1995; Smith et al., 2000; Ezzati and Kammen, 2001; Bailis, Ezzati and Kammen, 2005).[2]

The solutions to such ills are not strictly "technical" in nature, in the narrow sense of the term, for they encompass not simply scientific- and engineering-based medical measures but also the economic, political, and cultural developments necessary to change complex, entrenched systems of belief and practice. The integration of all of these elements is challenging, yet this is a challenge that has generally not been at the forefront of interest in science. The real-world messiness that creates the challenge also makes the problems less scientifically tractable, which makes scientists less interested. The problem is that these are "mundane" matters, which the *Oxford English Dictionary* (1999) defines as "belonging to the earthly world, as contrasted with heaven, worldy, earthy". For our purposes here, we define "mundane" as concerned with everyday life.

A prejudice against the study of the everyday, the mundane, is historically both cause and consequence of a conceptual *cordon sanitaire* within academia.[3] In energy and development research, it appeared as a disproportionate focus on advanced combustion systems, commercial fuels, and large centralized power facilities, even though more than three billion people rely on wood, charcoal, and other biomass fuels for the bulk of their energy needs (Casillas and Kammen, 2010). In the agricultural sciences, it appeared as an emphasis on genetic manipulation of crop varieties and idealized test-plot trials, in contrast to the relatively fewer on-farm studies of simpler technologies that reflect the actual constraints on subsistence and small-holder farmers, who still make up much of the global farming community (cf. Chapter 4).[4] In development and resource economics, it manifested itself in a focus on products traded in formal markets as opposed to those – often of more central importance to daily subsistence – produced and consumed locally. In conservation biology it is reflected in a disproportionate focus on the environmental impacts of indigenous peoples in protected areas, albeit surrounded by encroaching seas of industrial mining, ranching, and agriculture. In climate change studies, it is today reflected in the focus on abnormal places and things, including the Arctic, alpine glaciers, tiny islands, and polar bear populations (Orlove et al. 2015). Even in ecology, which has made important strides in practical conservation-oriented research, the prejudice was long reflected in the preponderance of studies of "natural" ecotypes as opposed to the complex successional mosaics associated with human influences. Everyday topics have not been not wholly neglected, but the attention they have received has long been limited relative to the critical role they play in actual human affairs.[5]

Scientific disinterest in the everyday is a modern phenomenon. It did not characterize most of the history of western scholarly thought. In classical times, for example, scholars did not make invidious distinctions between their views of weather and climate and folk views, which indeed they studied. In the "Weather Signs" of Theophrastus (1926, II:405, 421), thus, we find many passages like the following: "It is a sign of storm… when sheep or birds fight for their food more than usual, since they are then trying to secure a store against bad weather… ." Theophrastus (1926, II:393) also notes how important it is to find local informants from whom to glean such knowledge: "It is indeed always possible to find such an observer, and the signs learnt from such persons are the most trustworthy." "Weather Signs" is a celebration of fine-grained knowledge of the sort that environmental anthropologists and human ecologists have treated as major discoveries in recent decades. There is similar material in the writings on weather and climate of Hippocrates (1923), Hesiod (1914), Aristotle (1952), and Virgil (2004). Not until the nineteenth century, when many of the learned still subscribed to Hippocratic views of the relationship between climate and society, did the rise of scientific meteorology marginalize such views and create a clear divide between scientific and folk thought on this subject (Janković 2000). Although this seemed like the historic, final defeat of non-scientific thinking by science, it was also more complicated, for each needed the other. That is to say, modern scientific thinking constructed and defined itself in opposition to folk thinking and continues to do so, and the obverse is also true. As the current battle between climate change believers and deniers shows, the latter define their beliefs in explicit opposition to scientific beliefs (Oreskes 2010).

Any contest over knowledge is always in part political, for there exists a politics of knowledge. This was true in the nineteenth century, and it is true today, which partly explains the bias against studying the mundane. Hewitt (1995) has demonstrated how politics affects the classification of certain problems – like "natural" disasters, HIV/AIDS, and nuclear technology – as "special" dangers and others – like traffic "accidents", cancers induced by environment or lifestyle, and heart disease – as "ordinary" ones – a classification that bears vast implications for treatment and preventive measures. Everyday mundane problems tend, practically by definition, to be seen as less worthy of study, intervention, and the allocation of scarce resources – which gives this definition great political import, therefore.

The scientific bias against studying the mundane inevitably provoked a counter-effect. There are noteworthy examples of interest in folk or lay knowledge in the modern era, encompassing the French anthropologist Lévi-Strauss' (1966) concept of "bricolage" (a product of working with hands using "devious" means opposite to those used by engineers); the English philosopher Michael Oakeshott's (1962) concept of "practical knowledge" (which he

FIGURE 2.1 Studying the rich variety of biomass fuels exploited by a farm household in Pakistan's semi-arid *barani* districts

Source: Michael R. Dove

explicitly distinguishes from the technical knowledge of carrying out a scientific experiment and characterizes as not self-reflective and not capable of being formulated in rules); and the political scientist Scott's (1998) concept of mētis, which he defines as "situated knowledge." The field of anthropology has long distinguished itself by its interest in folk knowledge, dating at least from the work early in the twentieth century of Malinowski (1935). Bourdieu's (1977) work on "habitus" was a powerful later theorization of folk knowledge and practice. And there has been an extraordinary elevation of work on "indigenous knowledge" over the past several decades, not only within academic but also in policy circles, albeit at times problematic (Agrawal 1995; Dove 2000). Recent examples from the literature, specifically focusing on everyday dimensions of water (Sofoulis 2005; Anand 2011), land (Shipton 1994), and infrastructure (Star 1999; Carse 2014), show a continued interest in studying mundane (even "boring") dimensions of human life (cf. Figure 2.1).

The balance of this chapter will deal with three of the most prominent recent and ongoing efforts to address mundane ills with mundane solutions in the field of development: micro-credit schemes, cookstove improvement programs, and the expansion of off-grid and micro-grid electrification. We will summarize work in these areas and then analyze the lessons, first for micro-credit, cookstove improvement, and electrical grid development programs, and then for mundane science more generally.

II. Case studies

Here we examine the drivers, policies, outcomes, and reassessments of three high profile examples of mundane science: micro-credit, improved cookstoves, and off-grid/micro-grid projects. All of them have become over time important and agenda-defining activities worldwide, being now mainstays of the Davos conferences, the World Economic Forum, and the Clinton Global Summits. Indeed, improved cookstoves have become a cause célèbre, even being featured in White House events. President Obama's own late mother, S. Anne Dunham (2009), was a pioneer in the study and implementation of micro-credit programs in South and Southeast Asia. Off-grid and micro-grid development of electrification in Africa have the distinction of rising from spontaneous local initiatives and catching the top-down development establishment by surprise.

1. Mundane banking

An illuminating example of the application of mundane science to sustainable development is provided by the now often re-told story of Grameen Banking of Bangladesh, which pioneered the extension of small amounts of credit to the poor, beginning in 1976.[6] The bank was the brain-child of Muhammad Yunus, a professor of economics in Bangladesh. Yunus began by reversing the traditional relationship between the poor and large lending institutions: instead of asking how to make the poor more creditworthy, he asked how banks could be more responsive to their needs. Whereas the assumption in most poverty alleviation programs was (and often still is) that the poor cannot be trusted with money, Yunus assumed that they could and that society was at fault for not making this possible.

At the heart of the Grameen Bank's solution to the problem is the "lending circle," typically a group of five women who jointly manage and guarantee their loans (Yunus 1991). Through these circles, the bank first educates borrowers about money management and small-scale economic development and then makes small loans to them, usually no more than $20 (U.S.) per household the first time. When the borrowers have repaid these loans, they become eligible for larger and larger ones, culminating in housing loans of several hundred dollars. In all cases, however, borrowers proceed at a pace determined by their own capacity, not the needs of the lender. The combination of the Grameen Bank's trust in people, its education program, and its reliance on lending circles, resulted in a phenomenally high 98 percent loan repayment rate, a two percent default rate that contrasts with rates of over twelve percent for loans by both private and state-run banks to Bangladesh's business elites.

The Grameen Bank's approach to alleviating poverty has been one of the most successful in contemporary development history. Whereas the bank began with loans to some 20 families, estimates as of 2009 are that it now operates in one-half of Bangladesh's 30,000 villages, making loans of more than $400 million annually (Microfinance Information Exchange 2009:49). Furthermore, the bank's approach has been emulated in many other less-developed countries as well as some more-developed ones (e.g., there is now a Grameen U.S.). Although Yunus' idea of micro-lending initially met with skepticism from the World Bank and other mainstream organizations, his approach has now been championed by a number of agencies, and he himself was awarded the 2006 Nobel Peace Prize.[7]

When properly implemented, the Grameen model can serve as a basis for community development in which many of the recent advances in technology and participatory planning come together. This simple and classically mundane concept offers fresh insight into – as well as a theoretical challenge to – much of traditional development economics.

On the other hand, the Grameen approach has not been without its problems. Predictably, some of them stem from its perceived success and the tremendous interest it generated. Thus, early on the burgeoning interest in its approach led to a Microcredit Summit in Washington DC, in February 1997, which set a goal of "expanding microcredit to 100 million of the world's poorest families."[8]

While the Grameen Bank's own achievements showed that village-level organizing on this scale was theoretically possible, they also suggested that not just any organization could achieve it. The Grameen Bank itself grew slowly over a period of 20 years, and a number of the original borrowers became top managers. Then it attracted attention – and funding – from the World Bank, large commercial banks, and U.S., Japanese, and European aid agencies, whose desire to immediately inject hundreds of millions of dollars into small-scale lending lacked the patient, two-decade build-up of human capacity, public education, and local accountability that characterized Grameen's lending. Too often, these new loans came with demands for short-term returns and successes, which precluded the careful learning that was essential to Grameen's initial success. The logical alternative of putting NGOs in charge of new micro-credit programs was not without its problems. Microcredit must be approached as a socially responsible business, not as charity or social welfare, which requires most NGOs to dramatically change their approaches, capabilities, and systems if they are to be successful. It is difficult to incorporate a successful microcredit program into an institution that has a relief or social service approach to the poor.

Of most importance, Grameen's own operations in Bangladesh came to be criticized for overlooking the gender dynamics and politics of its household borrowers. As social scientists began to carry out long-term studies of the bank's customers, some found that its loans often played into, and exacerbated, gender-based inequities within households. The result was increased male demands on already over-burdened female labor and resources, even eventuating in a spate of female suicides purportedly related to micro-credit (Biswas 2010). In short, Grameen came to be criticized by some observers for a naive focus on female borrowers in isolation from the very real and constraining wider socio-economic context of their households.

2. Mundane cooking

Though rarely frontstage in policy discussions, the use of biomass fuels is one of the most important issues of sustainable development. Such fuels comprise 40 to 60 percent of total energy consumption, both industrial and domestic, in many developing nations. Household cooking alone accounts for more than 60 percent of total energy use in sub-Saharan Africa (exceeding 80 percent in several countries). Further, some poor families spend 20 percent or more of their disposable income on wood and charcoal or devote upwards of 25 percent of their household labor to collecting wood (Ezzati and Kammen 2001; Smith 2014). Environmental impacts and household energy budgets aside, there are other reasons why this subject is attracting attention. Cookstove research unexpectedly led to the discovery that indoor environments are the most important source of human exposure to pollutants in the rural areas of many developing nations.[9] Inefficient combustion of traditional fuels results in high concentrations of pollutants that cause acute respiratory infections. Indeed, 4.3 million people a year die prematurely from a suite of related illnesses attributable to the household air pollution caused by the inefficient use of traditional solid fuels (Table 2.1) (Smith et al. 2000; Woodward et al. 2014). The causes of death in Table 2.1 are all well-researched, "high profile" diseases, but their association with the quintessential mundane technology – cookstoves – has been very poorly studied.

Efforts to improve cookstove efficiency and reduce pollution, along with making the stoves inexpensive and easy to use, have a long and at times tortured history (Figure 2.2). Many of the classic problems with development efforts – the overemphasis on technology in isolation, the inapplicability of laboratory trials conducted under ideal conditions, and insensitivity to gender and household dynamics (as in the Grameen banking case) – were encountered in cookstove design and dissemination programs.[10] Some progress was made, however, by integrating the efforts of engineers, ecologists, anthropologists/sociologists, economists, government agencies, members of professional development organizations, and non-governmental and community groups.

TABLE 2.1 Breakdown of causes of death from indoor air pollution in less-developed countries

Percentage	Health outcome
34%	Stroke
26%	Ischaemic heart disease
22%	Chronic obstructive pulmonary disease (COPD)
12%	Pneumonia
6%	Lung cancer

Source: Ezzati and Kammen 2001; Woodward et al. 2014

FIGURE 2.2 An array of different cookstoves, both traditional (far left and center/back) and improved (those with clay and ceramic liners, second from left and far right) for sale in Kibera, the largest shanty town in Nairobi

Source: Daniel M. Kammen

From an engineering standpoint, an improved stove has to meet four requirements: maximize fuel combustion by maintaining a high temperature and an adequate supply of oxygen; maximize radiative heat transfer to pots by keeping them close to the flames; maximize convection by circulating as much of the hot gases over the pots as possible; and maximize conduction by adding insulation. Equally important, from a sociological/anthropological standpoint, to be acceptable to the end-users the stoves had to meet three additional requirements: inexpensive; easy to use; and adapted to local fuels, foods, and cooking methods.

The development of the *jiko* stove in Kenya (Figures 2.2 and 2.3) illustrates the difficulties inherent in meeting such diverse requirements. The *jiko* is a charcoal- or wood-burning metal stove shaped like an hourglass, the upper portion of which has a ceramic insulating liner. The current model costs roughly $2 (U.S.) to manufacture, uses 1,300 pounds less fuel per year than traditional Kenyan stoves, and saves urban households as much as $65 per year (one-fifth the average annual income in Kenyan cities). The initial designs had serious flaws, however: the stoves were unstable, burned too hot, and their openings did not match the size of most cooking pots. In addition, they were too expensive for the rural households to whom they were primarily being marketed.

Some of the earliest *jiko* designs were done not by engineers but by aid workers with little technical background and the mistaken belief that appropriate

FIGURE 2.3 A Pokot woman in Laikipia District, Kenya, examining improved efficiency cookstoves that are available for purchase at an educational session

Source: Majid Ezzati

technology was simple technology. As it turned out, an extensive research program was necessary to determine the physics and sociology/anthropology underlying such "simple" stoves, and even then the final successful design required much trial and error. Suggestions from actual end-users were critical to developing a more efficient, commercially viable model capable of performing as well in the home as in the laboratory. The problems were ultimately solved through a combination of additional technical research and consultations with local craftspeople and potential users. A less expensive, wood-burning version also was developed for rural households. Today, hundreds of local craftspeople manufacture some 20,000 stoves per month, and more than one million are in use throughout Kenya. Variants of the *jiko* are also finding their way into other African countries.

Since the 1970s, international aid organizations have promoted the development of cleaner, more efficient cookstoves for the developing world, and hundreds if not thousands of individual projects have been carried out in more than 50 countries. Worldwide, stove programs have led to the dissemination of more than 120 million stoves in China (reaching a remarkable 60 to 70 percent of all households), several million stoves each in India, Sri Lanka, and Bangladesh, and hundreds of thousands in a number of African nations. In Kenya, more than 50 percent of urban households and 10 percent of all households nationwide use improved stoves (Kammen 1995; Woodward et al. 2014). Whereas the most recent efforts have been exciting and in many cases reasonably successful, steady and sufficient funding for cookstove projects has been difficult to obtain: fewer than 200 projects have been undertaken during the last decade, most with budgets of only thousands or tens of thousands of dollars.

Funding constraints not withstanding, cookstove programs have been the focus of or impetus behind a remarkable array of scientific, economic, environmental, and methodological advances. Beyond the direct impacts on fuel use, indoor air pollution, household economics, and the environment (viz., forest cover), the in-depth household studies necessary to evaluate impacts and design adoption strategies have contributed to innovations in participatory rural appraisal and gender-sensitive interviewing, as well as to new theories of networking, communication, and the diffusion of innovations (Ruttan 1996; Smith et al. 2000; Global Alliance for Clean Cookstoves[11]).

3. Mundane lighting

The third case study of mundane science involves the expansion of electrical services in Africa. According to the World Bank, over 1.2 billion people worldwide lack access to electricity, which includes over 550 million people in Africa and 300 million people in India alone.[12] The development of off-grid and micro-grid lighting to address their needs is still evolving, but it paints a picture consistent with what we have seen so far of mundane science.

For people living beyond the reach of normal electrification grids, two paths of development are emerging. For those with no prospect for moving onto either a centralized or decentralized grid, a mixture of technological and marketing and outreach innovations have made lighting products far cheaper than was forecast only a few years ago (Zheng and Kammen 2014). Low-cost LED lights, small, reasonably effective batteries, and low-cost solar cells have opened up a wide range of products, which are both of interest to businesses and entrepreneurs seeking revenue and also may offer social empowerment to the "bottom of the pyramid" (Figures 2.4 and 2.5). Quality control remains a problem, as it did in the earlier generations of solar home system products (Acker and Kammen 1996; Jacobson and Kammen 2007), but these simple products are meeting a clear need, as evidenced by the rapid expansion of off-grid lighting from just a few countries in sub-Saharan Africa[13] to virtually all of sub-Saharan Africa. This includes not just lights but also other services (radios, cell phone charging, even direct current refrigerators and televisions) for poor and disenfranchised communities.[14]

For another segment of those living beyond normal electrification grids, micro-grids – distributed systems of local energy generation, transmission, and use – hold the potential to provide communities with electricity services,

FIGURE 2.4 Solar torches all sold under the banner of "Lighting Africa" products in East Africa, but with very widely divergent quality evaluations

Source: Daniel M. Kammen

FIGURE 2.5 An expanded range of off-grid lighting products, all certified by the Lighting Africa program

Source: Daniel M. Kammen

particularly in rural and in peri-urban areas of less developed countries. In many cases, the traditional approach to serving these communities has been to extend the central grid; but this approach is inefficient due to a combination of capital scarcity, insufficient energy service, reduced grid reliability, extended building times, and construction challenges to connect remote areas. Adequately financed and operated micro-grids, based on renewable and appropriate resources, are proving able to overcome many of the challenges faced by traditional lighting or electrification strategies (Schnitzer et al. 2014).

Unlike improved stove programs, for example, micro-grid development is driven largely by the market, sometimes successfully and sometimes not (Figures 2.6a and 2.6b). "Virtuous" development cycles are achieved through the production of (i) sufficient revenue to support the grid and (ii) service and schedule reliability to keep consumers as loyal customers. "Vicious" development cycles are characterized by a chain of poor maintenance, disappointed customers, insufficient revenue and dysfunctional community support. Whether micro-grid development follows a virtuous or vicious cycle depends upon such factors as tariff design, tariff collection mechanisms, maintenance and contractor performance, theft management, demand growth, load limits, and local training and institutionalization. This dynamic interplay between the scientific, technical, and social aspects of innovation and deployment offers theoretical insights into how mundane science (and indeed other) innovative systems operate. A deployed mini-grid system is seen in Figure 2.7.

The theory of vicious and virtuous cycles is predictive and offers clear guidelines for system assessment. As examples, consider two other promising mundane technologies: solar ovens (Kammen and Lankford 1990, 1991) and passive lights made from a plastic bottle and a drop of bleach (to prevent the water from growing algae or mold) inserted into a hole in the roof (Figure 2.8).[15] Both are outstanding products of mundane science that meet key needs but are given little research support.[16] Both are very promising and have achieved some significant success – tens to hundreds of thousands of deployments in each case. This is far from trivial, indeed one of us (DK) has worked on these technologies and finds them particularly valuable in specific niche applications. For all their benefits and low-cost, however, solar ovens not only require a significant change in cooking style (Kammen and Lankford 1991) but also present issues of food security, because meals must be left in the solar oven for hours. Similarly, the wonderfully simple – some would say transformative – nature of the bottle light presents its own challenges. First, it is so cheap that the technology is hard to commercialize; and second, cutting a hole in the roof and inserting a plastic bottle, while technically feasible, presents the challenge of adequately sealing the hole and making the roofing materials (today often corrugated metal) location-specific once the holes are cut. Although these technologies might succeed with sufficient further innovation (Table 2.2), the lessons of mundane science, and of vicious versus virtuous cycles, suggest that there is a high risk and potential for failure for each of these technologies. In short, an ingenious idea is not enough.

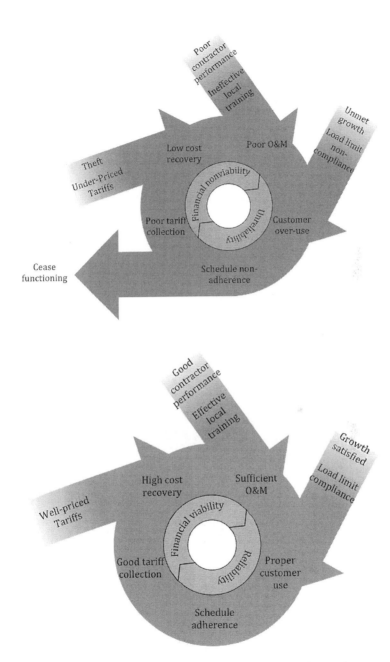

FIGURE 2.6 The theory of (top) destructive (vicious) or (bottom) constructive (virtuous) feedback leading to system failures or sustainable deployment of a technology, in this case mini-grids

Source: Daniel M. Kammen

FIGURE 2.7 A mini-grid deployed in the Crocker Highlands of Sabah, Malaysian Borneo. The system integrates solar power (shown), micro-hydropower, home and school electrification, and satellite-based communication (shown).

Source: Daniel M. Kammen

FIGURE 2.8 Liter of Light – a plastic bottle with bleach provides an excellent lighting source that requires virtually no maintenance (changing the water/bleach mixture roughly once every five years)

Source: Open Source

TABLE 2.2 Analysis of development prospects for solar ovens and solar bottle lights

Innovation	Description	Challenges	Potential solutions	Reference
Solar ovens	Passive insulated box to slow cook food	Food must be left in the oven for hours, often unmonitored/unprotected	Concentrating ovens cook more rapidly, but can be dangerous	https://www.solarcookers.org
Solar bottle light	Plastic bottle filled with water and a drop of bleach	While the 'Liter of Light' does work very well, it also presents technical and marketing challenges	Make this a village-based enterprise	http://aliterof light.org

Source: Daniel M. Kammen

III. Discussion: the six fallacies of mundane science

Our analysis of the three case studies, involving rural electrification, improved cookstoves, and micro-credit, offers a number of lessons regarding mundane science and its application. As attested to by the quotation from Benjamin Franklin in the epigraph to this chapter, scholarly aversion to mundane knowledge and practice is a long-standing problem. It shows up in contemporary research generally, and in environmental science and resource sustainability work in particular, in the form of six key fallacies: mundane science is anti-scientific in spirit; the greatest overall returns come from basic rather than applied research; mundane science is simply an application distinct from (and potentially in conflict with) basic research; mundane science is subjective, while basic science is objective; mundane science has more to do with society than science; and mundane research will not work because development must be centrally planned.

The first fallacy is that an emphasis on mundane science amounts to a rejection of scientific and technological progress. But the innovations in household economics, combustion, and lighting technologies, as outlined in the preceding section, belie such a charge. Mundane innovation does not necessarily mean innovation that is less challenging, less complex, or less elegant. We have known this since the "appropriate technology" (AT) movement spearheaded by E. F. Schumacher (1973) in the 1970s, which focused on the design and practical implementation of inexpensive windmills, latrines, bicycles, and other tools of everyday life, particularly to help the poor. Academics and development planners pursued AT in the years following the OPEC oil embargoes, but it later dropped out of the international development mainstream despite its great relevance and cost-effectiveness, in part because of the anti-mundane bias that we have been discussing. As a result, instead of emerging as a research and policy ally of development planners, AT evolved into primarily an opposition movement.[17]

Other developments around the world that belie the anti-progress charge against mundane science also have been documented. An example is the "peasant science" movement in the Philippines called MASIPAG (Frossard 2005). This alliance of farmers rejected the packages of rice varieties, fertilizers, pesticides, and directed development offered by the International Rice Research Institute (IRRI), because they gave the farmers too little control over the management, quality, and timing of their yields. Instead, MASIPAG farmers, in collaboration with researchers from the University of the Philippines in Los Baños, adapted IRRI's modern methods of crop hybridization to develop rice varieties that met their own criteria for cost, yield, disease resistance, soil impact, and taste. In other words, MASIPAG farmers employed IRRI's own technology to meet local needs and development concerns not satisfactorily addressed by IRRI itself. This example clearly shows that scientific development inputs are sometimes rejected not for their science but for the political and economic trappings that come along with it, a reality that is often difficult for the scientists involved – who may deny that their work has any political or economic trappings at all – to admit.

A similar example comes from Java, where post-Green Revolution rice farmers routinely produce their own custom mixes of different pesticides, aiming to strike their own personal balance between lower costs and higher potency. Such adaptation is not only not part of the prescribed technological regimen but actually violates government regulations. Because the farmers are not supposed to be doing this, this fascinating example of hybrid practice, of mundane science, has received little to no attention from researchers (see Winarto 2004 for an exception).

The second fallacy is that science is a zero-sum game where investment in anything but traditional basic research reduces the chance of true breakthrough discoveries in mainstream science. Again, the discoveries regarding latent entrepreneurship among poor women, the debilitating but preventable ill-effects of cookstove emissions, and alternatives to central development of electrical grids, as detailed in the previous discussion, do not support this assumption, which stems more from a culture of entitlement than from scientific reality. Moreover, greater applicability of scientific research has historically not only generated new hypotheses and research directions but has also increased financial and political support for research in general. The popularity of, and financial support for, most scientific fields rises and falls with demonstrations of their practical importance to everyday life. Examples include petrology and geology following the demonstration of accurate methods for locating subterranean natural resource deposits; nuclear physics following the Manhattan Project; and molecular biology and computer science following the commercialization of applications in both of these fields (Nemet and Kammen 2007).

The third fallacy – the perceived competition between basic and applied research – is partly a historical product of post-World War II research and development policy as formulated by Vannevar Bush (1945/1990: 18–19, 83; cf. Stokes 1997) in his landmark 1945 roadmap for post-war research, "Science – The Endless Frontier". In making the case for a dedicated federal research and development institution, which eventually became the National Science Foundation, Bush (ibid.), who was then director of the U.S. government's wartime Office of Scientific Research and Development,[18] argued that "basic research… is the pacemaker of technological progress" and "applied research invariably drives out pure." He argued that mission-oriented science should be conducted as a derivative operation, and generally by the private sector, as a sort of "mop up" operation to apply useful findings from the more exalted pure research.[19] In part because of this key mid-twentieth century policy directive, basic research has flourished in the years since, while applied research has lagged behind. The basic-to-applied funding ratio in the United States federal budget has increased from 1:3 50 years ago to roughly 1:1 by the end of the twentieth century (Nemet and Kammen 2007). This reallocation of funds from applied to basic research has doubtless contributed to the pervasive valorization within the academy today of the study of esoteric versus mundane subjects. With not increasing but decreasing funding for topics like microcredit, improved cookstoves, and non-grid-based lighting, research in the field of sustainable development is increasingly done not by academics but by professional practitioners and consultants with the support of a relatively small and fragmented research corps.

The fourth fallacy of mundane science is that development outcomes, both successes and failures, are generally determined by technological factors rather than sociological/anthropological factors. As this chapter showed, however, the initial – and to some extent continuing – challenges and failures of microcredit, improved stove, and rural electrification have been at least partly due to unanticipated or misunderstood social dynamics: the gender politics of the household, the economics and aesthetics of food preparation, and the cost versus reliability of micro-grid service. In general, when development efforts in the less-developed countries have failed to assist the poor and protect the environment, as has been the case more often than not, development analysts have interpreted these outcomes as due to accident, technical failure, or noncompliant subjects. But critics of development argue that when it fails to attain its goals, this is because it benefits a favored few rather than the majority, and because what it really does is open up new avenues for state control of natural resources and extend the reach of government bureaucrats and multinational corporations (Ferguson 1990; Escobar 1995). It is an article of faith in the international development community that development is a universal good, but in fact there are winners and losers in virtually every development intervention. This fact is anathema to development policymakers, given the imperative in international relations to treat the development process as apolitical.

The fifth fallacy is that the mundane aspects of development have more to do with society than with science. But as this chapter showed, even in the examples of micro-credit, improved cookstoves, and rural electrification, robust scientific questions could be asked regarding both the social and the biophysical dimensions of household life. The non-application of science to such topics is often dictated not by the untractability of the topic for study, but by either explicit or implicit political considerations. For example, the vast majority of Green Revolution-related research has focused on food production rather than post-harvest storage and distribution because the former is considered part of science while the latter is not (see Chapter 4) – even though as much as 40 percent of some harvests is lost to spoilage, corruption, and inadequate infrastructure (APHLIS 2014). The preference for research on plant hybridization and molecular biology instead of the mundane issues of food storage, equity, and security – all of which are, nonetheless, amenable to scientific scrutiny – epitomizes the preference for an apolitical, technical-fix approach to development science. Even more important, this helps to explain why the line between science and "non-science" has been drawn where it has: mundane questions like post-harvest distribution threaten the status quo, while esoteric issues like breeding rice to use more fertilizer do not and, indeed, may even strengthen it, by privileging those farmers with the capital to afford such inputs.

The sixth and final fallacy of mundane science is that successful development is necessarily etic (externally) versus emic (internally) driven. Although both the micro-credit and improved cookstove programs originated outside of the target societies, this is not always the case, as illustrated by the MASIPAG and Javanese rice farmer examples and, especially, the largely unplanned expansion of off-grid and micro-grid electrification in Africa. This latter, spontaneous development has largely outstripped the pace of either micro-credit or improved stove programs. It places in somber relief the picture of activists and scientists alike in the industrialized world, whether toiling in their labs or in "cookstove camps", while African societies forge ahead with blinding speed, local initiative, and no reference whatsoever to the work being done on their problems by northern actors. The off-grid and micro-grid electrification example raises some pointed questions: why haven't similar, spontaneous, emic developments overtaken the challenges of credit and cooking, for example? Does this mean that the needs here are less real, or less perceived, or more difficult to tackle? Why shouldn't northern development efforts simply focus on indigenous developments like the off-grids/micro-grids in Africa, aiming at accelerating and improving such native dynamics, rather than trying to initiate change where it is not already happening?

IV. Summary and conclusions

We began this chapter with a review of the concept and genesis of mundane science. We then presented three illustrative cases of the study and development of mundane subjects, involving micro-credit, cookstove improvement, and off-grid or micro-grid electrification. We then drew on these case studies to discuss the six fallacies of mundane science.

1. Policy recommendations

Mundane science, as illustrated by the three case studies, remains a timely, relevant subject in developmental circles. The persistence of poverty, along with the current dominance of neoliberal approaches to tackling it, ensures continued interest in micro-credit programs, not just in less-developed countries but in more-developed ones as well. And if pressures on local forest resources and deleterious impacts on the health of the user populations were not sufficient to ensure continued interest in improved cookstove programs, new knowledge of the impact on the global environment and society of climate change, given that cookstoves produce as much carbon dioxide as automobiles and much more of the much more threatening black carbon, would certainly suffice (Woodward et al. 2014). Finally, the combination of rising consumer demand for electricity in Africa, and the continuing development of the technology to make this both possible and attractive/useable, guarantees continuing expansion of off-grid and micro-grid electrification. So there will be great incentive to continue to think about and apply mundane science to these as well as other subjects.

There are a number of ways to give such initiatives a larger role in research and policy decisions. These include giving much more support to academic–industry and academic–practitioner partnerships; extending academic boundaries to encompass the entire range of human–environment interactions; breaking down the often antagonistic division between development professionals and academia; instituting a more open review process for development publications, projects, and institutions; removing the barrier between development planners and the intended beneficiaries or local populations; and addressing the frequently counterproductive tension between pure and applied research. The primary obstacles to implementing these proposals are cultural and institutional. Expanding our commitment to mundane science requires that we overcome a Catch-22 situation, however: mundane issues often generate little interest until a crisis emerges, at which point a solution is expected at once. Unless we overcome the bias against mundane science during non-crisis periods, we will be wedded to periodic, shortsighted, partial solutions to critical issues in the everyday lives of vulnerable populations. Serious promotion of mundane science requires a commitment to use-inspired basic research, with a clear focus on application and sustained periods of training, collaboration, and institution-building.

2. Wider theoretical implications

Mundane science is unique in the questions that it raises about the role of agency in the modern world. All of the mundane science casse studies discussed are remarkable in the way that they focus the attention of the more developed countries on the quotidian behaviors of marginal peoples in the less developed countries. Also remarkable is the fact that the success or failure of interventions in these behaviors, deliberated upon and planned by elites in the more developed nations, depends largely on the will of these same marginal actors. Unlike the case with many international development interventions – which can impose radical changes in lifestyle upon the unfortunate targets of development – the targets in the cases discussed here can generally "just say no". And when they do say no, as is the case more often than not with the improved stove programs, for example, this represents a highly public, uncontestable failure of development planning by northern elites. The interest to effect change, and the agency to actually carry it out, vary inversely in these cases – the northern elites having the interest and the southern actors having the agency – which, again, is a rarity in the realm of international development.

Mundane science is a quintessentially modern subject in its hybridity (Latour 1993). It not only spans basic and applied research, it also spans disciplines, north and south, scientist and activist, and analyst and consumer. This hybridity is the source of both the challenge and the promise of mundane science. It explains its untractability to the basic scientist; but it also explains its attraction to the activist, and to those fortunate individuals able to plant a foot in both camps, because in hybridity is where much creativity takes place.

Notes

1 The robust output of Benjamin Franklin – spanning the fields of architecture, fluid dynamics, physics, shipbuilding, navigation, and weather forecasting – is testament to the benefits of combining mundane and theoretical research.
2 Of course the proposition that a medical solution could be "technically correct" but incorrect on social grounds represents the very sort of dichotomy that this chapter is arguing against.
3 Contemporary academic structures and practices reinforce the anti-mundane bias. Much of the research and writing on mundane topics is done by the development community, and most of this appears only in a "grey" literature of internal project reports, which are not subjected to scrutiny and debate in peer-reviewed journals. This practice reinforces the mainstream view that mundane topics lie outside the proper scope of science. Over the past several decades, development-oriented journals have proliferated, but an academic/applied distinction and boundary still persists throughout most of U.S. academia.
4 To draw attention to the critical role small-scale farmers play worldwide, the U.N. Food and Agriculture Organization (FAO) declared 2014 the Year of Family Farming (http://www.fao.org/family-farming-2014/en/).
5 Robert H. Socolow, Director of the Center for Energy and Environmental Studies at Princeton University, has suggested another prejudice against mundane but pervasive environmental issues, namely that both the focus on "high technology"

issues such as biotechnology *and* the focus on the poorest segments of society represent a focus on the esoteric and an avoidance of the mundane. While the poor are largely affected by the environment, middle class people tend to have the greatest impact on the environment through their consumption patterns; and the latter are both politically much harder to study and, unsurprisingly, much less studied in practice (Personal communication, Princeton, NJ, 16 December 1996).

6 http://www.grameen-info.org.
7 Grameen's basic strategy of collective resource management is being extended beyond banking to meet a variety of other needs, including giving the poor access to modern telecommunications technology (e.g., cellular phones and the Internet) and providing solar and wind energy infrastructure to isolated or neglected communities. Grameen's expansion of the market for sophisticated technology among the poor could in theory stimulate a positive feedback cycle. Historically, every time sales of photocells, cellular phones, windmills, laptops, and so forth have doubled, unit prices have fallen roughly 20 percent. Opening the door to these and other technologies and services among the poor, combined with improved access to credit, could in theory spur locally controlled (as opposed to central, aid-driven) development and commercial activity.
8 For a summary of the many criticisms of microfinance, from the actual number of individuals and families involved, to the program costs versus benefits, see Bateman (2010) and the extensive academic literature about the degree to which microlending may impact other forms of entrepreneurship (Field et al. 2013).
9 These programs were part of a research effort to explore previously neglected small-scale or diffuse sources of trace-gas emissions, including rice paddies and the production of charcoal by pyrolysis – all of which turned out to be globally insignificant (Ezzati et al. 2004).
10 A leading combustion researcher at Yale University, for example, observes that articles on cookstoves are still conspicuously absent from the academic journals on combustion (Alessandro Gomez, Yale Climate and Energy Institute Conference, 09/27/11).
11 http://www.cleancookstoves.org. Two key elements of the Global Alliance stand out: first, the Alliance is focused on users and consumers; and second, their target is to "reach the last mile".

Regarding users as consumers: current challenges in promoting adoption of improved cookstoves include low awareness among potential consumers of the benefits in terms of health, time savings, and economic benefits; and the fact that cookstoves are a "push" product instead of a "pull" product such as a mobile phone or a computer, which present a service or address a need that had not been previously met. There are many ways to counter consumer skepticism about the benefits of investing in improved cookstoves, including developing public awareness programs that will resonate with the end-user.

Regarding reaching the last mile: many cookstove smoke-impacted households are located in rural or remote locations, in the so-called "last-mile", which are difficult to reach with clean cookstoves and fuels. The size, weight, and fragility of clean cookstoves often provide distribution and logistical challenges. Other factors such as consumer price sensitivity, cultural preferences, gender bias, and the need for both scalability and customization, must be considered when figuring out how to reach the end-user. To ensure successful adoption of clean cookstoves and fuels, training in the operation and maintenance of clean cookstoves is critical. Women can often play a central role in addressing these demand-side challenges, by taking the lead in entrepreneurial activities and by creating distribution and repair networks.
12 http://www.sustainability4all.org. Accessed 24 August 2014.
13 http://lightingafrica.org

42 The virtues of mundane science

14 The Global Lighting and Energy Access Partnership (Global LEAP) is a Clean Energy Ministerial initiative, and its mission is to encourage self-sustaining commercial markets that increase modern energy access worldwide.
15 The bottle light is wonderfully simple as well as an elegant application of Snell's thesis which states that the velocity of the incident light divided by the sine of the angle of incidence is equal to the velocity of the refracted light divided by the sine of the angle of the refracted light, $(v_1/(\sin\theta_1)) = (v_2/\sin\theta_2)$. This means that when light passes from a substance of lower optical density to a substance of higher optical density, slowing it down, the light ray is bent towards the normal of the boundary between the two media. Thus, a bottle light sticking out through a hole in the roof will collect more light than simply that which would pass through the hole as it receives both direct sunlight and scattered light from the outside. Once internally refracted, the light will then leave the bottle of water, with the light being spread out again into the room. Snell's law can also be written in terms of the refractive index, this in the terms of how optically dense the medium is. A medium's refractive index, n, is defined as the ratio of the speed of light in a vacuum, c, to the speed of light v in the medium, $n = c/v$, so that Snell's law can be written as $\sin\theta_1\, n = \sin\theta_2\, n_2$. Simply in summary, the bottle collects direct and indirect light from outside the room, and then re-refracts (scatters) the light inside the room.
16 The idea of using plastic bottles for daylight was pioneered by Alfredo Moser from Brazil in 2002. In 2011, this technology was further developed by students from the Massachusetts Institute of Technology (MIT) in the "Liter of Light" project. The students had the idea to build solar bottle bulbs when they were constructing a school classroom made out of recycled bottles in the Philippines and they noticed that the school walls made with clear bottles let light in during the daytime, and then they began to experiment with ways to use recycled bottles to bring in light through the roof. The first effort to use the technology as a social enterprise was made in the Philippines by Illac Diaz under the MyShelter Foundation in April 2011. The Foundation implemented a "local entrepreneur" business model, whereby bottle bulbs are put together and installed by locals who in turn earn a small income for their work. Beginning with one carpenter and one set of tools in one community in San Pedro, Laguna, within months the effort was expanded to encompass 15,000 solar bottle bulb installations in 20 cities and provinces around the Philippines, and it also began to inspire similar initiatives around the world. MyShelter also established a training center to conducts workshops with youth, business companies, and other groups interested in volunteering their time to build lights in their communities.
17 The Appropriate Technology movement eventually produced a journal (*Intermediate Technology*), a practitioner-oriented publication series from the Intermediate Technology Development Group, a website (http://www.oneworld.org/itdg/publications.html), and even the Schumacher College in Totnes, England, which is a center for the study of human–environment relations and non-traditional resource strategies.
18 In November 1944, President Franklin Roosevelt asked Vannevar Bush for guidance in four areas: how to foster dissemination of the scientific discoveries made during World War II; how to marshall medical resources to combat disease; how to stimulate and support research by private and public organizations; and how to expand the U.S. research community.
19 Bush's ideas stood largely unchallenged for almost five decades. In *Pasteur's Quadrant* (1997) Donald Stokes offers a new paradigm that places pure research and applied research (the latter a distant cousin to "mundane" research) on more comparable foundations, ones that are still far from equal but at least both are included in the same discussions of innovation.

3
NATURE, SOCIETY, AND SCIENCE IN ANTHROPOGENIC GRASSLANDS

Studying declensionist discourses

> We're tired of trees. We should stop believing in trees, roots, and radicles. They've made us suffer too much. All of arborescent culture is founded on them, from biology to linguistics.
>
> Giles Deleuze and Félix Guattari (1987)

> All people are grass, their constancy is like the flower of the field.
>
> Isaiah 40

Chapter 2 was an introduction to mundane science, the study of the everyday realities – household economics, cooking, and lighting – that often escape scientific scrutiny and the valorization that this bestows on a subject. The present chapter is devoted to an in-depth look at another such subject, a type of landscape that is important to hundreds of millions of people in the world today but has also been given short shrift by science: anthropogenic grasslands.

I. Introduction

Attention to how knowledge is produced, attention to the sociology of knowledge, is especially important with topics that manifestly cut across more orthodox ways of scientifically and institutionally dividing up the world, like anthropogenic grasslands. The production of knowledge in grassland ecology and management presents both stiff challenges and new possibilities for theoretical and also practical innovation.

Tropical grasslands were one of the earliest ecosystems to be exploited by humans and they remain one of the most important: grassy biomes – savannas and grasslands – dominate the terrestrial tropics and cover 20 percent of the

FIGURE 3.1 Linnaeus' drawing of *Imperata cylindrica*, initially named by him *Lagurus cylindricus*

Source: Linnean Society of London

global land area (Harlan 1982; Solbrig 1993; Parr et al. 2014). In some arid, semiarid, and arctic regions, and in perennially disturbed biomes like the slopes of volcanos (Dove 2007b), grasslands may form a natural climax vegetation; but in humid and subhumid tropical regions, grasslands are mostly anthropogenic in origin and character, meaning "having its origin in the activities of man" (*Oxford English Dictionary* 1999). In Southeast Asia, many grasslands are dominated by a single species, *Imperata cylindrica* (L.) Beauv. (Figure 3.1). Given the depth and breadth of their place on the human landscape, it is remarkable how inadequate and conflicted our understanding of such grasslands is. Indeed, tropical, anthropogenic grasslands are one of the most misunderstood human modifications of the earth's natural environments.

The earliest research on tropical anthropogenic grasslands consisted of brief commentaries in the colonial, ethnographic, and travel literatures, in the seventeenth, eighteenth, and nineteenth centuries. These commentaries were often quite insightful, because the observers' vision were less influenced by the orthodox beliefs concerning grasslands that dominated the initial, scientific research in the field. These beliefs were evident in the next wave of studies by specialists working in the second half of the nineteenth century and first half of the twentieth century, working mostly within the estate crop sector and focusing on how to eliminate grasses such as *Imperata*. This was followed by efforts late in the twentieth century by both natural and social scientists to interpret particular systems of grassland management and ecology in light of the actual social and biological evidence as opposed to prevailing orthodoxy. The current and still ongoing work consists of efforts to analyze this orthodoxy and to identify and try to overcome the gaps that it has left in our knowledge. According to the 1997 *Agroforestry Systems* special issue on *Imperata* (Garrity 1997), these gaps are greatest with respect to local smallholder grassland management systems and the wider political-economic forces that impact them.

Discussions of research and development in tropical anthropogenic grasslands have long been characterized by contradiction and contest. Local communities and central development agencies often hold diametrically opposing views of grasslands, with the former seeing them as an integral component of their agroecology and the latter seeing them as wastelands. Local villagers may see grasslands as fragile, whereas policymakers see them as tenacious. Scholars themselves have vacillated over the past two generations between seeing grasslands as models of equilibrium versus disequilibrium. As might be predicted from these conflicted views, development interventions intended to convert grasslands to other uses have been highly problematic. Nor is this pattern of conflicted intellectual and developmental engagement with grasslands new: its roots extend back into the colonial administrations of the nineteenth century and, in particular, to their concern for estate crop production and biases against extensive, subsistence agriculture.

This history has been largely ignored in most modern grassland research, which has focused on their biophysical dimensions, as noted by a number of the contributors to the *Agroforestry Systems* (1997) special issue. But the biophysical dimension alone comprises only a small part of the actual ecology of modern grasslands, thinking here of ecology in Bateson's (1972:504) wider sense of that which incorporates both the ecology that we study and the science that we use to study it (see Chapter 6). This is not to deny the biophysical reality of grasslands. Rather, it is to say, following Haraway (1992), that whereas nature is not a discourse, the discipline of ecology is. That is, whereas we do not produce nature, we do produce our ecological understanding of it – and this is an inescapable constraint. As Cronon (1992:1375–1376) writes, "However much we understand that an ecosystem transcends mere humanity, we cannot escape the valuing process that defines our relationship to it."

The purpose of this chapter is to discuss some of these self-imposed and unavoidable constraints, drawing largely on data – both primary and secondary – from Southeast Asia, which has some of the most extensive and most intensively debated anthropogenic grasslands in the world. We will first show how anomalous grasslands are within the forest-oriented environmental views of the Western, industrialized countries and how this view marginalizes both the grasslands and the people who live in and from them. Next we will discuss the grassland myths that dominate thinking in the conservation and development community, focusing on wildland fire, the perceived need for outside intervention, and the discourse of "helping". We will then examine how research programs support the misunderstanding of grasslands, and what an alternative research program might look like. We will conclude by discussing the implications of the interdisciplinary study of grasslands for our understanding of nature and culture, dynamism and stasis, and science and ecology.

II. The forest bias

Grasslands hold an anomalous place within Western environmental thinking, which has been prejudicial to their treatment within global conservation and development planning. This anomaly stems from the relative stature accorded to trees versus grasses in Western world views, and the related focus of Western environmentalism on perceived natural versus cultural landscapes, and forests to the exclusion of other habitats, all of which beliefs have ancient cultural roots.

1. Trees versus grasses in Western and non-Western thought

The tree and the forest occupy a powerful place in Western thought, one that is complex and at times conflicted. Harrison (1992:ix) calls forests the "shadow" of Western civilization, writing: "[T]he governing institutions of the West – religion, law, family, city – originally established themselves in opposition to the forests... ." Their role as "root metaphors" or central organizing images (Ortner 1973) is evident in pioneering works like Frazer's *Golden Bough* (1951), wherein tree beliefs are used as the central optic through which Western and non-Western religion are compared and contrasted. Even today, a writer like Friedman (1999) employs the olive tree as part of a dichotomy – the other half is the Lexus automobile – to describe the tension between local identity and globalization. Davies (1988) humorously summarizes the centrality of the tree to Western thought as follows: "In scaling the tree of knowledge without getting too far out on any limb, in exploring the many branches of thought, and in attempting to get at the root of the matter, we pursue a branching task". Davies (ibid.) attributes this centrality not to cultural or historical factors but to the "intrinsic suggestivity and the inherent attractiveness of trees as the basis for and evocative of symbolic responses." He argues that by comparison, "After all is said it remains true that grass, the most universal and successful of plants, has seldom fed the flames of creative thought to any marked extent. Trees have done so because they possess not only a variety of parts but because they stand over and against human generations in a way which demands acknowledgment."[1] A famous biblical reference to grass undercuts Davies' first point but supports his second one (Isaiah 40.6,7,8):

> A voice says, "Cry out!"
> And I said, "What shall I cry?"
> All people are grass,
> their constancy is like the flower of the field.
> The grass withers, the flower fades,
> when the breath of the Lord blows upon it;

surely the people are grass.
The grass withers, the flower fades;
but the word of our God will stand forever.

In a similar vein to Davies, Pollan (2006:125) writes, "For something people profess to like so much, grass is peculiarly hard for us to see… . Curiously, we seem to like grass less for what it is than for what it isn't – the forest, I mean – and yet we're much more likely to identify with a tree than a blade of grass."

This naturalization of tree symbols has come in for increasing critique among scholars, based in part on the comparative study of tree metaphors in non-Western societies and a more objective view of Western tree metaphors (Bourdieu 1977; Bouquet 1995; Dove 2011; Rival 1998). The impact of this scholarship has been to de-naturalize the tree metaphor and to alert us to the possibility of its historic, cultural, and even political loading. This latter point has been pushed perhaps furthest by Deleuze and Guattari (1987), who compare arboreally-oriented Western thought unfavorably with "rhizome-oriented" Eastern thinking, as noted in the epigraph to this chapter.

Such a sweeping dichotomization of Western tree-based thought and Eastern root-based thought is untenable, however. The central role of tree metaphors documented by Frazer in European folklore and religion is easily matched, as Frazer also found, by the tree-of-life, which is still a central cosmological symbol all over Southeast Asia (see also Chapter 4).[2] This ritual role parallels the centrality of trees in human economic and ecological history. The oldest trade-goods in the world may well be tree exudates. Camphor (*Dryobalanops aromatica* Gaetn. F.), "dragon's blood" (*Daemonorhops Blume spp.*), gum benjamin (*Styrax* spp.), and various pine resins (especially from *Pinus merkusii*) are the oldest trade products of Southeast Asia; and they fit into a trade niche that was originally created for the even more ancient traffic in the tree saps of the Middle East, the fabled frankincense (*Boswellia spp.*) and myrrh (*Commiphora spp.*). Equally important, one of the oldest and most successful forms of agriculture in the Southeast Asian region as well as globally, swidden cultivation, is based on the cyclic clearing, burning, and sowing of forest plots, with trees thus providing the essential environmental conditions for crop cultivation (see Chapter 4). Wherever and whenever swidden agriculture was replaced by more intensive, permanent-field forms of agriculture, the clearing of forest assumed a central role in cultural conceptions of social development and evolution. For example, a common Javanese term for development, *babad alas*, literally means "to clear the forest" (Horne 1974). In Southeast Asia, as elsewhere around the world, the historic valorization of forest-clearing has very recently been reversed. In Guinea in West Africa, modernization until recently meant bringing villages out of the forests into the open (Fairhead and Leach 1996). Forests were associated with primitiveness and open areas with modernity. Now the values have been reversed: modernity demands more forests/afforestation, whereas primitiveness is thought to lead to savannization and deforestation.

FIGURE 3.2 Central Javanese wedding paraphernalia, including *Imperata cylindrica* – on the floor at the feet of the bride

Source: Carol Carpenter

Whereas "arboreal" thinking is not absent from Asia, contra Deleuze and Guattari, "rhizomatic" thinking certainly is present.[3] Contra Davies and Pollan, and showing the cultural rootedness of their assessment of the creative deficit of grasslands, grasses have played an important role in traditional ritual throughout Southeast Asia (e.g., Dove 1986; Wessing 1992), For example, in Hadiwidjojo's (1956) notes on the prominence of *Imperata cylindrica* in traditional Hindu Javanese ritual, he quotes the traditional Javanese saying that "God lies in the tip of a stalk of *Imperata*," which refers to the fact that stalks of *Imperata* were used to sprinkle holy water during traditional Hindu ceremonies. To this day, *Imperata* is used in most domestic rituals in central Java, as in marital ceremonies (Figure 3.2). It is placed under the mat on which bride and groom kneel at one point in the ceremony (Carpenter 1987).

The traditional symbolic loading of grasses in Southeast Asia is also attested to by their role in myths pertaining to the origin of culture, for example among the aboriginal Batek of the Malay Peninsula (Tuck-Po 2004: 16):

> In the beginning, all *bangsa'* "races" were the same. All were Batek. One day, Adam, Tohan's younger brother, set fire to the *lalang* "grass" where the

Batek were living... One family fled into the forest. They left behind their *surat kitab* "religious books"... Another family was near the riverbank. They jumped into the river and took the *surat kitab* with them down river towards the sea. These became the Malays. The Batek looked for their *surat kitab* but the Malays had hidden them. This is why the Malays pray now. So the *surat kitab* belonged to the Batek first.

The prominence of grasses in the landscape of all-important cultural myth attests to their role as part of the basic cultural idiom for thinking about the world.

2. Forest focus of Western environmentalism

The historic dichotomy between forested and civilized spaces in the Western intellectual tradition generally led to analytic thought focusing on the latter. Since classical times, pastoral landscapes have been a greater focus of attention than wild ones, as in Virgil's (2004) *Georgics* and Hesiod's (1914) *Works and Days*. This emphasis has been reversed in the modern era. From its inception in the mid-nineteenth century, and until quite recently, modern ecological science has taken as its subject landscapes devoid of human influence. Although early environmentalists and natural historians like Henry David Thoreau (1964/1854) and Gilbert White (1937/1789) preached the study of proximate and human-impacted landscapes, this gave way to the idealization of distant and non-human landscapes as the most scientific objects of study. For more than a century, as a result, anthropogenic grasslands and perceived non-anthropogenic forests have fallen on either side of an academic *cordon sanitaire*, as discussed in the preceding chapter, with the latter being seen as a more legitimate and the former as a less legitimate subject of research. The distinction is based on two related characteristics: the perceived difference between natural and non-natural vegetation, and the perceived difference between forests and everything else.

The pioneering ethno-botanist Edgar Anderson (1971:45–46) was one of the first to identify the bias against purportedly non-natural vegetation and argue for a different path:

> Once he is in the field, the average taxonomist is an incurable romantic. Watch him take a group of students on a field trip. The nearest fragments of the original flora may be miles away and difficult of access but that is no barrier. With truck, bus, train, jeep, or car, on foot if need be, the class is rushed past the domesticated and semi-domesticated flora among which they spend their lives to the cliff side or peat bog or woodland which most nearly reflects nature in pre-human times.

Anderson argued that the theoretical questions pertaining to human-influenced vegetation are just as interesting and important as those pertaining to so-called "pre-human" or natural vegetation.

The focus of ecology on purportedly non-human ecotypes was reproduced in the younger field of conservation ecology. Buttel (1992) memorably terms this emphasis, in a critique of the focus of international environmentalism on Third World forests, "forest fundamentalism". Stott (1991) similarly writes that "With a few notable exceptions... the 'green' debate in the tropics nearly always focuses on the forests." As Parr et al. (2014) also write, tropical grassy biomes have attracted little of the public interest and conservation attention given to tropical forests. This forest bias is not confined to the exercise of international policy in the tropics; it holds in Western industrialized nations as well. As the environmental historian Cronon (1995:73) writes of the U.S., "[T]o this day there is no national park in the grasslands."

"Forest fundamentalism" can be critiqued on a number of grounds beginning, firstly, with its conception of untouched nature. It is now recognized that the perceived dichotomy between natural and human-impacted landscapes is much more problematic than was once supposed. Work over the past generation in historical ecology and allied fields has demonstrated that what was once thought to be natural or virgin forest has in most cases been modified by human behavior, however subtly (see Balée 1994; Denevan 1992; Raffles 2002 on the Amazon; see Ellen 2008, Neidel 2006, and Puri 2005 on the Indonesian archipelago). The past conception of virgin and unchanging forest is now seen to reflect the premises of an equilibrium-based model of the environment, which has been largely discredited. As Worster (1990:8) says, the forest is now seen as "an erratic, shifting mosaic of trees and other plants." Considerable academic interest has shifted from traditional studies of so-called climax vegetation to fallow dynamics and secondary forests (e.g., Coomes et al. 2000; Chokkalingam et al., 2001; Cairns 2007).

Not only is the natural forest ideal of "forest fundamentalism" chimerical, but also it tends to direct conservation attention away from the mundane landscapes on which people live and work, which can have far-reaching political consequences. As Stott (1991:18) writes of the focus of the global conservation movement on forests: "The dominant forest ideology is most unfortunate because it blinds us to the facts that the rain forests are not, and never were, the most widespread formations in the tropics, and that the majority of people eking out a living in the tropical world do so in lands derived from other, non-forest, formations, above all the savannas." In short, the forest bias is depriviledging for other land covers like savannas and grasslands and for the peoples who live in them. The lack of attention to these non-forest biotas in policy circles is implicitly or explicitly delegitimizing and thus inimical to their continued existence.

Alternative conservation visions were and are possible. There is a growing literature on conservation in human-modified landscapes (Dove, Sajise, and Doolittle 2011). It is at least in part historical contingency that kept the U.S. from taking this direction to begin with. Stewart (2005) suggests that if Muir had studied the pastoral landscape of the American south, instead of the western wilderness, the trajectory of American – and later global – environmentalism might have been very different. McWilliams (2011) supports this thesis with his inspired study of what grasses and weeds meant to the American colonists, who had to reconcile Old World intolerance of weeds with a New World human ecology in which living with weeds was unavoidable.[4] Truett (2010), in his recently published *Grass*, also directly challenges the basis for forest fundamentalism by arguing that we humans and our culture and identity evolved with grasslands and thus have an innate affinity for them. Parr et al. (2014) critiques contemporary programs like Reducing Emissions from Deforestation and Degradation (REDD) that are premised on the goodness of replacing grassland with forest.

3. The morality of vegetative trajectories

Forest fundamentalism affects the way that the biophysical evidence of environmental change – what Latour (1993) calls "the testimony of non-humans" – is interpreted. It predisposes observers to see grasslands as statements not just about environmental relations but specifically about failed environmental relations. As Potter (1988: 129) writes of Dutch colonial views of the extensive grasslands of Southeast Kalimantan: "The very existence of the Hulu Sungai... with its *sawah* [irrigated rice] fields in close proximity to grass-covered uplands dominated by *Imperata cylindrica* and followed at a distance by swidden sites in secondary forest, was felt to be an object lesson to all" (cf. Table 3.1). Colonial officials ignorant of and unreceptive to local traditions of grassland management did not read this landscape as an intentionally "patchy", diversified, and productive one. Instead, they read the proximity of grassland and non-grassland as a moral story about the unwanted spread of grasslands, about environmental decline.

There is a teleology to all stories about environmental change, with a specific directionality, and this is central to their moral dimension (Cronon 1992:1370; Braun 2002:216). The presence of grasslands is commonly interpreted as a "lesson" about what could happen to non-grassland covers if sufficient care is not taken; but the reverse and ecologically equally likely lesson is rarely if ever

TABLE 3.1 Spatial patterning of Banjarese land use in south Kalimantan

Village center	←————————————————————→				Village periphery
River bank	River bank	Ravines	Grasslands	Young forest	Older forest
Gardens	Rubber	Irrigated rice	Rain-fed rice	Swiddens	Rattan etc.
Dwellings	Other trees	Cattle		Fallowed forest	

Source: Michael R. Dove

drawn. That is, observers almost never interpret non-grassland covers – e.g., forest – as a lesson about what could happen to grasslands. Vandenbeldt (1993:3) states the conventional wisdom as follows: "*Imperata cylindrica* grasslands are a fire-climax vegetation type derived from cleared forest lands." Yet it would be equally ecologically valid, but unheard of, to describe *Imperata* as "an unstable vegetation type often terminating in closed forest" or to describe tropical rainforest as a "climax vegetation type derived from unmanaged grasslands". Indeed, the possibility of a spontaneous succession from grassland to non-grassland may be politically unwelcome in certain circumstances. For example, Fairhead and Leach (1996) suggest that the historic progression from grassland to forest in Guinea is interpreted by the government as just the opposite, in part to attract more funding for afforestation projects.

Increasingly, however, grassland history is being interpreted not in terms of an equilibrium model, which assumes a static condition that is only periodically and unnaturally upset, but in terms of a non-equilibrium model in which ongoing perturbation is assumed to be the natural state of affairs. The equilibrium model, which was based on work from Clements' (1916) research on vegetative succession to Odum's (1953) research on homeostasis, has been supplanted by the non-equilibrium model over the past generation in much of the natural and social sciences. Worster (1990:3,11) writes that "Odum's ecosystem, with its stress on cooperation, social organization, and environmentalism" has been replaced with an image of "nature characterized by highly individualistic associations, constant disturbance, and incessant change". Worster (1990:3) summarizes the change as one from "a study of equilibrium, harmony, and order" to a study of "disturbance, disharmony, and chaos." Our understanding of grassland ecology has dramatically changed as a result of this shift in explanatory paradigms. Whereas most scholars once saw grasslands as exemplars of ecological stability, they now see them as just the opposite, as models of instability and disturbance (Worster 1990). The older paradigm prevails to this day in much of the policy and development community, however, where it is still assumed that grasslands are a stable and tenacious climax community, which will not disappear unless dramatic steps are taken to make them disappear (Truett 2010).

Scholars now agree that many grasslands depend for their existence upon continued human perturbation of the environment, without which they will in fact disappear. This is well illustrated by Laris' (2008) study of the role of human activity as one of the buffering agents in maintaining the balance between grasses and trees in the unstable savannas of southern Mali. In Dove's (2008) study of the Banjarese of South Kalimantan, similarly, he found that continuous management inputs were critical to the maintenance of grasslands (Figures 3.3 and 3.4).[5] This is reflected in the fact that if grassland is left alone for so many years that the signs of such inputs begin to disappear and a natural process of afforestation commences, tenure to that patch of grassland lapses and it is considered to be a free good. To understand the dynamics of such a system, it is necessary to ask what reasons local communities may have to

FIGURE 3.3 Banjarese oxen and plough for cultivating grasslands
Source: Michael R. Dove

FIGURE 3.4 Banjarese livestock grazing on *Imperata cylindrica*
Source: Michael R. Dove

continue or discontinue the burning that typically accounts for the appearance versus disappearance, respectively, of the grasslands. This is a key question that conservation and development planners typically fail to ask.

III. Grassland myths and development interventions

A critical component of the "practical ecology" (Dove 1986; see Sahlins 1976a) of the grasslands of Southeast Asia is the extent to which local peoples and non-local policymakers perceive them differently. Such differences are a decisive factor in the repeated failure of government efforts at grassland "reclamation"; yet they are resolutely left out of even the most insightful analyses of grassland development (see Vandenbeldt's volume [1993] on *Imperata* in Southeast Asia as an example). As De Foresta and Michon (1997:106) write:

> The reforestation problem is still too often viewed as a pure forest plantation problem. If this approach was correct, reforestation could successfully be achieved by forestry services through technical programs. The numerous failures (caused by fires, encroachment by farmers) encountered by this kind of program show that this approach is too narrow, mainly because it fails to address the roots of the problem, namely the causes for *Imperata* grasslands' existence.

The fact that local and extra-local parties often systematically disagree about grasslands is regarded as an obstacle on the path to tackling the problem of grasslands, whereas it should be regarded as the central problematic itself.

1. "Wild fire" and "unmanaged grasslands"

One of the principal differences in the perception of grasslands by local versus non-local actors is that they are unmanaged. Outside observers usually recognize the role of local communities in grassland succession, but they usually do not recognize that this role is an intentional one. In fact, grassland succession is normally not an accidental or unavoidable transformation of the landscape. Rather, it is a recognized, anticipated, and desired part of the local "built landscape". In contrast, official views of *Imperata* and other grasslands tend to assume that they are unintended deviations from the intended landscape.

Prejudices against burning are central to the official view of grasslands as unmanaged. Burning of grassland (or forest or brush) usually signifies to officialdom the absence of rational community resource management; whereas it typically represents for local communities the foremost tool of grassland management. Fire is one of the chief means by which succession from forest to grassland is precipitated and by which succession from grassland back to forest is inhibited.[6] This may be the most misrepresented aspect of the ecology of tropical grasslands, and it is also the most ancient. Fire, which is the main evolutionary factor in the establishment of grasslands and savannas (Bond and Keely 2005), is also the linkage in an ancient co-evolutionary relationship between human society and grasslands. Komarek (1967:154) suggests that early humans were an evolutionary product of fire environments and were, indeed, "fire selected" in evolutionary terms. Stephen J. Pyne (1993:246), perhaps the leading contemporary researcher on fire and human society, similarly argues that the domestication of fire was integral to the development and spread of human society:

> Everywhere that humans went – and they went everywhere – they carried fire. The hominid flame propagated across the continents like an expanding ring of fire, remaking everything it touched. Within that ring lived humans; outside it, the wild still reigned... Much as humans killed wolves and propagated dogs, so they drove back the domain of wildfire and substituted a regime based on anthropogenic burning.

Facetious remarks to the effect that some traditional groups lived off fire were not as far from the truth as their speakers may have thought. As Ernest Giles observed of the Australian aborigines in 1889 (cited in Hodgkinson et al. 1984:141):[7] "The natives were about, burning, burning, ever burning; one would think they were of the famed salamander race, and lived on fire instead of water."

Human beings do not just use fire environments, they also reproduce these environments through the use of fire. This makes humans, in ecological terms, "pyrophytes", meaning a species whose traits include those that make fire more likely. Pyne (1982:69) argues that humans are foremost among pyrophytes in that they can "project fire rather than endure it." Among plants, grasses are a major pyrophyte. D'Antonio and Vitousek (1992:73) write that grassland and fire can be considered to be an "identity" and we can speak of a "pyrophytic grass life form." Referring to *Imperata* in Southeast Asia, Fosberg (1962:121) wrote one-half century ago: "It may be thought of as the true 'climax' of the *man-shifting-cultivation-burning complex* in this part of the world. *Imperata*, with the tough matted wiry buried rhizomes, is about as near as nature comes to producing a really fire-proof plant." In the fire-climax grasslands of Southeast Asia, two major pyrophytes, people and grasses, come together in a mutually supportive relationship. People and grass both promote fire, they both benefit from it, and they both benefit from the other's involvement. The association of people, grass, and fire is far from accidental, therefore. The strong tendency in officialdom to insist otherwise is reflected in this explanation of the great 1997 fires in Indonesia by the manager of a para-statal plantation on Pulau Bangka: "There are some types of tall grasses which in strong winds catch fire" (Agence France-Presse 1997).

The predisposition of officialdom to misunderstand fire's role in the peasant agricultural tool kit is not confined to Southeast Asia and less-developed countries. Not so long ago a debate raged in the United States over the use of fire in local community management of grasslands and forests. Thus, in 1939 the U.S. Forest Service commissioned a staff psychologist, John P. Shea, to find out why the residents of the South burned the forests. The results of the study were published one year later in the infamous article, "Our Pappies Burned the Woods" (Shea 1940). Shea's principal finding was that burning by rural dwellers was due to "emotional satisfaction." He wrote, "The sight and sound and odor of burning woods provide excitement for a people who dwell in an environment of low stimulation and who quite naturally crave excitement" (Shea 1940:162). Shea (1940:160) ascribed the persistence of fire burning in the face of government proscription to the strength of tradition, saying that "Their strongest law is the custom of their forefathers." He quoted one of his informants as saying, "Woods burnin' is right. We allus done it. Our pappies burned th' woods an' their pappies afore 'em. It war right fer them an' it's right fer us" (Shea 1940:159). Shea refused to accept his informants' own ecologically-oriented explanations for burning. Thus, he subsequently quoted the aforementioned informant as saying, "Fires do a heap of good, kill the' boll weevil, snakes, ticks, an' bean beetles. Greens up the grass. Keeps us healthy by killin' fever germs" (1940:159). In response, Shea (1940:162) wrote, "Their explanations that woods fires kill off snakes, boll weevil and serve other economic ends are something more than mere ignorance. They are the defensive beliefs of a disadvantaged culture group."

With the benefit of hindsight, we can see that the forest psychologist's views of forest fires were really his views of rural people. Similarly, official mainstream views of Southeast Asia's grasslands are really, in part, views concerning the people who dwell in them. As Raymond Williams (1980:67,70–71) said in an oft-quoted passage, arguments about nature are often really about culture: "The idea of nature contains an extraordinary amount of human history... . What is often being argued, it seems to me, in the idea of nature is the idea of man; and this not only generally, or in ultimate ways, but the idea of man in society, indeed the ideas of kinds of societies." Thus, government critiques of local grasslands often amount to critiques of the local communities; and government efforts to "rehabilitate" grasslands often amount to efforts to restructure economic or political relations with the local communities. This dimension of grassland ecology has been overlooked by even the most astute observers. Clifford Geertz's famous characterization (1971: 25) of *Imperata* grasslands as Southeast Asia's "green desert" shows that even one of the most famous social scientists of the twentieth century failed to see the political bias in the reports of *Imperata*'s perniciousness (Sherman 1980:126). The view of local peoples that is reflected in many official views of Southeast Asia's grasslands is a view of the quintessential "other." The grasslands and their inhabitants are together seen as unmanaged, unproductive, and – in Scott's term (1998) – worrisomely "illegible."

2. Interventions and failures

This view of grasslands as the "other" is associated with a particularly hostile developmental stance toward them. From the colonial to the postcolonial era, most government policies have problematized tropical anthropogenic grasslands and sought to replace them with other land-uses, albeit with very limited success. The persistence of such unsuccessful policies can be attributed to the opportunities that they create for development intervention in local resource governance.

The basis for development interventions in grasslands lies in the way that they are classified. During colonial as well as post-colonial times throughout Southeast Asia, anthropogenic grasslands have been labeled "wastelands" or something similar, a term that is inherently supportive of alternate land-uses (as are terms like "green desert"). The connotation of an unchanging and degraded ecosystem is prejudicial both to recognition of any existing active management of the land and to any local claim to the land. This connotation helps to construct an official landscape, which can be contrasted to what Jackson (1984) calls the "vernacular" landscape. Jackson writes (1984:148), "A landscape, like a language, is the field of perpetual conflict and compromise between what is established by authority and what the vernacular insists upon preferring." The gap between the former and the latter has been marked in the case of Southeast Asia's grasslands.

Beginning in colonial times and extending throughout Southeast Asia, national governments have typically viewed grasslands – especially those dominated by *Imperata* – as an unproductive and undesirable land-use that should be replaced with something seen as more productive, such as forests, plantations, or permanent agricultural fields. A generation of research before World War II and another following it has been devoted to promoting such replacement. These efforts have been characterized by an emphasis on technological innovation with limited consideration for economic costs, except on plantations, and/or social costs (cf. Whyte 1962). The perceived need to reclaim grasslands has persisted to the present day. For example, in the waning years of Suharto's "New Order" regime, the Indonesian Ministry of Forests designated grasslands as one of five priority land-use types for conversion to industrial tree plantations (Hamzah 1993); and up to the present day, *Imperata* is seen as a prime candidate for reclamation by tree crops (Mulyoutami et al. n.d.).

Modern efforts to reclaim grasslands have been remarkably problematic. They have seldom succeeded at any large scale and without subsidies, beyond the test plots and pilot projects, especially where there are proximate farming communities. Such chronic failures of development planning have prompted scholars over the past couple of decades to re-think the concept of "failure" itself. That is, if interventions always fail, then what does "failure" mean? The development community itself has typically blamed failure on recalcitrant rural peoples, sometimes on poor project implementation, but rarely if ever on misguided development policy or planning. But even the most accurate explanation, misguided policy and planning, is naive, because it treats grassland reclamation failures as aberrations as opposed to normal phenomena that are deeply embedded in wider social and historical processes. As Hecht and Cockburn (1989:99) write of development failures in the Amazon: "To take 'poor policy' as the precipitating factor in deforestation is to see 'policy' as something conceived and executed by technocrats secluded from a country's political economy, and is an extraordinarily naive assumption." Such assumptions result in an inability to correct, and thus a tendency to perpetuate, development failures.

Some light is shed on what failure means in the reclamation of Southeast Asia's grasslands by examining the occasional examples of success. The historic development of the famous Deli tobacco cultivation system in Sumatra in the second half of the nineteenth century is one such example (Pelzer 1978a; cf. Bartlett 1956). During the early decades of the industry, *Imperata* spread like wildfire in the tobacco fields. It consumed the tobacco fields after the initial harvest, but the planters little cared because they were abandoning their fields after each cropping. But then the planters' attitude changed, and the *Imperata* simply disappeared, as summarized by Pelzer (1978a:29–30):

> So long as the planters believed that their land could produce only *one* tobacco crop, they did nothing to combat the spread of grasses. Once they realized, however, that they had been far too pessimistic and that tobacco could be planted repeatedly provided the land lay fallow under the second-growth forest, or *blukar*, for not less than seven or eight years, they took measures to prevent the burning of the grasses and the concomitant killing of young trees... . These actions greatly altered the physiognomy of the tobacco plantations, as second-growth forest smothered the grasses and spread steadily at the expense of the savannas.

In short, then as now, the appearance and disappearance of *Imperata* is much more a function of human wishes than the outcome of a fierce battle between people and nature. This is drolly attested to by Bartlett's (2008: 88) observation that *Imperata* was replaced, "regardless of economy", whenever Europeans wanted to establish golf courses in the tropics (cf. Bartlett 1955, I: 401).

There are apposite and equally surprising case studies of successful grassland management from elsewhere in the tropics. One of the most famous of these is the study by James Fairhead and Melissa Leach (1996) from Guinea, in West Africa, the landscape of which is today dominated by forest islands in the midst of savanna. This landscape has been interpreted by outsiders for a century or more as natural forest remnants in a sea of human-altered vegetation. The orthodox premise is that this land was all once forested, and that these forest islands are all that is left due to human abuse. The forest islands are interpreted, thus, as evidence of vanishing nature at the hands of local people. Fairhead and Leach persuasively argue, however, that this view represents a backwards misreading of the environmental history. They marshal a complex set of data to argue that the forest islands actually represent portions of the savanna that have been tipped from grasslands into forest as the result of human activity. They also argue that the number and size of these islands have been increasing, not decreasing over time, in association with increased human settlement. They see a completely different trajectory, thus: they see a pattern of afforestation not deforestation.[8] And they see the role of people as diametrically reversed: they see people as crucial agents in spreading the forest, not diminishing it.

3. Development logic

The Deli tobacco example demonstrates that successful management of *Imperata* grasslands is not technologically difficult. This is also obvious from a number of studies that have been conducted of traditional peasant management of *Imperata* in Southeast Asia, which reveal systems even more sophisticated and successful than that of the Deli tobacco planters (Clarke 1966; Conklin 1959; Dove 1986, 2008; Potter 1997; Sherman 1980). With few exceptions, however, these local successes have been ignored by developers, who treat local communities as incapable of managing grasslands on their own. This raises the question: What are the implications of portraying skilled, indigenous resource managers as needy victims, as people confronted with resource degradation that they cannot cope with? In short, what are the implications of outsiders asking, "How can we help?"

The representation of a situation as one in which help is needed is empowering of the one doing the helping and dis-empowering of the one being helped (Edelman 1974). It is critical to its own self-interest for any development agency to be able to publicly portray potential development subjects as needy, in particular with respect to the resources that the agency offers (Escobar 1995). It is critically important for any development agency, in short, to create a conceptual welcoming niche for itself, as Ferguson (1990) demonstrated in his pioneering analysis of the development programs of the World Bank and the Canadian Agency for International Development in Lesotho. These agencies, in order to create a niche for themselves in Lesotho, portrayed a nation that was essentially a labor reserve for the South African mines as an autonomous, subsistence-oriented agrarian society. Reality, in short, was upended. The larger the potential niche, the greater the self-interest of the development agency in making this effort. Estimates in Indonesia, for example, have suggested that *Imperata* grasslands alone cover over 10 million hectares, which is an area so large as to give to its conversion to alternative uses profound economic, social, and political implications.

Anthropogenic grasslands are one of a complex of perceived resource development problems – including swidden cultivation, wildland fire, etc. – that appear to be insoluble; but this very insolubility raises questions about the validity of the problem (Thompson et al. 1986). There often is no grassland problem in the sense as conceived by the development agency, which is thus in

FIGURE 3.5 Javanese transmigrant grazing cattle on *Imperata cylindrica* in South Sumatra

Source: Michael R. Dove

the position of offering a solution in search of a problem. Often the only real problem in grassland landscapes is the conflict between the local community and central policymakers. For example, Javanese transmigrants in South Sumatra say that *Alang-alang hanya menjadi persoalan kalau dilihat petugas proyek* (*Imperata* only becomes a problem [for the transmigrants] if it is seen by the transmigration project officials) (Dove 1986) (Figure 3.5).

The reverse of this is also true: officialdom only becomes the "solution" to *Imperata* if they can depict it as a problem. A startling example of this comes from the southern U.S., where in 2009 the state government of Alabama secured $6 million in federal stimulus money to initiate "Alabama's War on Cogongrass", "cogongrass" being the Philippine name for *Imperata*. According to a *New York Times* reporter who wrote a story about the new program, *Imperata* is thought to have come into the state early in the twentieth century as packing material is shipments from East Asia, but had come to be seen as an environmental threat to the state and indeed the entire country (Barry 2009). The administrators of the project see cogongrass as useless: "Its serrated leaves and grainy composition mean that animals with even the most indiscriminate palates – goats, for example – say no thanks." They also see it as aggressive: "It can take over fields and forests, ruining crops, destroying native plants, upsetting the ecosystem. It is very difficult to kill." As one of the directors of the program said, "People think this is just a grass, they don't understand that cogongrass can replace an entire ecosystem." The program's proposed solution is massive state-wide use

Nature, society, and science in anthropogenic grasslands   **61**

FIGURE 3.6 Braving volcanic hazards on the slopes of Mt. Merapi in Central Java to cut *Imperata cylindrica* for stall-fed cattle

Source: Michael R. Dove

of potent herbicides (Arsenal and Roundup). All of the premises of the program appear to be completely uninformed by a century of study of *Imperata* in Asia, specifically relating to the facts that it is very palatable (when immature) to livestock (Figures 3.4, 3.5, and 3.6), and also wild herbivores (Figure 3.7); it does not spread, indeed will not even persist, if not burned; and it can be destroyed by simply turning over the clods with a digging stick or hoe and exposing the roots to the sun. Most important, and characteristic of a century of anti-*Imperata* programs in Asia as well, there appears to have been no effort in this program to ask what land-use practices were driving the spread of the grass. The program accorded all agency to *Imperata* itself and none to humans, except for the government and its contractors with their herbicides.

IV. Understanding and mis-understanding anthropogenic grasslands

The study of how knowledge of anthropogenic grasslands is produced and managed affords new insights into the roles played in everyday life by knowledge and ignorance. Fairhead and Leach (1996) urge a Foucaultian approach to the

FIGURE 3.7 Banjarese hunting wild cattle on grasslands near the last Banjarese *kraton* 'palace'

Source: Schwaner (1853–1854)

mis-reading of environmental histories of forest-grassland change, viewing it not simply as an absence of correct reading but as an actively constructed mis-reading in its own right:

> While technicists might see the problem lying in "bad science", and its solution in "good science" and training, we have argued that there are much broader and more intransigent reasons why the degradation view has made sense, which impinge on – or condition – any scientific endeavor. In this sense, one can speak of a Foucauldian discourse of degradation.

Braun takes this critique one step further, by suggesting that all representation has partisan dimensions. He writes (Braun 2002:218), "[T]o assume that power operates through *mis*representation (or mystification) is to leave re-presentation itself unquestioned; it is to forget that truth is not prior to, but always an effect of, its representation." Fairhead and Leach (1996:261) distinguish between passive ignorance and active misunderstanding by the state: "The degradation position has been sustained... not on the basis of ignorance, but through the continual production of supportive knowledge." One of the ways of amassing supportive knowledge is through not amassing *un*supportive knowledge: "In Kissidougou, assessments of vegetative changes [by government and development agencies] have never drawn on historical data sets in more than a cursory way" (Fairhead and Leach 1996:50).

1. Grassland studies

Considerable research has been done on Southeast Asia's grasslands; but it has rarely been so directed as to challenge the dominant developmental myths (see Dove's 2008 edited compendium of the exceptional cases). The most common research topic is the elimination of grasslands. Abundant experiments have been done on the eradication of grasslands through the planting of replacement grasses, mechanical tillage, and especially the use of herbicides (Bagnall-Oakeley et al. 1997). Some research has focused on the conversion of grasslands to agroforestry systems (e.g., Garrity 1997); but the value of these latter studies has been limited by the lack of additional study of the economics of such conversions. As Tomich et al. (1997) write, "There has been almost no economic analysis of agroforestry approaches to conversion of *Imperata* grasslands."

The indifference to the realities of local systems of resource-use that is reflected in this neglect is also seen in the absence of study of local grassland management systems and ways of building on them. As Bagnall-Oakeley et al. (1997:100) write: "There has been relatively little research into integrated *Imperata* management practices for Smallholders... There has been even less participatory on-farm research that takes account of Smallholders' views in the development of technologies for their use." Aspects of these smallholder systems that are inconsistent with the dominant grassland myths are almost never empirically examined. This applies to the myths pertaining to grasslands' purported (1) infertility, (2) lack of conservation of soil and water, (3) uselessness for agriculture and animal husbandry, and (4) irrationality of local management practices, especially those involving the use of fire. Bagnall-Oakeley et al. (1997:100) write:

> The relationship between *Imperata* in smallholdings, its control, and the risk of fire have not been researched at all as far as we are aware... Its neglect can probably be explained by the fact that fire-related issues are not normally addressed by agricultural research programmes. Consequently, fire is not recognised by researchers as a research issue; not recognised by research institutes as being within their mandate...

As Bagnall-Oakeley et al. also note, the research lacunae extend to some of the most obvious agroforestry topics. They write, "It is well known that *Imperata* competition can have a severe retarding effect on rubber trees during the first few years after planting, although there has been only one published piece of research on this subject" (Bagnall-Oakeley et al. 1997:85). This lack of research on subjects of such importance is remarkable, but see Mulyoutami et al. (n.d.) for a recent exception. As Bagnall-Oakeley et al. (1997:101) conclude, "One would expect that this subject would have been well-researched. It appears, however, that it has not."

When data that do not support the orthodox views of grasslands are gathered, they are resolutely ignored – which can lead to tell-tale, schizophrenic statements.

For example, one leading scholar of Southeast Asian grasslands (Vandenbeldt 1993) wrote in a single publication:

> *Imperata* grasslands in SEA are a "wasteland" *and* its value as fodder "appears not to be inferior to that of [improved] grasses".
>
> The soil under *Imperata* is "considered infertile" *and* it "may occur in all kinds of soil".
>
> "[*Imperata*] has poor value in reducing runoff and adds to the risk of erosion and flooding" *and* it "can be useful as a ground cover to preserve soil condition, prevent soil erosion, and consolidate dikes and dams."

One could not hope to see a better example than this of the power of a hegemonic discourse to unwittingly deflect the production of knowledge about a natural resource away from reality.

There is a marked lack of study regarding the role of policymakers toward grasslands. Policymakers characteristically problematize the grassland landscape and proximate communities; but they do not question their own premises that these grasslands are unmanaged and unproductive or that their rehabilitation is economically feasible. Yet Tomich et al. (1997) maintain that given current technologies, markets, and government policies, it is unprofitable or at best marginally profitable to convert large areas of existing grasslands in Southeast Asia to other uses (cf. Vandenbeldt 1993). The general lack of critical reflection regarding development policy in grasslands is clearly at least partly responsible for the failure of so many of these same policies.

The fact that needful grassland research has not been done, or has been done in error, or has been done correctly but without impact, is sociologically meaningful. As Thompson et al. (1986) have written, repeated developmental mistakes are development "signposts," which point us toward important development truths. The truth being pointed toward in this case is that the misunderstanding of anthropogenic grasslands is integral to their "practical ecology". Such misunderstanding is not a simple function of the challenge of understanding Southeast Asia's natural environment. Rather, it is a function of past and present structures of political and economic power in the region. Systemic misunderstanding of grassland dynamics is not an accident but rather a determined product, following Weber (1946), of particular political-economic institutions. This is reflected in the fact that the misunderstandings are not random: they are consistent in both content and implication. This is reflected, for example, in patterns of grassland research that systematically avoid critical topics like local land uses and rights. Thus, the dominant views of grasslands in policy circles in Southeast Asia tend to privilege the science, policy, and resource-use regimes of the region's states and their elites, as opposed to the knowledge and resource-use systems of local communities, many of which are politically and socially marginal.

2. Implications for future studies

The most obvious insight for conservation and development planning from this review of anthropogenic grasslands in Southeast Asia is that many such lands are integrated into and valued within local systems of agriculture and animal husbandry. Such grasslands are managed and maintained, therefore, they are not simply unmanaged climaxes. The corollary insight is that such grasslands will be valued far more highly in the eyes of local peoples than by extra-local observers and administrators.

In any development plan to eradicate or replace anthropogenic grasslands, therefore, the first question to ask – one that is remarkably rarely asked – is whether local valuations of these lands and local roles in their dynamics have been given due consideration. In particular, simplistic schemes to reforest such grasslands, based on exogenous views of their lack of utility, should be critically examined. The niche for tree cultivation in such lands – when they are being locally managed and exploited, and when conversion to other uses may be rightfully viewed with antipathy – may be nonexistent.

One of the most important but overlooked dimensions of anthropogenic grasslands, and one that should be at the forefront of planning of any development intervention, is their political character. These grasslands are typically contested landscapes, the focus of diametrically opposed assessments of existing and alternative land-uses. As a result, any proposed reforestation of anthropogenic grasslands is politically inflected. The cultivation of trees in such lands often undermines local tenurial relations and enhances external control by the state and/or its elites, which may foredoom any intervention before it even begins.

Research priorities for anthropogenic grasslands include the on-farm research of such topics as the economics of grassland conversion and the dynamics of grass–tree interactions such as that between *Imperata* and rubber (*Hevea brasiliensis*). Fire management is a particularly important research topic for grasslands. In any anthropogenic grassland, fire tolerance is the foremost criteria for successful tree growth. The possible role of fire-tolerant trees within local schemes of grassland management is a greatly understudied topic.

V. Summary and conclusions

Anthropogenic grasslands, meaning grasslands that owe their existence to human activity, are one of the most important land covers of the tropics, but their management is dominated by conflicted and contested views, which is reflected in the problematic record of grassland development intervention. This chapter analyzes the historic, cultural, political, and institutional factors that affect the way grasslands are viewed, drawing largely on data from Southeast Asia. These data suggest that perceptions of grasslands are colored in part by the marginal place that they occupy in the cosmologies of Western industrialized societies, which have idealized forest covers in the modern era. Consequently, national and international agencies view grasslands not as a common land cover but as a conservation and development problem. The agendas of conservation and development agencies are often not grounded in a proper understanding of the local human and bio-physical ecology of grasslands or of successful local grassland management practices. And research on many of the most important dimensions of grassland management is absent or poorly conducted and/or utilized.

The greatest gaps in our understanding of grasslands are a function of the past research emphasis on natural as opposed to social dynamics of anthropogenic grasslands, a curious emphasis given the obvious fact that the grasslands in question are a human product. This emphasis reflects a still persisting difficulty in science in bridging natural and cultural arenas, which is the raison d'être of the present volume. Ironically, the success of local, smallholder grassland managers rests precisely upon such a bridge – articulating field and forest, culture and nature. Interdisciplinary research, with a mandate to cross this same divide, is uniquely suited to studying grasslands and offering ways to improve their management. How are the dynamics of succession of ligneous and herbaceous species balanced and managed in the grasslands? How do the economics and ecology of grassland management fit into wider land-use systems often comprising both annuals and perennials and both more- and less-intensive cultivation methods? And how and why do different actors – local as well as non-local – see the grasslands in different ways? These questions, and others like them, are well-suited to interdisciplinary perspectives and approaches.

This analysis of tropical anthropogenic grasslands also raises a number of points of relevance to the wider natural resource management issues of the day. It shows that how we draw the line between natural processes on the one hand and cultural processes on the other is often highly subjective and self-interested. It shows that whether we view the environment as dynamic or static has enormous implications for both environmental and social relations. It shows that where we locate agency, in both society and environment, is fraught with implications for state projects of intervention.

Notes

1 The longevity of trees does seem to impress itself on human thought in many societies, both Western and non-Western. For example, among the Kantu' of West Kalimantan, Indonesia, there was traditionally a proscription against the use of Borneo's foremost timber, from the ironwood tree (*Eusideroxylon zwageri*), in house construction. The Kantu' rationale for this proscription was that the durability of this wood and anything constructed from it surpassed and thus challenged the life-span of the people using it.
2 See Schärer (1963) on the tree of life among the Ngaju of Indonesian Borneo.
3 Cf. Mosko's (2009) interesting analysis of "fractal" tubers as metaphors for human social action in Melanesia.
4 Runk (2009), drawing on the aforementioned work of Deleuze and Guattari (1987), has critiqued the "arboreal" focus of conservation NGOs in Panama, based on

her analysis of the riverine focus of indigenous peoples in the region. Cf. Carse's (2014: 217) analysis of water hyacinth in the Panama Canal: "Seeing an iconic canal through a weed illustrates how profoundly our infrastructures are entangled with our political ecologies."
5 In South Kalimantan, Dove (2008) found a system of active local management of the grasslands, of which people said "We could not live without them." The Banjarese were cultivating the grasslands using brush-sword, fire, and cattle-drawn ploughs, and they reaped an average crop of 2,200 kilograms of rice per hectare, for up to seven years in a row followed by a three-year fallow. They also were burning the grasslands to create graze for their livestock.
6 There are additional complexities to the human ecology of grasslands, of course. Grazing cattle on grasslands reduces the fuel load and thus reduces the severity and extent of fires (Bond and Keely 2005). It is ironic, therefore, that policymakers, in their perennial search for successful fire-management techniques, have been so resistant to acknowledging the grazing potential of *Imperata* grasslands.
7 The Australian aborigines are still famous for their sophisticated use of fire in land management (Lewis 1989).
8 There are other unexpected cases of tropical afforestation (e.g., Hecht 2010).

4

HIGH MODERN VS LOCAL FOLK VIEWS OF DEARTH AND ABUNDANCE

Studying failure vs success in resource management systems

> Alice looked round her in great surprise. "Why I do believe we've been under this tree the whole time! Everything's just as it was!" "Of course it is," said the Queen. "What would you have it?" "Well, in *our* country," said Alice, still panting a little, "you'd generally get to somewhere else – if you ran very fast for a long time as we've been doing." "A slow sort of country!" said the Queen. "Now, *here*, you see, it takes all the running *you* can do, to keep in the same place. If you want to get somewhere else, you must run at least twice as fast as that."
>
> Lewis Carroll (1960:210)

> All progress in capitalism is a progress in the art, not only of robbing the laborer, but of robbing the soil.
>
> Karl Marx (1887)

The preceding chapter dealt in part with the perceived morality versus immorality of differing trajectories of vegetative succession: forest to grassland versus grassland to forest. This chapter deals with the perceived morality versus immorality of different resource-use systems, and the linkage of this especially to differences in whether the boundaries of the system are drawn – are conceived of – narrowly or broadly.

I. Introduction

Every four to five years on average, the upper canopy trees of Borneo's rain forest experience a mast flowering and fruiting, which is the synchronized or so-called "gregarious" fruiting of a number of different tree species at the same time. This phenomenon is eagerly awaited by Borneo's indigenous, forest-dwelling tribesmen, the swidden-cultivating Dayak, who exploit it for both subsistence and commercial purposes. The tribesmen believe that this bounty comes with a price, however: one group, the Kantu', say that the spirits of the forest demand a tribute of *s'igi' kolak mata mensia* "one basket of human eyes"[1] in exchange for every mast season.[2]

We suggest that this belief is about precisely what it appears to be about, namely an exchange of resources between people and the environment (between culture and nature).[3] In particular, we suggest that this belief is about the morality of this exchange, about the morality of environmental relations. This belief, in other words, is the basis for a "moral ecology." We base the phrase "moral ecology," in part, on James C. Scott's (1976) concept of "moral economy" , which is itself derived from the work of E. P. Thompson (1963, 1971). According to Scott's work, the moral economy is one that guarantees basic subsistence through the social investment, as opposed to extraction, of agricultural surplus. We suggest that the moral ecology is one that guarantees the basic sustainability of both society and environment through investment in exchange relations of great time-depth and spatial-breadth.

Time and space are important issues in the discussion of moral ecology, because the "morality" of a given ecological system is expressed in when and where one draws its boundaries and, thus, in when and where moral strictures apply or cease to apply. This is, in short, a question of boundaries. The question of how to bound the unit of analysis has been a subject of interest within anthropology since its inception, beginning with the work of Wissler (1922), Kroeber (1963), and Steward (1955) on culture areas. In the 1950s and 1960s, scholars like Barth (1956/2008) and Rappaport (1968/1984) suggested that the boundaries of social systems are like the boundaries of ecosystems. Such parochial scales were subsequently repudiated by neo-Marxist and world systems scholars, and then by political ecologists, who suggested that the concept of the autonomous local community was a pernicious myth (Netting 1990/2008; Wallerstein 1974, 1980; Wolf 1982). A succeeding generation of scholars have taken issue with world systems perspectives, however, on the grounds that they depict local peoples as having less agency than they really have and also privilege the idea of a removed, all-knowing observer (Ingold 1993/2008).[4]

We propose to illustrate the concept of moral ecology by contrasting the exploitation of mast-fruiting and swidden agriculture in Borneo on the one hand, and on the other hand the cultivation of high-yielding variety (HYV) "green revolution" rice in Java and elsewhere around the globe. Mast-fruiting and swidden agriculture illustrate our concept of moral ecology; green revolution agriculture illustrates its opposite. Most if not all ecologies, like all economics, have a foundation in moral thinking, but there can be important distinctions in the logic involved.[5] The two moralities under review here differ principally in the way they account for bounty versus shortfall. Thus, the Dayak tribesmen of Borneo view mast-fruiting and bountiful swidden harvests as a recurring but unpredictable and definitely temporary boons, which are the product of good relations between human society and the spirits of the forest. In contrast, green revolution scientists view the elevated harvests of HYV crops as the continuing norm, the natural result of getting the technology right. According to the moral ecology of the Dayak, any benefit that comes in must be reciprocated with one going out; any benefit – like mast fruiting or a good swidden harvest – bears a cost. In contrast, the doctrine of the green revolution denies that its benefits bear a cost; it views any problems attending the cultivation of HYVs not as systemic costs, but as ad hoc technical problems. Whereas past commendations and critiques alike of the green revolution have focused on its direct agronomic, economic, social, and environmental impacts, we suggest that a different but equally important dimension of the green revolution is conceptual not technological and that its real failing is ideological.

We begin with a description and comparison of mast-fruiting, swidden cultivation, and green revolution agriculture, all of which we consider to be "root metaphors" for the wider social, economic, and political systems that encompass them (Ortner 1973). Exploitation of mast-fruiting in the tropical forest is central to the way that tropical forest people like the Dayak think about their relations with the natural environment: the beginning and end of the world is represented in some Dayak cosmologies by the mast-fruiting of the great "tree of life" (Dove 1993; Schärer 1963). And swidden cultivation is not just relevant to the worldview of the Dayak; in many respects it *is*, or traditionally was, their worldview. The Kantu' – a Dayak group in West Kalimantan – say that someone who does not engage in *bumai betaun* "making yearly swiddens" is not human. Similarly, the green revolution is lauded as one of the few development successes of the massive post-World War II investment in development in the Third World (the Nobel Prize was conferred on one of its pioneers, Norman Borlaug, in 1970); its technology has dominated the post-war development of a number of less-developed countries; it still dominates thinking within the major international venue for agricultural research and development, the Consultative Group on International Agricultural Research (CGIAR), and indeed the Gates and Rockefeller Foundations are currently calling for a new Green Revolution for Africa.[6]

Our data on mast-fruiting and swidden cultivation were gathered from first-hand observations in West Kalimantan, Indonesia, and our data on green revolution agriculture were culled from first-hand observations on Java and from second-hand reports on the situation in Indonesia and around the world.

II. Mast-fruiting, swidden cultivation, and green revolution agriculture

There are underlying similarities in mast-fruiting, swidden agriculture, and the cultivation of HYVs, based on shared developmental origins, but there are also enormous differences in the way the three systems are perceived today, especially by central planners and policymakers.

1. Mast-fruiting

The mast-fruiting of the dipterocarps of Borneo is one example of a phenomenon of synchronized timing of flowering and fruiting found all over the world.

Masting characterizes not just tropical forest trees and bamboos (Janzen 1976), but also temperate zone trees such as oaks, beeches, and conifers. The *Oxford English Dictionary* (1999) gives as one substantive form of "mast:" "A collective name for the fruit of the beech, oak, chestnut, and other forest trees, especially as food for swine." The term has Old English, Dutch, and Germanic cognates and is originally derived from related terms in Old Teutonic, Aryan, and Gothic (ibid.). Tropical forest masting has been described as follows (Ashton, Givinish, and Appanah 1988:44):

> At irregular intervals of 2 to 10 years several species of dipterocarps... come into flower more or less simultaneously. Over a period lasting a few weeks to a few months, nearly all dipterocarps and up to 88% of all canopy species can flower after years of little or no reproductive activity. The region over which such a mass-flowering event occurs can be as small as a single river valley or as large as northeastern Borneo or peninsular Malaysia.

The mast year appears to be triggered by fluctuations in climate that reduce the minimum night-time temperature by 2°C for three or more nights (Ashton, Givinish, and Appanah 1988:64). In eastern Borneo these fluctuations are associated with the El Niño Southern Oscillation (ENSO) phenomenon (Curran et al. 1999), but in western Borneo, where we have done most of our work, they appear to be chance fluctuations in the subtropical monsoonal circulation system (ibid.).

It is theorized that mast-fruiting represents an evolutionary mechanism for overwhelming (viz., satiating) predators during fruiting, while denying them food during the intervening years and thereby suppressing their population growth (Appanah 1985; Ashton, Givinish, and Appanah 1988; Janzen 1974). There is some fruiting during the intervening non-mast years, but much less, involving fewer species, and less intra- and inter-species synchronicity. Mast-fruiting was traditionally of great importance to forest-dwelling human populations in Borneo, both directly through consumption and indirectly through the game animals that also are supported by the mast (Redford, Klein, and Murcia 1992). But it is not attractive to extractive industries. As a result, the mast and indeed all other non-timber forest products have been completely eclipsed on the global resource landscape by first timber, even though timber may have been the less valuable resource overall (Peters, Gentry, and Mendelsohn 1989), and now estate crops like rubber and especially oil palm.

2. Swidden agriculture

Swidden agriculture in Borneo both mimics and manipulates the principle of mast-fruiting. It mimics it by synchronizing the timing of swidden planting and thus harvesting, so as to minimize crop predation. If a particular Kantu' household is late in planting, then it also will be late in harvesting, compared with other households. As a result, when this tardy household's crop begins to ripen, it will be the lone target for the area's pest populations and it accordingly will bear a disproportionately large pest load. The consequences of this are reflected in the Kantu' statement that even the all-important bird omens are not efficacious if the timing of swidden-making is off. They say, "If planting is [too] early or late, the omens no longer count" (cf. Dove 1985b:209).

Swidden agriculture manipulates the principle of mast-fruiting in its production, in the first place, of an annual grain harvest. As Janzen (1976:382) has written, "Man has simply replaced the mast crop with farms and their annually masting fields of grain." The long-fallow swidden rotation overcomes the constraint of the inter-mast, non-productive years, by allowing cultivators to start new swiddens each year in different forest plots, until the earlier-cultivated swidden plots are ready to cultivate again. If we count the fallow years as well as cropping years, we see that the periodicity of individual swiddens is not unlike the periodicity of the mast-fruiting.

Swidden agriculture yields high returns per unit of labor; it is the most sustainable agricultural technology ever developed for tropical rain forests; and by the end of the twentieth century it was supporting as many as one billion people – 22 percent of the population of the developing world in tropical and subtropical zones (Thrupp et al. 1997) – although it is increasingly in retreat due to urbanization, industrial plantations, population growth, and other dimensions of modernity (Mertz et al. 2009; Padoch et al. 2010).[7] Like mast-fruiting, however, swidden is not conducive to extraction by supra-local entities (Scott 1998; Dove 2011). As a result, it has been heavily sanctioned by national governments and international development agencies, because of its high ratio of fallow time to cropping time and its purportedly destructive environmental impact and "nomadic" character.[8]

3. HYV agriculture

The principle of synchronized maturation is even more critical in green revolution agriculture than in swidden agriculture, and it also is manipulated more profoundly. The overall timing of this agriculture is intensified because of a shift with the HYV package to more intensive cropping, two to three times per year instead of once or twice with traditional varieties. Timing also is intensified within each cropping cycle (Cassman et al. 1995:183). A heightened reliance on mechanization, precise water control, and intense and precisely timed chemical inputs, in addition to the increased threat of predation, all necessitate greater synchronization both within and among fields. This is achieved by breeding greater synchronization into each variety, by cultivating fewer varieties overall, and by requiring greater synchronization among farmers. It also is achieved by replacing traditional patterns of labor exchange with mobile labor gangs.

Green revolution agriculture is eminently suited to centralized control and extraction and thus has received unparalleled support from national and international institutions, with praise focusing on its high production per unit of land. Yet it yields relatively low returns to human labor in particular and energy in general; it favors larger, capital-rich, mechanized farms and thus exacerbates local socioeconomic inequity; it bears costly externalities of environmental pollution; and it is challenged by long-term trends of rising inputs, falling yields, and degradation of its resource-base.

III. Systemic logic

In spite of some shared ecological underpinnings, there are major differences in how mast-fruiting, swidden agriculture, and green revolution agriculture are conceived. A critical distinction between the three resource systems is not just the incidence of success versus failure but the expectation of success versus failure. There is a lengthy anthropological literature on external perceptions and misperceptions of abundance versus dearth in non-western societies – e.g., on "primitive affluence" (Sahlins 1972), the "wild yam debate" (Headland and Bailey 1991), the scarce protein thesis (Gross 1975:538–539; Rappaport 1984/1968), and the "counterfeit paradise" of the wet tropics (Meggers 1971) – but there has been much less study of how these societies themselves perceive these matters.

1. Understanding success and failure

A. Mast-fruiting

The Dayak perceive the natural bounty of mast-fruiting to be outside the norm, and so they invoke special cultural institutions to deal with the bounty of mast years, institutions not invoked during other times. Thus, among the Kantu', the cultural rules that traditionally govern the collection of fruit during mast-fruiting years are less restricting than the rules that prevail during non-mast years. During non-mast years, collection focuses in or near village territories and on trees that are individually owned, whose fruit can be taken, by their owners, by climbing. But during mast years, collection focuses on trees in the forest that are thought to be owned by spirit ancestors, and whose fruit cannot be taken by climbing but only by gathering from the ground, which is permitted to anyone (Figure 4.1). These rules considerably enlarge the pool of potential fruit gatherers.[9] In short, when unusual and short-term concentrations of resources eclipse society's normal capacity to exploit them, the Dayak have developed institutions that suspend the normal practices of exploitation and invoke special practices to maximize the overall community benefit from the event.[10]

There also are special cultural institutions for marketing the products of mast-fruiting. For example, the pattern of local, market-oriented exploitation

FIGURE 4.1 A Kantu' man carrying a basket of jackfruit and durian home from the forest during the mast season

Source: Michael R. Dove

of the illipe nut (*Shorea spp.*) during mast-fruiting years is clearly based on the assumption of episodic, not continuous (viz., annual), abundance. Thus, the proceeds from illipe nut sales in mast years traditionally are not used to fill regular subsistence needs; rather, they are used to fill periodic needs for one-time purchases of special items, such as heirloom property (e.g., ceramic vases, copper gongs), an outboard motor, a mechanical rice-huller, or school entry fees. As a result, the absence of an illipe nut harvest in non-mast years does not jeopardize basic subsistence. Other resources – primarily the rice swiddens and secondarily the rubber gardens – guarantee subsistence needs in those mast years.

B. Swidden agriculture

Recognition of the inevitability of dearth as well as abundance is also built into the Dayak swidden system, in the form of extensive cultural mechanisms for coping with harvest failure. The principal mechanism is a complex of institutions for redistributing rice from households and longhouses that have reaped swidden surpluses to households and longhouses that have experienced

High modern vs local folk views of dearth and abundance **75**

FIGURE 4.2 A bountiful swidden rice harvest gathered at a Kantu' longhouse
Source: Michael R. Dove

swidden shortfalls (Figure 4.2). Among the Kantu', most harvest surpluses were traditionally redistributed in this manner. The principle that governs all such redistributions is reciprocity: today's donor is tomorrow's recipient. Refusal to participate in such redistribution is socially sanctioned.[11] This system of redistribution represents insurance against the certainty of a time in the future when a household or longhouse – no matter how industrious – will experience a harvest shortfall. The existence of this system of reciprocal aid is thus a cultural statement that swidden fortunes, bounty and shortfall will inevitably fluctuate.

Other major mechanisms for coping with harvest shortfalls include the cultivation of cash crops like pepper (*Piper nigrum*) and, especially, rubber (*Hevea brasiliensis*), the gathering and marketing of non-timber forest products like rattan, and the capacity to shift under duress from the rice staple to non-rice famine foods like cassava (Dove 2011). The existence of these mechanisms for coping with swidden failure is evidence both of the frequency of such failure and also of cultural recognition of this frequency.

C. HYV agriculture

No such recognition, in contrast, is associated with green revolution agriculture (Table 4.1). This is explicitly reflected in the generic term for the crop varieties associated with the green revolution: "high yielding varieties." The very terminology for these varieties carries the promise of high yields, not

TABLE 4.1 The conception of abundance in mast-fruiting, swidden cultivation, and HYV agriculture

	Systems of resource exploitation		
	Mast-fruiting	Swidden cultivation	Green revolution
View of abundance			
Abundance seen as norm?	No	No	Yes
Scarcity seen as inevitable?	Yes	Yes	No
Systemic understanding			
Failure seen as systemic characteristic?	Yes	Yes	No
Benefit seen as entailing cost?	Yes	Yes	No
Secondary/feedback effects recognized?	Yes	Yes	No

Source: Michael R. Dove

sometimes but every time. The fact that high yields often are not attained is not recognized, or addressed, within this management model. The premise is that bounty is constant and reliable, not periodic and unreliable. As Barker, Gabler and Winkelmann (1981) wrote early on in the development of the green revolution, the scientists and institutions involved initially predicted that this new technology would reduce yield instability, but the evidence shows that this prediction was often not accurate. The instability of yields in green revolution agriculture is now generally recognized; yet the premise of stability as well as bounty is still reflected in the failure of development planners to provide a safety net for green revolution programs.

Green revolution scientists and planners recognize that "high-yielding variety" harvests often fail; but they do not associate this failure with the technology per se. They may blame failure on either the participating farmers' failure to use the technological package correctly, or on the emergence of new environmental problems, especially new pests. Much green revolution research was devoted to isolating one immediate environmental cause after another for HYV crop failures: thus, if the problem one year was locust infestations, then a locust-resistant variety was developed; but then next year the problem might have been weevils, and so a weevil-resistant strain was developed, and so on.[12]

Green revolution scientists and planners have been even less open to the possibility of long-term systemic failure. However, studies on both rice and wheat have discovered unmistakable evidence of long-term unsustainability in yields.[13] Scientists at the International Rice Research Institute (IRRI) in the Philippines, for example, years ago documented a decline in the "total factor productivity" of rice production (Cassman and Pingali 1995:301), meaning that the rate of growth in rice yields was not keeping up with the rate of growth in cultivation inputs, in particular increases in nitrogen fertilizer and continual improvements in genetic stock. Scientists associated with the Centro Internacional de Mejoramiento de Maiz y Trigo (CIMMYT) in Mexico reported a similar situation with HYVs of wheat: Byerlee and Siddiq (1994:1354) suggested in a study of Pakistan that the increases in fertilizer inputs and improvement in genetic stock over the prior two decades were virtually canceled out by continually declining yields.

2. Scope of the system

The Dayak belief, that the spirits of the forest demand in exchange for every mast season a tribute of enough human dead to fill a basket (*kolak*) with their eyes, links the state of human communities with the state of the forest. We can read this belief as the folk expression of a perceived statistical correlation – the *kolak* is an indigenous unit of measure, which thus connotes some sort of quantitative relationship – between spikes in forest productivity and human mortality.[14] There is some scientific basis for such a correlation. Although most past research on the ENSO cycles that drive forest masting have focused on agricultural and forest ecology, some researchers have begun to examine the impact of ENSO on human health and they conclude that there are clear impacts on human morbidity (e.g., Gagnon, Bush, and Smoyer-Tomic 2001; Woodruff and Guest 2000).[15]

We can also read implications of scope in the Dayak beliefs. The reference to the basket of eyes, with its denotation of dozens of individuals, enlarges the scope of analysis beyond the local household or community. In addition, it is not the fruit trees themselves that are said to demand a basket of human eyes, but the spirits of the forest. The mast, and the principles of exchange that govern it, are thereby situated within a wider moral landscape. For some Dayak, the landscape of mast-fruiting encompasses the entire cosmos: the Ngaju Dayak of Southern Borneo, for example, believe that when the "tree-of-life" flowers in what amounts to the mast to end all masts, sacred hornbills will eat and destroy it and from this destruction the cosmos will be renewed (Schärer 1963:128; cf. Dove 1993). There is some ecological basis for this wider scope: given the mobility that some of the forest's fruit-eaters possess,[16] the pest-saturating mechanism of mast-fruiting can only be understood in relation to the wider forest ecosystem – perhaps indeed the global ecosystem, given the involvement of the El Niño Southern Oscillation phenomenon in triggering mast-fruiting.[17]

The Dayak similarly interpret their system of swidden agriculture within a wider moral and cosmological context. The Kantu', for example, interpret swidden harvest success and failure in terms of a moral pact between themselves and the spirit world.[18] According to this pact, if the Kantu' honor the ritual proscriptions laid down by the spirits, especially against certain types of illicit sexual congress (viz., adultery, incest, and illegitimate birth), they will reap good harvests; and if they don't, they won't. Thus, one year when incessant rains led to destructive flooding of all low-lying swiddens in one of the valleys where we worked, the Kantu' blamed the disaster on a rumored case of father–daughter

FIGURE 4.3 A flooded river in front of a Kantu' longhouse, following a distant case of incest

Source: Michael R. Dove

incest in another Kantu' community some 135 kilometers distant (Figure 4.3). The fact that it is an act of incest that brings down the wrath of the spirits reflects the centrality of exchange to the human–spirit relationship, because incest is the very antithesis of social exchange. The ultimate and most ancient of social exchanges is of spouses between different, exogamous families or groups, and this is obviously undercut by taking sexual partners within the family or group.

Although empirical analysis of Dayak swidden agriculture does not support the view that the social behavior of far-flung communities affects swidden outcomes, it does support the idea of an explanatory context that transcends the local community. Research over the past several decades has demonstrated that the political-economic character of swidden communities cannot be explained except in reference to more central political-economic structures (Friedman 1975), just as the economics and ecology of the swidden system itself cannot be divorced from their age-old involvement in global markets through forest products and cash crops. Thus, it is not isolation from political-economic centers that forces people to practice swidden cultivation, it is swidden cultivation that permits people to distance themselves from such centers (Dove 1985a). Activities like the smallholder rubber cultivation of the Kantu' and other Dayak can be productively reinterpreted in this light (Dove 2011; Gouyon, de Foresta, and Levang 1993; Pelzer 1978b).

The breadth of the explanatory framework needed to understand swidden agriculture and mast-fruiting applies equally to the green revolution. Over the years social scientists studying green revolution successes and failures have progressively enlarged the scope of their analysis, from the crop to the farm, then the rural community and its region, then the nation-state and the world-system. Many analysts now argue that the development of green revolution agriculture was driven not by the needs of farmers but by politicians interested in promoting technological rather than social change; by central government bureaucracies interested in asserting more control over rural populations; and by international agribusiness and chemical firms interested in stimulating demand for their genetic, chemical, and mechanical products.[19]

Rejecting the narrow focus on the local farmer, farm, and crop of green revolution proponents, many scholars have argued that there was a latent, unacknowledged, but powerful geo-political dimension to this development (Perkins 1997). Beeman and Pritchard (2001:95) write, "To critics of the green revolution, misguided technology forced on developing nations by the American agricultural and foreign policy establishment was a form of cultural imperialism that disrupted rural social patterns and made poorer nations ever more dependent on energy for irrigation and machines and on capital for seeds and chemicals." Yapa (1993:257) reminds us that the phrase "Green Revolution" was first coined in explicit opposition to "Red Revolution" as a label for the technological revolution that the U.S. was promoting as an alternative to social revolution in the poor agrarian regions of the globe, most immediately as an alternative to land reform in Mexico. And Blaikie (1985:18) writes of the green revolution, "This was undoubtedly a breakthrough of major significance, but it was developed with particular strategic and world political objectives in mind: the containment of communism by increasing food production, and the reduction of US food-aid, were major impelling factors."

IV. Exchange and the system

Very different relations with the natural environment are implicated in the Dayak systems for exploiting mast-fruiting and forest swiddens on the one hand, and the system of green revolution agriculture on the other hand.

1. Exchange between society and environment

A. Character of relations with nature

The Dayak expectation that the forest spirits will exact a toll of one basket of human eyes for every mast-fruiting is part of a more general set of beliefs regarding relations of exchange between humans and their physical environment, which we are calling their moral ecology. The premise behind this conceptual linkage of society and environment is that whatever happens in the one, or passes from the one to the other, must be reciprocated.[20] The reference to the *kolak* measuring basket in the aforementioned belief underlines the fact that the Kantu' have,

FIGURE 4.4 A Kantu' man sacrifices a pig to the spirits as thanks for a good swidden harvest

Source: Michael R. Dove

in effect, a "deal" with the spirits who govern their environment: thus, a mast-fruiting entitles the spirits to no more, and no less, than one measuring-basket of human eyes.[21] This principle is also explicit in the swidden system: at the start of each annual swidden cycle, every Kantu' household with the wherewithal to do so traditionally sacrificed a domestic pig to ensure a good harvest (Figure 4.4). Such a sacrifice entails a significant economic cost to the tribespeople, but it is one that they justify by saying that "Any family that makes this sacrifice is certain to reap better harvests as a result; and at the very least, that family can count on reaping better harvests than other families that do not make the sacrifice." Alternatively, the Kantu' say that whatever they expend on ritual sacrifice will increase their favor with the spirits and this will in turn increase their swidden returns sufficient to, minimally, surpass their initial expenditure. Similar notions of the morality of exchange are common throughout Southeast Asia. Jorgenson (1989), for example, writes that the Pwo of Thailand periodically compensate the forest for the bounty that it provides them by turning over to the forest and the forest fauna an entire swidden, complete with standing crops.[22]

The pig sacrifice is the symbolic return made to the spirits of the forest for a good harvest; the real return is the long fallow that they give their swiddens after

FIGURE 4.5 Natural afforestation of the previous year's swidden in front of a newly burned swidden

Source: Michael R. Dove)

each cropping (Figure 4.5). A defining characteristic of the Dayak or, indeed, any system of swidden agriculture is its reliance on a fallow period that is longer than the period of cultivation (cf. Conklin 1955:1), which serves to restore levels of exploitable nutrients in the environment after their depletion by each period of cropping. This long fallow gives swidden agriculture its unparalleled returns to labor: the benefits of the fallow have been insightfully termed by Alcorn (1993) the "subsidy from nature." The Kantu' see this not as a subsidy from nature, however, but as a boon from the forest spirits, and one that must be recompensed. Both symbolically and actually, the Dayak expect to be sustained by their environment, by the forest spirits, only in return for some sacrifice on their part.

A very different principle underlies the green revolution paradigm (Table 4.2). Whereas the Dayak system expects to make sacrifices for what is taken, the green revolution tries to optimize the difference between what it takes out and what it puts back in, the difference between "outputs" (crops) and "inputs" (fertilizer, etc.). Similarly, one of the principal objectives of green revolution agriculture, and modern agricultural development in general, has been to eliminate the fallow period and achieve continuous cropping of the land through the use of external inputs like chemical fertilizers. Another contributing factor has been the development of HYVs with such short maturation periods that they can be cropped two to three times per year, thereby practically eliminating even the brief fallow period between cropping cycles. The fallow period's "subsidy from nature" is replaced, thus, by a petro-chemical subsidy.

TABLE 4.2 The conception of exchange in mast-fruiting, swidden cultivation, and HYV agriculture

	Systems of resource exploitation		
	Mast-fruiting	Swidden cultivation	Green revolution
Exchange between society and environment			
Relations with environment seen as:	2-way	2-way	1-way
Environment seen as:	Reciprocal	Reciprocal	Giving
Local versus extra-local exchange			
Level focused on in exploitation of abundance:	Local	Local	Extra-local
Level focused on in dampening fluctuation:	Local	Local	Extra-local

Source: Michael R. Dove

These aspects of green revolution agriculture exemplify broader developments of post-World War II agriculture in the United States. The mid-twentieth century development of industrialized agriculture based on extraction of resources from the soil entailed a shift from a partnership with nature to a battle against it, from emulation of nature to defiance of it – to an industry based on extraction of resources from soil. Here is a government scientist's critique of the opposing ideal of organic agriculture: "We cannot have our cake and eat it. We cannot put what grows on the soil back into it and still raise enough food to feed the people of the country." What came to reign supreme was the core logic of capitalism famously articulated by Marx one century earlier: "All progress in capitalism is a progress in the art, not only of robbing the laborer, but of robbing the soil." This is indeed what twentieth-century modernist agriculture policymakers explicitly advocated, and this represents a real break with traditional agriculture. Whereas swidden agriculture as among the Dayak idealizes exchange, modern industrial agriculture, exemplified by the green revolution, idealizes *escaping* exchange; swidden ideology strives for symmetry, the green revolution strives for *a*symmetry – the green revolution seems to strive, in short, for a "free lunch". But is a free lunch possible? The physicists say "No" (see Chapter 6), Dayak cosmology says "No", activists like Vandana Shiva (below) say "No", but high-modern green revolution agriculture says, in effect, "Yes".

B. "Miraculous" agriculture

This agronomic sleight-of-hand, this idea of something for nothing, this belief that the natural order can be cheated, has been explicitly reflected in the green revolution discourse of "miracle crops". More for less is what the term "miracle" connotes. The *Oxford English Dictionary* (1999) variously defines "miracle" as "A marvellous event occurring within human experience, which cannot have been brought about by human power or by the operation of any natural agency, and must therefore be ascribed to the special intervention of the Deity or of some supernatural being" and "as applied hyperbolically to an achievement seemingly beyond human power, or an occurrence so marvellous as to appear supernatural". Vandana Shiva (1991: 46), in her pioneering critique, "The Violence of the Green Revolution", writes "The Green Revolution has been offered a miracle…[But] One way in which agricultural research went wrong was precisely in saying… that some miracle was being produced."

The whole notion of "miracle" crops is based on the belief that these crops give higher yields with lower inputs. But as Shiva (ibid.) continues, "[T]he term *'High Yielding Varieties'* is a misnomer because it implies that the new seeds are high-yielding in and of themselves. The distinguishing feature of the seeds, however, is that they are highly responsive to certain key inputs such as fertilizers and irrigation." Many analysts suggest that this responsiveness, which could also be called a dependency, transformed relations between the local farmer and the wider society; and that this was the real distinguishing feature of the new seeds. That is, these industrial inputs made local labor inputs less necessary at the same time as it made them less affordable, because more and more of the surplus production had to be expended beyond the local level to pay for these inputs. Note how different it would sound, however, if these seeds were named for certain other of their characteristics, such as their vulnerability to pests, their bias toward large-scale agricultural operations, their ignoring of community welfare, and so on (Table 4.3). Farmer discourses come much closer to reflecting the realities of green revolution dynamics, exemplified by the joke that circulated in the wake of the introduction of high-yielding varieties to Pakistan, that the introduction of "miracle rice" had produced a "miracle locust" to eat it.

Shiva deserves credit for focusing critical attention on seemingly benign terminology like "miracle agriculture" and in pointing out that the miracles in question were really the products not of scientific breakthroughs but of obfuscation of production realities, which made transformative socio-economic development not less but more difficult. As Michael Pollan (2001) writes in *The Botany of Desire*:

> We need a new silver bullet, an entomologist with the Oregon Extension Service told me, and biotech is it. Yet a new silver bullet is not the same thing as a new paradigm. Rather, it's something that will allow the old paradigm to survive. That paradigm will always construe the problem in [the] fields as a Colorado beetle problem [e.g.], rather than what it is: a problem of potato monoculture.

TABLE 4.3 Alternative names for high-yielding varieties

Actual focus	Actual names
Grain & outputs	High-yielding variety
Alternative focus	*Alternative names*
Pests	'High predation, high risk variety'
Inputs	'Big farmers' variety'
	'High-input variety'
	'Industry-friendly variety'
	'Credit/debt-dependent variety'
Social impacts	'Market sale-oriented variety'
	'Household- vs community-focused variety'
	'Anti-traditional morality variety'
	'Me-first variety'
Political impacts	'High political-economic integration seeds'
	'End of autonomy variety'
Metaphoric	'Miracle crop' vs 'Trojan horse'

Source: Michael R. Dove

C. Pest relations

The difference in environmental relations between the tribal and green revolution management systems is reflected in their respective attitudes toward crop pests. Dayak diversification of crops and agricultural strategies typically keeps pest populations relatively low, in what amounts to an indigenous, integrated pest-management strategy. For example, each Kantu' household traditionally planted an average of 17 different varieties of rice and 20–21 different non-rice "relishes," made an average of 2.3 separate swiddens each year – each located in a different micro-environment – and also owned and exploited an average of 4–5 separate rubber gardens, each containing (in addition to rubber trees) a wide variety of non-cultigens, many of economic use, such as edible bamboos and ferns (Dove 1985b:97,159–160,173; 2011). Some crop pests, like the bearded pig (*Sus barbatus*) and sambhur deer (*Cervus unicolor*), are even welcomed in Dayak fields and gardens, where they are more easily hunted (Dove 1993; cf. Redford, Klein, and Murcia 1992). Nearly one-half by weight and two-thirds by number of the deer and pig taken in hunting by Kantu' are killed in or near swiddens (Dove 1985b:239) (Figure 4.6). Dayak subsistence ecology is not, thus, premised upon the complete eradication of pest populations.

Pests are a more prominent de facto feature of green revolution agriculture than swidden agriculture, although, ironically, the green revolution ideology has been less tolerant of their presence. In fact, the initial inability of the green

FIGURE 4.6 A Kantu' hunter with a wild pig (*Sus barbatus*) shot in a rubber grove near the longhouse

Source: Michael R. Dove

revolution paradigm to accept the existence of pests greatly exacerbated its pest problem. Everything that the green revolution technology did to enhance the ecological niche for the HYVs – decreasing inter-cropping, genetic diversity, and maturation periods; and increasing crop homogeneity, density, and synchronicity (cf. Altieri 1987:161–166) – also, albeit unwittingly, enhanced the niche for HYV pests. Moreover, the nature of the initial green revolution response to pest outbreaks – namely, to redirect the genetic and pesticide defenses of each year's new HYV package to meet the latest threat – only made matters worse. For example, before the advent of the green revolution, the brown planthopper was a minor, untroubling element within the Southeast Asian rice agro-ecosystem, but the green revolution transformed it into a super-pest. As Atsatt and O'Dowd (1976:27) insightfully wrote at the time of the initial outbreaks, in any "arms race" between a crop and a pest, the "short-generation-time, rapidly evolving pests and pathogens are almost sure to win." The instrumental linkage between pesticide use and pests became so obvious to farmers in some parts of the world that they concluded that the pesticide manufacturers themselves were somehow putting the pests in the pesticides (Bentley 1992:10) – a conclusion that is, speaking metaphorically, very close to the truth. Pests may not be in pesticides, but they *are* in the system of which pesticides are part. Thus, we can read the folk statement that "Manufacturers put pests in pesticides" as "Manufacturers are ensuring the proliferation of pests in the agro-ecological system", an empirical, causal relationship that scientists, policymakers, and the business sector were obfuscating. We can read this farmer belief, thus, as re-writing the boundary of the green revolution system to include its pests, contra the green revolution ideology that excluded them.[23]

In short, the green revolution management model, by refusing to accept the principle of any exchange between pests and crops, actually exacerbated the terms of the exchange. This exchange became so bad that it resulted in one of the most prominent "roll-backs" in the green revolution model to date, involving Indonesia's pioneering – albeit partial – turn away from strictly chemically based pest management toward so-called "integrated pest management" (Fox 1991:75–76; Winarto 2004, 2011).

2. Local versus extra-local exchange

Just as the two management models differ in their exchanges with the natural environment, so do they differ in their exchanges with the social environment. Both models engage in exchange, but in the Dayak case, it is local and social in character[24] – an example is the Dayak custom whereby kinfolk come to visit and share in the good fortune of a household that reaps an exceptional harvest – whereas in the case of the green revolution, it is distant and economic in character (Figure 4.7). Both management models are concerned with fluctuation in production, but whereas the Dayak model focuses on fluctuation at the local level and addresses it through exchange at that level, the green revolution focuses on global food supplies, which it addresses by exchange at that level.

In the Dayak case, agricultural surpluses are supposed to be used to cover agricultural shortfalls (within the community) and, by and large, they are used for this purpose. Households that violate this norm are socially sanctioned. The Kantu' (e.g.) regard the storage of rice by one household for so long that it rots (as will happen after a year or two in this climate) as a sign of both that household's swidden success and its social failure, because such grain should have been used – as either reciprocal gift or wage labor-in-kind – to tide other households over temporary shortfalls. This obligation is, in a broad sense, part of the pact of reciprocity with the spirit world that determines the success or failure of the harvests. The norms governing exchange in the green revolution model are just the opposite; they are outwards-looking not inwards-looking. Green revolution technology depends on much greater use of market inputs and, in consequence, much greater marketing of outputs, than does non-green revolution agriculture. Involvement in exchange with wider economic systems is viewed not just as a necessity, but as a good in its own right. The green

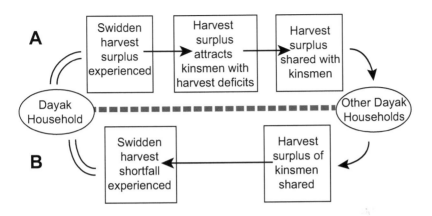

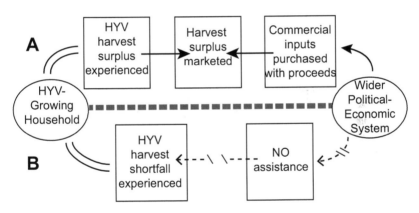

FIGURE 4.7 The use of surplus in swidden cultivation versus green revolution agriculture

Source: Michael R. Dove

revolution management model implicitly honors the oft-stated principle that development does not occur unless produce enters a system wider than the local one in which it was produced – hence the common invisibility in development thinking of resources like cattle dung, fuelwood, and so on that are vitally important but do not enter formal markets.

V. Conclusions

This analysis demonstrates that the Dayak systems for exploiting mast fruiting and swidden agriculture on the one hand, and on the other hand the green revolution system of agriculture, differ profoundly in how resource surpluses or shortfalls at particular times and places are related to broader patterns of surplus and shortfall. The Dayak systems of resource management that have been discussed – mast-fruiting and swidden agriculture – systematically relate surplus and shortfall to each other in a model of exchange. In contrast, green revolution agriculture introduces a discontinuity between surplus and shortfall through a particular contextualization of its activities. The green revolution ideology artificially isolates its benefits in time and space – viz., the good harvest and the immediate field that produces it – while displacing its costs onto other times and spaces – viz., the failed harvests and the wider social and physical environment that is impoverished and degraded by its technology.[25] As Yapa (1993) says, this amounts to a dichotomization between those who benefit from green revolution technology and those who pay its costs. This dichotomy fundamentally challenges the core tenet of green revolution ideology, that high yields = low scarcity of food. Instead, the spatial reorganization and disciplining that the green revolution in fact brings about explains what Yapa (1993:255) refers to as the seeming "paradox of how improved seeds can provide high yields and create scarcity at the same time."

Just as the problem of poverty is partially generated by our conception of poverty (Yapa 1993:255, 271), so are the problems of agriculture generated, in part, by our conceptions of agriculture: what is agricultural success as opposed to failure, what does the term "agriculture" encompass or not encompass, what indeed *is* agriculture? The dichotomization between costs and benefits that characterizes the green revolution belongs to a wider set of phenomena that is drawing increasing attention from both physical and social scientists, namely the artificial isolation of the poor, the sick, and the disaster-ridden from the wider society that is implicated in their impoverishment, illnesses, and catastrophes. There is an analogy between the artificial abundance of the green revolution harvest and the artificial scarcity of famine, for example (Sen 1981). A major albeit implicit achievement of the green revolution model of resource management is to create an illusion of abundance through concentrating resources in time and space and then publicly representing these concentrations as not merely legitimate but as naturally given.[26]

Whereas the green revolution has been popularly represented as a technological revolution, it was in fact also a conceptual revolution, one that redrew the boundaries of "agriculture". Placed outside the new boundaries were farmers having little or no land, upland or non-irrigated land, and limited capital and mechanization. This is just one example of a more general research bias in conservation and development, which Chambers (1983:76–77) has referred to as "the concentration of research, publication, training and extension on what is exotic rather than indigenous, mechanical rather than human, chemical rather than organic, and marketed rather than consumed." A generation ago in Indonesia, officials openly debated whether swidden cultivators were farmers or not, and in Pakistan anyone who did not have the thousands of acres deemed necessary for optimal cultivation of HYVs was not considered to be a "farmer" at all (Dove 1994). Equally important, the boundaries of "agriculture" were redrawn in a way that separated the newly-bounded agricultural system from many of its social and ecological costs. Removed beyond the boundaries of agriculture was the social and environmental degradation that occurred as a direct result of the green revolution technological package.

Perhaps the most important boundary-remaking project of all in the green revolution was the redrawing of the boundary between production and consumption. Most notably, what precedes the harvest is deemed part of "agriculture" and thus part of agricultural research and development; and what follows it is not. There are many illustrations of this, one of which involves the attention devoted in green revolution research to pests: pre-harvest, in-field predation has received a great deal of attention, but post-harvest, extra-field losses to pests have not.[27] But most far-reaching in its consequences has been the attention given to pre-harvest production as opposed to post-harvest distribution and consumption. Whereas the current size and projected future growth of the global population was reflexively cited in all green revolution literature as the underlying rationale for the development of HYV technology, the actual delivery or distribution of HYV crops to this population went virtually unexamined. This inattention to the issue of distribution, in a program designed to "feed the world", occurred at the same time as an academic consensus was developing that famine is precipitated not by absolute shortages of food but by localized shortages, created by political and economic forces (e.g., Sen 1981; Watts 1983) – this paradigm shift ultimately being reflected in the award of a Nobel prize to Amartya Sen.

The green revolution paradigm addresses production losses because this is deemed to be a scientific, biological issue. It does not address issues of mal-distribution because these are deemed to be not scientific but rather "political" issues. Post-harvest problems are accepted as inevitable social facts, whereas pre-harvest problems are contested as modifiable biological facts. The development in the past several decades of the post-modern critique in the humanities and social sciences has illuminated the way that scholars customarily focus attention on a removed "other" and thereby not only deflect attention from themselves, but indeed categorize and thus privilege themselves as above and beyond critical study. From this perspective, the attraction of the green revolution focus on production problems, like pests and recalcitrant farmers, is that they are ready-made "others", clearly distinguished from the scientist and his or her own society. In contrast, other problems, particularly those involving post-harvest issues of distribution, are less distant, involving as they do such "close" subjects as class and ethnic divisions, market regulation, international trade, and even research policy and scientific careers. That is, a study of these topics often implicates and thus has the potential to jeopardize the scientist's own socioeconomic reality, in a way that narrowly focused studies of losses to invertebrate crop pests, for example, can never do.

Critical to the success of this boundary-making dimension of the green revolution is the fact that it was implicit. The new boundaries were not explicitly articulated or defended: rather, they were presented as given, as "natural", although they were not drawn from nature; they were cultural constructs. The green revolution was in this sense a highly "cultured", highly ideological project. As Wright (2005) has written in his definitive study of the green revolution in Mexico, this system of agriculture is characterized by a distinct "belief system, ideology, world view" – consisting of faith in science, belief in human dominion over nature, and a disconnect from it – although it self-presents as having no belief system, ideology, or world view, but as being strictly science-driven. A key characteristic of the ideology of the green revolution, in short, was to self-represent as having no ideology. This is not, as it might seem, a neutral stance, rather it is just the opposite. As Stanley Fish puts it, "So it would seem, finally, that there are no moves that are not moves in the game, and this *includes* even the move by which one claims *no longer* to be a player." Placing oneself above the fray is an extremely powerful political move. Disguising its partisan dimensions has been critical to the attainment by the green revolution model of a hegemonic position in global agricultural production because, as Bloch (1974) has so astutely written, "It is precisely through the process of making a power situation appear a fact in the nature of the world that traditional authority works."

Those who have immediately suffered from this implicit exercise of power within the green revolution have not necessarily been fooled. In keeping with the Marxist adage that the oppressed perceive what oppressors might obfuscate, small farmers the world over have recognized and resisted much of the boundary-making project of the green revolution. This resistance has ranged from social unrest that followed its initial introduction in many places, such as the rioting that broke out in Java when mobile labor crews replaced the use of traditional village work parties, to more subtle acts like the continued, surreptitious cultivation of traditional land races.[28] More interesting and perhaps of more long-lasting impact has been the pervasive farmer manipulation of green revolution technology – and the conceptual boundaries implicit in this technology – including the adaptation of the technological package to local cultural threats (Bebbington 1993), the construction of hybridized systems of cultivation (Gupta 1998), the adaptation of integrated pest-management packages to local conditions (Winarto 2004, 2011), and the unilateral adoption and re-working of breeding technologies to suit the farmers' own priorities (Frossard 2005).

The issues involved here continue to be relevant ones. The ongoing controversy over so-called "terminator seeds" shows that global agri-business continues to see a principal avenue of development as the manipulation of critical agricultural boundaries – in this case between farmers, seed reproduction, corporations, patent laws, and the legal system – and continues to reconceptualize what agriculture is all about, with ever increasing intrusion into and surveillance and disciplining of the lives of the farmers. More broadly, there continues to be continued dichotomization and frank misunderstanding of the relationship between agricultural production and consumption. On the occasion of the death of Norman Borlaug in September 2009, for example, David Beckmann, president of the anti-hunger group "Bread for the World", was asked to address the question, Why are so many people in the world hungry when global agriculture produces in theory sufficient food to feed everyone? Beckmann replied that the existence of hunger alongside food abundance was due to "a lack of give a damn". "It's mainly neglect", he said, "political neglect". In short, he seemed to see the problem as a sort of accident, as opposed to the inevitable product of existing institutional forces. Beckmann sees the problem as something not done versus done. This ignores Sen's work on famines; it ignores our Weberian understanding of how institutions work; and it ignores the insights presented here into the actual versus imagined workings of high-modern, green revolution technology.

Notes

1 The *kolak* "basket" that is mentioned here is a regional unit of standard measure (of volume) (cf. Wilkinson 1959:607,621), which averages 5.9 liters among the Kantu'. Since the human eye has an average volume of 6.37 cubic centimeters, one *kolak* could hold approximately 157.0 eyes or the eyes of 78.5 persons.
2 An alternative version of this belief is that the spirits only demand a "basketful of human eyes" when the mast occurs two years in a row. The principle is the same in either case, however: unusual bounty is thought to bear a cost that complements its benefit.
3 We follow Taussig (1980) in trying insofar as possible to accord native beliefs a literal as opposed to exotic and metaphorical reading.
4 All of these discussions might be said to concern "perimetrics", following Stone's (1994) coining of this term to describe the demarcation of agricultural boundaries and perimeters.
5 We are grateful to Donald Worster for this point.
6 http://www.gatesfoundation.org/nr/downloads/globaldevelopment/Africas
7 Swidden agriculture was prevalent in Europe and North America through the nineteenth century (Sigaut 1979; Otto and Anderson 1982).
8 See Li et al. (2014) for a recent review of the state of swidden agriculture in Southeast Asia.
9 Similar cultural institutions deal with other instances of episodic bounty, like the killing of large game. Among the Kantu', most deer (*Cervus unicolor*) and pig (*Sus barbatus*) traditionally had to be shared with the other members of the hunter's longhouse. Another example is fish runs: when fish spawn in the interior rivers and streams, normal household-based fishing technologies are temporarily replaced with technologies that involve the whole longhouse.
10 Compare Hardin and Remis (2006: 275) on the link between cycles in forest phenology and human settlement in the Congo basin.
11 In addition, rice does not store well in this equatorial, rainforest climate, which makes its "social storage" all the more sensible.
12 Green revolution scientists fell victim to what has come to be called "the Red Queen syndrome" in evolutionary theory, which refers to the famous exchange between Alice and the Queen of Hearts in Lewis Carroll's *Through the Looking Glass* (Gardner [1960:210n.9] says that it is the most oft-quoted line from the

Alice books – although the reference is typically not to evolutionary but political systems). After Alice discovers that she and the Queen have been running furiously without moving, Carroll writes (Gardner 1960:210): "Alice looked round her in great surprise. 'Why I do believe we've been under this tree the whole time! Everything's just as it was!' 'Of course it is,' said the Queen. 'What would you have it?' 'Well, in *our* country,' said Alice, still panting a little, 'you'd generally get to somewhere else – if you ran very fast for a long time as we've been doing.' 'A slow sort of country!' said the Queen. 'Now, *here*, you see, it takes all the running *you* can do, to keep in the same place. If you want to get somewhere else, you must run at least twice as fast as that.'"

The implications of the Red Queen syndrome are especially problematic for users of technology who are not at the "high end" of the system. Well-off and well-connected farmers receive the latest technological releases and have some chance of staying one step ahead of disaster; but farmers who are less well-off and less well-connected are likely to wind up using already outmoded technology; and in this system, meeting this year's environmental challenges with last year's rice variety (e.g.) is courting disaster.

13 Evidence also is emerging of not just physical or ecological unsustainability but social unsustainability: Kato (1994) has documented the seemingly permanent "abandonment" of 50 percent of the wet rice fields in one Malaysian state between 1970 and 1990.
14 The eyes in the basket represent people in one sense, but in another sense they represent the specific organ that enables a privileged class of people – *manang* "shamans", who have undergone the ritual insertion of placing gold dust into their eyes – to see the spirits who are otherwise invisible to ordinary human beings.
15 See Sandweiss and Quilter (2008) on the study of the general association between ENSO events and human social evolution.
16 The mast was historically associated with one of the most spectacular seasonal phenomena of the tropical forest, the mass migration of the bearded pig (*Sus barbatus*), which followed the staggered peaks of the mast from one river valley to the next (Caldecott 1990).
17 Janzen (1976:383) cautions that it may be impossible to prove that the function of mast-fruiting is pest satiation, because "The species may not yet be extinct, but the interaction is." Janzen (1974:84) elsewhere writes that "Just as we can no longer examine the coevolution of the passenger pigeon and mast-fruiting by oaks in North America, the reduction of big mammal populations in Malaya and Borneo by hunting make this question [of the function of mast-fruiting] very difficult to examine directly."
18 Cf. Von Heland and Folke (2013) on the moral contracts with the spirit ancestors that underpin socio-ecological stability and delivery of ecosystem services in Southern Madagascar.
19 Beeman and Pritchard (2001: 95) write, "In the ecologists' view, the green revolution miracle of Mexican wheat production was a triumph only of monoculture agriculture, was affordable only to elites, and was devoted primarily to producing livestock feed for the export market, not to feeding hungry Mexicans."
20 Cf. Pœrregaard (1989) on ritual sacrifice and relations of reciprocity with nature in the Peruvian Andes; and compare Clay (1991:266) on the Tukano of Brazil (e.g.): "Tukano also believe in reciprocity; in the case of fishing taboos, they believe that if fish are taken from restricted areas, the ancestors of the fish will take infant children – one child for one fish."
21 We are indebted to Carol Carpenter for this insight.
22 Cf. Stewart and Strathern (2008) on concepts of exchange between the cosmos and society in Melanesia.
23 An early and famous statement of the arrogance and folly of attempting to "control nature" through use of pesticides came from Rachel Carson (1962:261–262).

24 This is not to say that the Dayak have no extra-local economic linkages: they have long been involved in production for regional and even global markets – for the past century through cultivation of export crops and for centuries if not millennia before that through the gathering of forest products (Dove 2011).
25 Cf. Hornborg's (2007) point, discussed in Chapter 6, that when technological advances under capitalism save time and space for one actor in one part of world system, other actors somewhere else in the world system must lose time and space.
26 The economic viability of the green revolution model depends on this rigid separation between abundance and dearth, benefits and costs, causes and consequences. The economic calculus of many development programs only makes sense if real costs are obfuscated. Rich (1994) suggests that this is why the World Bank has systematically ignored the environmental externalities of its projects.
27 This difference in attention is not explained by differences in the magnitude of the problem. Pimentel (1991:646) estimated that whereas pre-harvest losses to insects, disease, and weeds account for approximately 35 percent of global crop production, an additional 20 percent is lost during post-harvest transport and storage.
28 There has been an ongoing debate as to whether farmers who adopted green revolution technology became better or worse off as a result (Freebairn 1995), but there is little question as to the negative impact on landless laborers who were displaced from the agricultural system as a result of the widespread adoption of this technology.

5

DIFFERENCES IN PERCEPTIONS OF CLIMATE CHANGE BETWEEN AND WITHIN NATIONS

Studying science, scientists, and folk

> Even though it may burn my tongue to say that global warming is a fact whether you like it or not.
>
> Bruno Latour (2004:227)

> [T]he problem of how to transmit our ecological reasoning to those whom we wish to influence in what seems to us to be an ecologically "good" direction is itself an ecological problem.
>
> Gregory Bateson (1972:504)

> The inhabitants of the zones that are far from temperate... are also farther removed from being temperate in all their conditions.
>
> Ibn Khaldûn (1958, 1:168–169)

Just as there is a clear morality to local environmental relations, so too is there a morality to global ones, albeit often obscured by the complexity and time delays of the system. Global climate change is the largest-scale environmental phenomenon of concern to human society today. From one perspective, it is a factual, geophysical phenomenon without moral implications. But from another perspective, the way that climate change is perceived, studied, experienced, mitigated, and adapted to is relative, varying with the stance of the observer. In short, a physical process has a subjective, partisan, and ultimately moral dimension. The object of this chapter is to explore this dimension of climate change.

I. Introduction

We will begin by recounting a conversation that one of us had with a noted climate scientist, during the time that we were working on this book, on the topic of the social science of climate change. We were attempting to draw attention to this subjective dimension of climate change and to the fact that this dimension, whether we judge it to be accurate or not, helpful or not, is itself a social fact; and this difference is therefore part of the problem of climate change, if we consider its human perception and response as part of the problem.

Author: If the implementation of climate science findings about climate change was straightforward, then we would be close to solving the problem. Not only is this not the case, but the problem of implementing climate science findings in the real world are manifestly so great that I would argue that they are part of the problem of climate change itself. I would argue, that is, that the problem of global climate change is partly a problem of how all of the actors involved conceive of the climate change, its origins and solutions, its winners and losers, heroes and villains, and so on (I am particularly thinking here of differences in conceptions between more- and less-developed countries).

Climate Scientist: Thanks very much. I think these are very important points. But there is another huge problem, really the 400-pound gorilla, which is that we've already changed the physical/chemical landscape, and political, social and economic efforts to reduce CO_2 emissions is at this point closing the barn door after the horse (and cow and chickens) have left.... One might continue to argue that we need further study because we don't entirely understand how the climate system works. But that's a red herring and at this point you have to assess how dire the situation is and take medical response, i.e., go in with the best but admittedly incomplete information you have and act before the patient dies on the table, rather than take another 6 weeks to run every scan imaginable.

Author: I am not sure that we disagree as I will attempt to illustrate using your metaphor of the 400-pound gorilla in the room. The 'gorilla in the room' represents the fact that CO_2 build-up has progressed so far that modest changes no longer suffice and there is no time for further study. Your point is that the only solution, given the severity of the problem, is for the gorilla to leave the room ASAP (viz., implement aggressive global policies to deal with CO_2 emissions). My point is not that the gorilla should not leave the room ASAP, my point is simply that the gorilla is in fact *not* leaving the room, your imperatives notwithstanding, due to an ongoing debate over its species, size, ownership, cost of eviction, etc. Whereas stating that there is a 400-pound gorilla in the room might seem to us both like a sufficient statement of the problem and its obvious solution, in practice it is not. Many of our fellow global citizens have shown themselves quite capable of living in a room with a 400-pound gorilla, the obvious hazards to their health notwithstanding. My point is that it is insufficient to simply draw attention to the gorilla in the room, because the problem is not just the gorilla. The problem is also that we have been slow to take offense at his presence and slow to think about evicting him. This is the human dimension to which I wish to draw your attention: the 'human–gorilla dynamic' if you will. We need to understand and address some of the counter-intuitive features of this dynamic if we are to succeed in evicting the gorilla.

The point that the climate scientist seemed to be trying to make here is that the physical facts of climate change are sufficient unto themselves as a justification for action. The point that we were trying to make is that, regardless of whether we agree that the physical facts should be sufficient, it is obviously the case that they are not sufficient, since the needed action is not taking place. The climate scientist suggested that the reason for the lack of action is the "incompleteness" of our knowledge of climate change, but he argued that we could not afford to wait for complete knowledge. In fact, we do not think that the problem is incomplete knowledge, rather we think that the problem is contested knowledge. That is, where the climate scientist sees a problem of science, we see a problem of politics. Put otherwise, and to return to the language of the gorilla, we do not dispute the compelling presence of the gorilla (of climate change) in the room. But we are asking, what else is in the room besides the gorilla – for example, poverty, uneven development, political-economic inequity, and environmental injustice (Sustainable Energy for All 2012)? We might call these things the "invisible 400-pound gorilla in the room".

II. Initial North–South fault line: the WRI–CSE debate

In the course of the "gorilla debate", we refer to the difference between more- and less-developed countries in their conceptions of climate change. A divide between the former and latter, between the global "North" and "South", was prominent early in the global discourse of climate change. This was epitomized in a famous 1990–1991 exchange between the World Resources Institute (WRI) of Washington DC and the Center for Science and Environment (CSE) in New Delhi, which has ever since been cited as the textbook example of North–South divisions over climate change (e.g., Demeritt 2001; Jasanoff 2004a; Lahsen 2004).

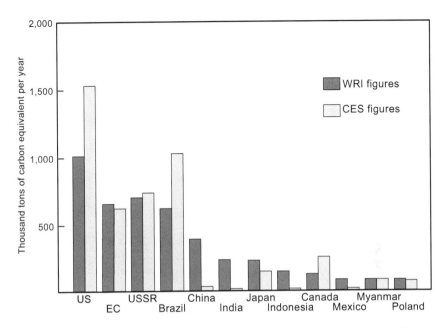

FIGURE 5.1 Countries with the highest net greenhouse gas emissions, according to the WRI versus the CES. The WRI figures are taken from WRI (1990:349–350, Table 24.2); the CES figures are taken from Agarwal and Narain (1991:34–35, Appendix 7). "EC" refers to the European Commission, the forerunner of today's European Union, which contained the following countries at the time of the WRI–CSE exchange in 1990–1991: Belgium, Denmark, France, Germany, Greece, Ireland, Italy, Luxembourg, the Netherlands, Portugal, Spain, the United Kingdom.

1. The debate

In 1990, the World Resources Institute (WRI) of Washington DC published its bi-annual report on *World Resources*, with two of its twenty-five chapters focusing on global climate change. The publication of this material (in this report and subsequently elsewhere as well[1]) initiated a sharp debate. The most pointed contribution to it came from two researchers at India's Center for Science and Environment (CSE), Anil Agarwal and Sunita Narain (1991), who accused WRI of "environmental colonialism". They were particularly critical of WRI's conclusion that the developing countries of the "South" shared some responsibility for global warming, which had previously been assigned largely to the developed countries of the "North". Agarwal and Narain's analysis of greenhouse gas emissions found the latter to be more culpable and the former to be less culpable than appeared from the WRI report (Figure 5.1).[2]

The primary reason for the difference between the CSE and WRI analyses was that they emphasize different aspects of the same phenomenon (Table 5.1). For example, whereas research on global warming had previously focused on

TABLE 5.1 The early lines of the global warming debate

	WRI/North	CES/South
Emission emphasis	Fossil and biomass fuels CO_2 and CH_4	Fossil fuel CO_2 CO_2 and CH_4
	Combustion & burning	Combustion
	Long- and short-lived gases	Long-lived gases
Spatial emphasis	Suitability of low latitudes to be CO_2 sinks	Responsibility at high latitudes, vulnerability at low latitudes
Temporal emphasis	Present/future	Past
	Future threat	Past damage
	Addition to problem	Cumulative problem
	Avoiding past environmental mistakes	Repeating past economic successes
Problem	Environmental protection	Economic development
	Southern greed	Northern hegemony
	Efficiency of emissions	Morality of emissions
Solution	Index based on total emissions	Index based on total population
	Global environmental accord	Structural change in global economy

Source: Michael R. Dove

combustion of fossil fuels and the release of long-lived CO_2, the WRI report directed some attention toward the burning of biomass and the release of shorter-lived gases like CH_4. The significance of this shift lies in the fact that while the former is more associated with the energy regimes of the developed countries, the latter is more associated with that of the developing countries.[3]

In many respects, this debate reduced to differences between the self-interests of the North and those of the South. While the WRI report proposed to allocate shares in global carbon sinks based upon each country's total emissions (Table 5.1) – which the North has a lot of – the CSE report counter-proposed to allocate them on the basis of each country's population – which the South has a lot of (Brookfield 1992; Redclift 1992). The CSE report spoke of WRI's "legerdemain" in making a virtue out of the North's excesses (of emissions), but it was equally deft in making a virtue of the South's population growth (Agarwal and Narain 1991).[4] Redclift (1992) noted that the CSE report was strangely silent on the role of population growth in global warming, despite the fact that some predicted that this growth would account for one-half of the increase in emissions in developing countries between 1985 and 2100 (Bongaarts 1992). The WRI report paid some heed to "efficiency" of emissions (in terms of amount of emission per dollar of GDP), which is a measure

Perceptions of climate change between and within nations **99**

FIGURE 5.2 Yo! Amigo!! We need that tree to protect us from the greenhouse effect!
Source: Scott Willis 1989

where the North enjoyed clear superiority over the South; this measure was ignored in the CSE report (Table 5.1). And while the CSE report distinguished between "survival emissions" – such as those from cattle and irrigated rice fields, which predominate in the South – and "luxury emissions", such as those from automobiles, which predominate in the North – the WRI report made no such distinction (Figure 5.2).[5]

The rival positions of North and South also have spatial and temporal dimensions (Table 5.1). Regarding space, for example, the CSE report claimed that the North's campaign to halt forest clearance in the South was motivated by a desire to utilize the South as a "carbon sink" to cope with excessive emissions from the North. It claimed that this geographical division of functions would preserve the current imbalance of political-economic power between North and South. As regards time, the CSE report accused the WRI of focusing on present and future as opposed to past greenhouse gas emissions, as reflected in increased attention to short-lived gases and in the concept of a nineteenth-century baseline (Agarwal and Narain 1991; Smith 1991a; Subak 1991).[6] The CSE – with its emphasis on past emissions and long-lived gases – had just the opposite orientation. Whereas the CSE accused the WRI, in effect, of attempting to deny history, the CSE itself was trying to deny the future. In fact, both orientations were self-serving: the focus on the past served the interests of those countries with grim "emission futures" but little in the way of culpable "emission histories"; while the focus on the future served the interests of those countries in the opposite position, namely those whose emissions futures were brighter than their pasts.

2. Historical synchronicity and asynchronicity

The different perspectives on climate change of the CSE and WRI, of South and North, are to some extent a function of history and geography. Because technological transitions around the globe during the modern era have not been "synchronous", the transitions relevant to global warming have taken place in some nations or regions before others. This is reflected in the choices, alternatives, and constraints that the contemporary developing nations face that the developed nations historically did not have to face at a similar stage in their development. For example, today's developing countries must make choices between, on the one hand, cheap but dirty technologies that have long been available, and on the other hand, expensive but clean industrial technologies that have been recently invented. The technology and critical awareness that is being brought to bear on the greenhouse gas budgets of today's developing countries is the product of the greenhouse gas histories of the developed countries, although it was not brought to bear on these earlier histories.

The developed countries, in contrast, historically enjoyed an absence of choice – or at least of awareness – that is no longer available to their developing counterparts: they could make all of their greenhouse gas-related decisions on strict economic grounds. And today the developed countries enjoy a presence of choices (in mitigating global warming), by virtue of the economic and technological advantages of their historical position, that is denied to the developing countries: the five strategies for reducing global warming listed in the 1990 WRI report were all within greater economic and technological reach of the developed than the developing nations: (1) increasing the efficiency of energy production and use, (2) switching from carbon-intensive fuels such as coal to hydrogen-intensive fuels such as natural gas, (3) encouraging the rapid development and use of solar and other carbon-free energy sources, (4) eliminating the production of most CFCs and developing the means to recapture those now in use, (5) reducing the rate of deforestation. By virtue of historical antecedence alone, therefore, the developed countries enjoy the moral high ground: they can elect to be "good" today, and they do not have to worry about having once been "bad." In contrast, the developing countries are bad today, at a stage when it may cost them to be good.

The antecedence of the developed countries vis-à-vis the developing ones seemed oddly coercive in other ways as well. The future development of the developing countries cannot follow the same path once taken by the developed ones: the future of the developing countries must differ from the past of the developed ones. The developing countries must follow a different path than the developed countries, precisely because they were preceded by the developed countries, and this is part of the problem. If a path from the past is followed, it will have different consequences – e.g., use of dirty combustion technologies will have a different impact on global warming today (*ceteris paribus*) than it did when the developed countries were themselves developing – so in a literal sense the past cannot be repeated even if the attempt is made. The challenge, in fact, is the reverse of this: it is to achieve the benefits achieved by past paths while not following them. As Hayes and Smith (1993) wrote at the time:

> The challenge facing humanity, therefore, is to find ways that the many benefits accompanying economic development can be attained by the world's poor without simultaneously emitting the amounts of greenhouse gases that have accompanied such economic development in the past.

Should the developing nations be punished for being among the last to deforest, at a time when the carbon consequences of deforestation are least tolerable? Arguably they are already on the front lines of paying for environmental damages (Farbotko and Lazrus 2012). On the other hand, should the developed nations be punished for deforestation that their ancestors carried out and at a time when the consequences were more tolerable?

3. "One world" versus many

One of the main conclusions that the CSE reached in its analysis of the WRI report was that there were "political motivations" behind it (Agarwal and Narain 1991). Similarly, the editor of a journal issue devoted to the WRI–CSE debate characterized it as a debate about "equity issues" (Mitchell 1992). And Ahuja (1992) thanked the CSE for making clear that dividing up the resource pie is a "political act" – an act of partisan pie-slicing of which the CSE itself was guilty, however. On the other hand, some claimed to see just the opposite. Thus, the WRI scientists, as one observer commented (Thery 1992), "were pleased to show that everybody shared responsibility for the build-up of greenhouse gases in the atmosphere". Even those who were suspicious of WRI's report, or of CSE's response, urged those involved to rise up above politics. For example, Ahuja (1992) admonished all participants in the debate to "assume" that each side is motivated by "concern for the earth and our collective well-being", not by narrow self-interest aimed at "perpetuating disparity" on the part of the North or "extracting resources from rich countries" on the part of the South. Another observer simply urged "no more cold-blooded colonism [*sic*]; no more narrow-minded nationalism; but only warm-hearted globalism" (Songqiao 1992).

This is an enduring tension. There is a compelling anti-political, "universalist" bias in environmental discourse in general, which valorizes commonality versus difference, and which has also characterized the discourse of climate change. As Lahsen (2004:153–154) writes, the "Temptation to gloss over these persistent differences and unresolved tensions [both within and between nations] is considerable, not the least in the environmental arena where various actors – whether politicians, environmental activists, and academic scholars studying international regimes – seek to consolidate support for their vision of social reality and social change." This "one world" vision is a powerful tool for mobilizing people to address challenging environmental problems, but it also has a downside, which has drawn the critical attention of many prominent scholars (e.g., Lahsen 2004; Jasanoff 2004a; Ingold 2008).

The problem with a universalist framing of climate change is that it is not strictly accurate – as many have said of the "lifeboat earth" metaphor, not everyone is *in* the lifeboat – and its draws attention away from important non-universalities, from differences. As Lahsen (2004:167) says, the idea of a shared global vision (e.g., the purported global "epistemic community" of climate science) can "fail to capture and threaten to obscure" important divisions. It can obscure historic divisions – like unequal national histories of, and thus responsibility for, carbon emission – and it can obscure contemporary ones as well. As Demeritt (2001: 313) notes, some critics of the global discourse of climate change argue that "the threat of future climate change holds little meaning for developing nations and the poor people in them struggling daily in the face of crippling structural-adjustment policies with more basic and immediate needs of sanitation, health, and hunger". Not only does the globalist vision marginalize non-climate issues, but even with respect to climate change it is selective in what it problematizes. Here again is Demeritt (2001:313, cf. Gallagher 2009): "The specifically global scaling of climate change highlights more general concerns about the effects of increasing GHG concentrations in the earth's radiation balance at the expense of other ways of formulating the problem, such as the structural imperatives of the capitalist economy driving those emissions, and indeed of other problems, such as poverty and disease."

A universal framing can produce a discourse of climate change that, with its universalist pretensions but actual particularities, serves problematic political functions. Its political power is all the greater because it is cloaked in apolitical universality. The result can be an exacerbation of existing political-economic inequity. Indeed, the field of environmental justice was developed to study the discriminatory impacts on disadvantaged segments of society of assumed non-discriminatory environmentalist regimes (Bryant 1995; Pellow 2004). The result can be an aggravation of North–South relations with respect to assessing climate change blame and responsibility (Lahsen 2004:153–154; Roberts and Parks 2007; Lahsen 2010a). Finally, none of these ill-effects can be divorced from the way that climate change science is planned, carried out, and communicated. Perhaps the most damaging consequence of a naive universalist discourse of climate change, in short, is that it ignores the way that climate change science and climate change geopolitics co-produce one another (Lahsen 2004: 168).

III. Complications in the North–South divide at the global level

Given the way that the emerging global discourse of climate change shaped up in the early 1990s, as exemplified by the acrimonious WRI–CSE debate, it seemed like the North–South opposition would completely dominate this discussion, marginalizing all other fault lines. And indeed, prominent scholars like Jasanoff (2004a) and Roberts and Parks (2007) continue to see a prominent North–South dimension to the climate change debate. However, the evolution of the international climate policy regime in the decades following the WRI–CSE exchange did not in fact strictly follow a North–South fault line (Tables 5.2 and 5.3).

In contrast with the other environmental-related international policy regimes like those formed on acid rain, hazardous waste trade, or the protection of the Antarctic, the climate change regime was not pioneered by specific nation-states. Instead, the leading role was assumed by two international organizations within the United Nations system: the UN Environment Program (UNEP) and the World Meteorological Organization (WMO). During the late 1970s, these two institutions organized key events and promoted key publications that defined global warming as an international issue and political priority, culminating in the First World Climate Conference held in Geneva in February 1979, primarily organized by the WMO (Sagar and Kandlikar 1997).[7]

The process of defining and describing climate change accelerated in the mid-1980s due to the availability of more accurate and reliable research. With the purpose of providing an institutional scientific global framework for the climate change issue, the WMO and UNEP created the Intergovernmental Panel on Climate Change (IPCC) in 1988, with the mandate to "assess the magnitude and timing of climate changes, estimate their impacts and present strategies for how to respond" (IPCC 2007). In immediate response and opposition, an industry coalition of British and American multinationals established the "Global Climate Coalition" (GCC) a few months later in 1989. A network of NGOs working on climate change, the "Climate Action Network" (CAN), taking a political stance reflective of the interests of developing countries, was also founded in 1989.

With states and non-state actors already active in a contest over the climate policy regime, the UN General Assembly legitimized climate change as a priority issue in international politics by adopting Resolution 45/53 in December 1988, which recognized that "climate change is a common concern of mankind", and determined that "necessary and timely action should be taken to deal with climate change within a global framework". The successful negotiation process of the "Montreal Protocol on Substances that Deplete the Ozone Layer", which went into force in January 1989, encouraged hopes for a constructive negotiation process on climate change between developed and developing nations.

During the 1990s and the early discussions of the Kyoto Protocol, developing countries viewed global warming, like the ozone layer, as a "Northern" problem

TABLE 5.2 Major events in the development of the international climate policy regime, 1979–2010

1979	First World Climate Conference takes place in Geneva, Switzerland.
1992	United Nations Framework Convention on Climate Change created. Under the international treaty, countries agreed to stabilize greenhouse gas emissions in the atmosphere.
1994	UNFCCC comes into force.
1995	Countries begin to negotiate binding agreement to require reductions in greenhouse gas emissions.
1997	Kyoto Protocol signed, laying out legally binding emission targets for developed countries to reduce emissions by an average of 5.2% below 1990 levels between 2008 and 2012. The treaty also requires developing countries to track and report emissions and develop national climate change policies.
2002	Canada's Parliament ratifies the Kyoto Protocol February 2005. After enough countries have ratified the treaty, the Kyoto Protocol comes into force. The United States, which signed the treaty, declines to ratify the agreement and is not bound by any targets.
2007	Bali Road Map adopted, laying the foundation for new efforts to adapt to a changing climate while helping both developed and developing countries reduce their emissions.
2008	First Kyoto commitment period begins.
2009	A climate summit in Copenhagen collapses without a binding agreement. But many countries draft an agreement with voluntary emission reduction targets.
2010	Cancun Agreements create a Green Climate Fund to help developing nations deal with the effects of climate change and reduce their global-warming causing emissions.
2011	Durban conference ends with countries agreeing to new climate change regime to be finalized by 2015.
2012	Leaked draft of Intergovernmental Panel on Climate Change assessment report on latest scientific research says scientists are "virtually certain" human activity is upsetting the balance in the atmosphere and causing most of the planetary warming observed in recent decades.
2012	Canada withdraws from the Kyoto Protocol.
2013	Beginning of second Kyoto commitment period.
2015	International deadline to finalize new agreement on emission target reductions.
2020	New global climate change regime slated to come into force.

Source: Daniel M. Kammen

TABLE 5.3 The North–South dimension during the evolution of the international climate policy regime

Date	Event	Geo-political fault line
1988–89	IPCC, GCC, CAN established	Global vs Industry vs South
1991	INC, Washington D.C. Ministerial Conference – Beijing Declaration	North responsible, South needs help
1991	INC Geneva	North must limit emission, though contested
1992	Earth Summit RIO, FCCC	Differentiates Annex I & II (North) vs Non-Annex nations (South)
1997	Kyoto Protocol	Kyoto "surprise", CDM developed, relaxing North-South division
2001	COP-bis Bonn	EU (North) and G-77+China (South) cooperate, North and South also form EIG
2001	COP-7 Marrakesh	EU (North) and G-77+China (South) vs Umbrella Group (North)
2007	COP/MOP-3 Bali	EU (North) and G-77 (South) cooperate, U.S. vs China
2008	COP/MOP-4 Poznan	South vs Umbrella Group (North)
2009	COP-15 Copenhagen	U.S. vs BASIC (South), differentiation within South

Source Michael R. Dove

for which they had no causal responsibility. Their agenda prioritized poverty and development issues like sanitation, urban pollution, and desertification. However, once the climate community began reporting on the potentially catastrophic impacts of climate change in the South, some developing countries took sides and assumed leadership roles. Marked divisions also erupted between the cartel of the Organization of Petroleum Exporting Countries (OPEC), whose economies were completely dependent on hydrocarbons and hence hydrocarbon emissions, and the Association of Small Island States (AOSIS), who saw their very survival at risk and who consequently favored ambitious emissions reductions (Prum 2007:225). The AOSIS was the first group to propose that the less-industrialized countries take a position in favor of legally binding emissions, which the G-77/China then adopted as its official stance. At this stage, the perceived strategic need for unity outweighed internal differences, allowing for a quite unified Southern bargaining position (Najam 2004:227). Among the Northern nations, on the other hand, there were divisions. The major emission nations – the United States, Japan, and the Soviet Union – all rejected the idea of explicit targets and timetables. This contrasted with the position of several European countries that had strong domestic environmental movements – particularly Denmark, the Netherlands and Germany – which chose to acknowledge global warming as a real threat and espoused the need for a legally binding international agreement (Grubb, Victor, and Hope 1991).[8]

The political negotiations began at a conference in Toronto in 1988, "The Changing Atmosphere: Implications for Global Security", which was attended by government officials, scientists, and representatives of industry and environmental NGOs from forty-six countries, and concluded with a proposal for a reduction in carbon dioxide emissions. After several subsequent conferences and changing negotiating positions among the actors involved, at the end of 1990 the UN General Assembly established by Resolution 45/212 the Intergovernmental Negotiating Committee for a Framework Convention on Climate Change (INC) as a single intergovernmental negotiating process. For the next fifteen months, nations gathered in five different sessions to discuss the coming shape of the international climate regime.

During the first INC session in Washington in February 1991, the discussions partly reflected a North–South struggle. This tension became more explicit by the second INC session in 1992, when just days beforehand China organized a widely attended "Ministerial Conference of Developing Countries on Environment and Development". The outcome was the "Beijing Declaration", which explicitly framed the climate regime negotiations process in North–South terms by asserting that: "The FCCC [Framework Convention on Climate Change] currently being negotiated should clearly recognize that it is developed countries, which are mainly responsible for excessive emissions of greenhouse gases, historically and currently…. Developing countries must be provided with full scientific, technical and financial cooperation to cope with the adverse impacts of climate change" (*Yearbook of International Cooperation on Environment and Development*; Prum 2007:230).

In the subsequent INC session in Geneva in June 1991, the main principle of the Beijing Declaration was adopted, namely the limitation and reduction of CO_2 emissions by the Northern countries, despite resistance and counter-proposals from the Northern parties themselves. For example, the U.K. and Japan proposed a "pledge and review" process that would allow countries to set their own targets and encompassed not only the developed but also the rapidly developing nations, which was rejected by China and India (Grubb, Victor, and Hope 1991). After several more INC sessions, the FCCC was finally signed by 154 countries at the Earth Summit in Rio de Janeiro in June 1992, with the goal of restoring greenhouse emissions by 2000 to "earlier levels". The FCCC did not commit any nation to hold emissions to a specific level, despite an effort by the European negotiators to persuade the U.S. to accept a binding commitment. By December 1993 enough countries had ratified the Climate Convention to make it operational, entering into force in March 1994.

In terms of framing the dynamics of future negotiations, the most important outcome of this early bargaining process was that it established a commitment, albeit a non-binding one, for the developed countries to stabilize their greenhouse gases emissions at 1990 levels by 2000. It formalized a North–South divide by separating the signatory countries into two categories. The developed countries were classified as either "Annex I" or "Annex II" parties, which included both Organization for Economic Cooperation and Development (OECD) members and countries with economies in transition (CEITs), each of whom was expected to "adopt national policies and take corresponding measures on the mitigation of climate change, by limiting its anthropogenic emissions of greenhouse gases" (FCCC/INFORMAL/84).[9] Conversely, of the developing countries were classified as "Non-Annex" countries, with no commitments in terms of either finances or policy reform.

This North–South division was addressed in the "Principles" section of the FCCC text, in a now-famous statement: "The Parties should protect the climate system for the benefit of present and future generations of humankind, on the basis of equity and in accordance with their common but differentiated responsibilities and respective capabilities. Accordingly, the developed country Parties should take the lead in combating climate change and the adverse effects thereof." The principle of "common but differentiated responsibilities" would play a unique role in the subsequent evolution of the international climate regime, framing asymmetric environmental obligations at all levels, with no obligations from the South and allowing for differentiated obligations within the North. Many observers have argued that this principle one-sidedly benefited developing countries.

This seeming division between developed and developing countries was not as straightforward as it may have appeared at first glance, however, since the FCCC also differentiated responsibilities within the developed country bloc, namely between Annex I and Annex II Parties, stating: "a certain degree of flexibility shall be allowed by the Conference of the Parties to the Parties included in Annex I undergoing the process of transition to a market economy". The text of the Convention is explicit in assigning financial commitments only to the Annex II Parties. Therefore, some of the dynamics of the North–South divide were reproduced within the Northern bloc.

The EU had originally proposed a 15 percent cut by the year 2010 of a basket of three gases (carbon dioxide, methane, and nitrous oxide); Japan proposed a cut of 5 percent by 2010 of all three gases combined; and the G-77/China called for a gas-by-gas reduction of 7.5 percent by 2005, 15 percent by 2010 and 35 percent by 2020, for the same three gases. Ultimately, the Kyoto Protocol, adopted by the COP-3 in December 1997, imposed on developed countries a legally binding reduction of their overall emissions of six greenhouse gasses (CO_2, CH_4, N_2O, HFHs, PFCs and SF_6). The reduction targets, to be achieved between 2008 and 2012, were tied to a baseline of 1990 emission levels. The specific targets varied from country to country. Some countries, like Russia,

Ukraine and New Zealand, managed to avoid any commitment on emission reductions; while Australia, Iceland and Norway were even allowed to increase their emissions.

The Kyoto Protocol also established three flexible implementation mechanisms: an Emissions Trading System, allowing countries that have emission units permitted but not "used" to sell this excess capacity to countries over their targets, effectively creating the "carbon market"; Joint Implementation of emissions-reduction projects among Annex I Parties, meaning developed countries and countries with economies in transition, including Russia; and the Clean Development Mechanism, which proposed emissions reduction projects for developing countries. The Clean Development Mechanism was labeled "the Kyoto surprise", because it seemed to represent an unexpected relaxation of the North–South structure of blame and responsibility for mitigation established by the UNFCCC in Rio in 1992. While the Kyoto negotiations mainly focused on struggles within the Northern bloc, there were some North–South dimensions as well. For example, the United States' negotiating stance was circumscribed by the Byrd–Hagel Resolution, passed by the U.S. Senate in July 1997 by a vote of 95–0, which stated that the US would not honor their Kyoto commitments unless key developing nations "meaningfully participated" in climate mitigation efforts.

Negotiations resumed at the Bonn Meeting (COP-6 bis) in July 2001. With the new Bush Administration refusing to ratify the Kyoto Protocol, the dynamics shifted considerably. Ironically, exclusion of the U.S. from the process increased the motivation of the remaining parties to reach an agreement, because some negotiators were now willing to accept provisions that they had opposed when they saw the U.S. as the principal beneficiary. Remarkably, this stage of negotiations also witnessed substantive North–South cooperation, largely between the European Union and the G-77/China, which together pushed for strong and ambitious implementation mechanisms. Another example of North–South cooperation was the formation of the "Environmental Integrity Group", a coalition consisting of the Republic of Korea, Switzerland and Mexico, again showing that the negotiation of the international climate policy regime at this stage was more than a simple North–South struggle.

To the surprise of many observers, the Bonn negotiations were relatively successful, satisfying a majority of both developed and developing countries regarding the thorny issues of carbon sinks, finance, implementation mechanisms, and a compliance system. One representative of an otherwise potentially obstructive state, Peter Hodgson, New Zealand's Energy Minister, said "we have delivered probably the most comprehensive and difficult agreement in history" (ENB Vol.12 No.176). Nevertheless, many problematic and arguably regressive concessions were made by the EU and the G-77/China to seal the deal in Bonn, in an effort to appease a veto coalition led – in the absence of the United States – by the Russian Federation and including Australia, Canada, and Japan (ENB Vol.12 No.176). This coalition's leverage stemmed from the fact that the Kyoto Protocol had to be ratified by at least 55 Parties accounting for at least 55 percent of 1990 emissions, which made the support of at least Japan and Russia absolutely necessary.

In the subsequent Marrakesh meeting (COP-7) held in November 2001, the EU, which was again supported by the G-77/China, pressed for an ambitious deal, although it also had to preserve enough consensus to ratify the Kyoto Protocol. On the other hand, the Umbrella Group continued to seek flexibility in fulfilling their emission commitments and, with veto power, they pushed back against the position of the EU and the G-77/China; they lowered the eligibility requirements for implementation mechanisms, weakened requirements for public participation and transparency, weakened requirements for providing information on sinks, and weakened the compliance system (ENB Vol.12 No.189). Notwithstanding these painful compromises, satisfactory agreements for all parties involved were reached on the issue of flexible mechanisms and financing, with the creation of three new climate funds that would mainly benefit the developing countries. These included two new financial mechanisms: the Special Climate Change Fund to finance projects relating to adaptation, technology transfer, energy, forestry, economic diversification, etc.; and the Least Developed Country Fund, which has mainly been used to finance National Adaptation Programs of Action. An Adaptation Fund also was nominally created, although it would have to wait until the next phase of negotiations to be approved.

With the U.S. absent from the negotiation process and the most sensitive operational issues having been defined, after Marrakesh the bargaining continued in the next COPs in Delhi (2002), Milan (2003), and Buenos Aires (2004), leading up to the ratification of the Kyoto Protocol. By May 2002, the EU and its member states had ratified it, but two more years were needed in order to satisfy the clause requiring approval by parties accounting for at least 55 percent of emissions. After a painstaking negotiation process and under very favorable terms, the Russian Federation finally ratified it in November 2004, formally entering into the Kyoto Protocol in February 2005.

The COP/MOP-3 in Bali, Indonesia in 2007 marked the culmination of a year of extremely high levels of political, media and public attention to climate change science and policy. It produced a two-year "roadmap" called the Bali Action Plan (BAP), which outlined five key themes: (1) a shared vision for long-term cooperative action, including a long-term global goal for emission reductions; (2) enhanced national/international action on mitigation emphasizing Measurable, Reportable and Verifiable (MRV) objectives, Quantified Emission Limitation and Reduction Objectives (QULROs), mitigation commitments by developed countries and Nationally Appropriate Mitigation Actions (NAMAs), and a program for Reducing Emissions from Deforestation and Forest Degradation (REDD) in developing countries; (3) enhanced action on adaptation, especially in the most vulnerable countries; (4) technology transfer and diffusion of green technologies, and (5) the provision of financial resources to support implementation of the plan (Grubler, Nakicenovic, and Victor 1999).

At the heart of the Bali roadmap were two parallel negotiating tracks: the Ad Hoc Working Group on Long-term Cooperative Action (AWG-LCA) to carry out the BAP agenda; and the already existing Ad Hoc Working Group on Further Commitments for Annex I Parties under the Kyoto Protocol (AWG-KP). The Bali conference established an Adaptation Fund Board, the majority of whose members came from the South, but this did not simply reflect the usual North–South division of interest. There was a deep division between different visions of how to administer the fund: one view was that joint management by Northern and Southern nations would bring shared understanding; and another view was that equity would only be achieved by establishing separate "Northern" and "Southern" funds – precedent for the latter approach being the United Nation's establishment of the UNDP based in New York city and the UNEP based in Nairobi. The potential polarization was eased when the EU decided to relax their negotiation stance, by issuing a pre-Bali declaration that they would accept whatever model the G-77 endorsed, thus reflecting yet another instance of EU/G-77 collaboration.

One of the most significant developments of the Bali conference was development of a proposal to ensure that all mitigation actions undertaken by developing country parties would be supported by technology, financing, and capacity building, subject to Measurable, Reportable and Verifiable procedures. The fact that this was one of the key points under discussion illustrates that the international climate regime was moving into new policy territory, by involving developing countries in mitigation actions. However, this proposed involvement was attended by controversy and division, particularly within the Southern bloc. Bangladesh proposed inclusion of a reference acknowledging "differences in national circumstances", which failed due to vehement opposition by China and India. In a direct challenge to China, the United States similarly insisted that the responsibility to mitigate must be differentiated "among developing countries in terms of the size of their economies, their level of emissions and level of energy utilization, and that the responsibilities of the smaller or least developed countries are different from the larger, more advanced developing countries" (IEA 2012).

At the subsequent COP/MOP-4 in Poznan, Poland in December 2008, there was more urgency in the political atmosphere than was the case in Bali. The negotiations were carried out against the backdrop of the rapid deterioration of the global financial system; and in spite of the election of a more climate-friendly Obama Administration in the United States, the U.S. negotiators came with good intentions but without anything substantive to put on the negotiation table. The South did allow for some minor progress on Measurable, Reportable and Verifiable provisions and the idea of a registry for Nationally Appropriate Mitigation Actions in developing countries. However, all suggestions for differentiation among developing countries in terms of responsibility for mitigation were, again, firmly rejected by the major developing countries, while being endorsed by the Umbrella Group.

In the much-awaited COP-15 in Copenhagen in December 2009, the largest environment-related meeting in history (Bodansky 2010: 3), the bargaining remained stalled almost until the end of the conference. The developed countries in Annex I were generally reluctant to accept a new round of emission targets under the Kyoto Protocol for the post-2012 period, unless other major emitters including the United States and the major developing countries accepted legal commitments as well. Their expressed preference was for a single, new, comprehensive legal agreement that would replace the Kyoto Protocol. However, the developing countries were united in opposing such a one-track approach. They feared losing one of the Kyoto provisions most important to them, namely the legally binding emissions commitments for the developed countries. Consequently, the G-77 nations repeatedly insisted during negotiations that the negotiating track from Kyoto (AWG-KP) receive the same attention as the negotiating track from Bali (AWG-LCA).

In the end, the attendance by 115 Heads of State in the last days of the Conference changed the dynamics of the negotiations. A "Friends of the Chair" group, consisting of roughly 25 countries consulting with one another at the highest political levels, produced an agreement, the final wording of which was decided by the U.S. and the four major developing economies of the BASIC group, Brazil, South Africa, India and China (Hamilton, 2009). This signaled a significant change in the structure of negotiations, from the EU and G-77/China versus the Umbrella Group in the Marrakesh Accords, to a new geopolitical contest primarily between the U.S. and the major developing countries.

Ultimately, with the facilitation of UN Secretary-General Ban Ki-moon, it was agreed at COP-15 to "take note" of this Copenhagen Accord and establish a procedure, without precedent under the UNFCCC, for countries to register their support for it, and submit their mitigation targets and actions, by a deadline of 31 January 2010. Because of the circumstances under which the Copenhagen Accord was drafted, it included some ambiguity and confusion in substance and form (Muller 2010: 7). But it did clearly signal a redrawing of the long-standing fault line between Annex and non-Annex parties in the international climate regime, by unmistakably differentiating responsibilities within the South: "Non-Annex I Parties to the Convention will implement mitigation actions.... Least developed countries and Small Island developing States may undertake actions voluntarily" (Paragraph 5).

In summary, whereas North–South tensions have always been present in the international climate policy regime, this particular opposition has not defined many of the most important policy debates and outcomes. A North–South dimension was most clearly observed in the early stages of the international climate negotiations. Under the then-leadership of China, and negotiating through a fairly united G-77, the developing countries exerted great influence on the development of the climate regime by focusing on questions of distributional equity. This was made clearest in the FCCC principles dating from 1990, and the official separation between developed countries as Annex I parties and developing countries as non-Annex parties in the 1992 Rio accord.

To date, the Kyoto Protocol negotiation process is perhaps best understood as a North–North struggle, where the countries responsible for bearing the costs of the regime (the Annex I parties) fiercely fought over this responsibility at the negotiation table. The EU consistently promoted an ambitious protocol, partially reflecting the political influence of their domestic environmental movements; while the veto coalition consistently sought maximum flexibility in both emission targets and implementation mechanisms, reflecting domestic political pressures from their fossil fuel-dependent industries. Although the South, under the umbrella of the G-77, continued to be actively engaged in the process, it mainly defended what it had initially gained under the FCCC.

IV. Non-North–South dimensions

The complications of the international climate policy regime do not solely involve inter-nation differences within either the Southern bloc or the Northern one. There also are differences within individual countries in both South and North, which point to the existence of additional, often unanticipated, and in some cases even unseen dimensions of climate and society.

1. Complications within Southern nations

The early prominence of a North–South fault line in debates over the science of climate change prompted some scholars to study communities of climate change scientists in the South, and what they have found has been surprising (Kandlikar and Sagar 1999; Mwandosya 1999; Lahsen 2004; Thaker and Leiserowitz 2014). Myanna Lahsen, an American anthropologist working at the Brazilian Institute for Space Research, is one of the leading scholars worldwide of this subject (Lahsen 2004, 2007, 2009, 2010). She found in the Brazilian community of climate scientists some continued affinity for a Southern stance like that of the CSE, which defied their easy placement within a so-called global "epistemic community" (Haas 1992). On the other hand, Lahsen also found that it was problematic to simply locate these scientists within a monolithic Southern bloc. As she writes, "On second glance, not only does the transnational epistemic community appear internally fractured along geopolitical lines; important fractures also reveal themselves at the national level and even within the subjectivities of individual scientists, at the most intimate level of personal commitments and understandings of self and the world" (Lahsen 2004: 168; cf. Thaker and Leiserowitz 2014).

Some similar differences within the climate science communities in individual Northern countries have been found as well. There is a small but vocal cadre of scientists in Western Europe and North America who have been critical of the evidence of climate change put forth by the majority of the international climate science community. One of the most interesting studies of scientist skeptics is Lahsen's (2008) study of a small group of aging nuclear physicists in the U.S., whose critique of the thesis of global climate change traces back to their critique of the "nuclear winter" thesis (viz., another thesis of global-scale climate change), which they saw as unnecessarily undermining the strategic value of the nuclear weapons that they helped to develop. But the most interesting, and likely the most important development of difference within individual Northern nations, involves a divide between all scientists, on the one hand, and on the other hand the lay masses who are engaging in a wholesale rejection of scientific authority. This difference has deep historic roots.

2. Complications within Northern nations

Human thinking about the relationship between climate and society, is ancient. In the second millennium B.C., sages in India contemplated the relationship between humoral oppositions within the human body and the divide of India into wet and dry zones and laid down corresponding prescriptions and proscriptions for a healthy life (Zimmermann 1987). In the classical era of Greece and Rome, folk beliefs and practices regarding weather and weather prediction were studied and enumerated by the great thinkers of the time, as noted in Chapter 2. This folk tradition of climate knowledge persisted well into the nineteenth century, when it was challenged by the rise of the modern scientific paradigm. An "epistemic contest" resulted, ending with a seemingly decisive victory for the scientific paradigm, which completely supplanted and marginalized folk theories of climate (cf. Jankovic [2014/2007] on the case of wind). This seemed to signal the end of the millennia-old history of folk theories of climate and its impact on human society. Modern climate science is dominated by highly complex, quantitative, predictive modeling, which is not only beyond the capabilities of most non-climate scientists, but is also beyond the capabilities of most of the world's national scientific communities. So determinate is the role of this type of climate science, indeed, that Hulme (2011:247) calls it "climate reductionism" or "neo-environmental determinism". But the waxing of hegemony of this variant of climate knowledge within the academic community has been matched, whether coincidentally or not, by a waning of its influence in the wider society.

A lay critique of the scientific thesis of anthropogenic climate change roared into being during the first decade of the twenty-first century, in particular in the United States. Its virulence and ubiquity can be seen in the phenomenon of public criticism of scientific articles on climate change (or the synopsis of them in news media), when published in journals or other media that invite on-line comment. The Yale legal scholar Dan Kahan (2012) is one of the few academics to seriously study this phenomenon. He rejects the idea that critiques of climate change science simply stem from "irrationality", arguing that the problem is not that the public is irrational, but rather that their "reasoning powers have been disabled by a polluted science-communication environment" (ibid.). Scientific belief or disbelief has come to be associated with group identity, Kahan argues, and this pollutes the science-communication environment with "divisive cultural meanings" (ibid.).

As suggested by the debate over the "gorilla in the room" with which we began this chapter, climate scientists generally regard this popular critique and debate as a luxury that the world cannot afford, as climate change – and the difficulty of redressing it – advances with every passing year. These scientists see this debate as an obstacle to solving the problem of climate change, but as something fundamentally apart from climate change. Thus, they categorize the phenomenon of denial as an educational problem or a political problem, but not as a scientific problem demanding scientific scrutiny. There has been some public opinion-type study of climate change denial (notably by Leiserowitz 2005, 2006, 2010); but there has been little if any attempt to interpret it as part of the problem of climate change itself. Indeed, its status external to the problem of climate change is reflected in Kahan's own characterization of denial as "pollution" (ibid.).

Social scientists have been as constrained as natural scientists with respect to addressing the issue of climate science and its critics. Scholars who have spent a generation studying the social reproduction of science often baulk when it comes to climate change science, because most regard climate change as such a serious threat to society. Bruno Latour (2004:227), in a famous article, suggests that even though it may "burn my tongue to say that global warming is a fact whether you like it or not", given a career spent assailing just such statements, he feels that the looming environmental crisis is so serious that he must say it. In short, a truce was called in the so-called "science wars" of the 1990s (Gross and Levitt 1994; Ross 1996), which often pitted natural scientists against social scientists and humanists, once all of science – all of academia in fact – came under attack from outside the academy. Latour admitted that he would hesitate to critique the methods by which climate scientists claim authority for their findings, because he deems those findings so important – and he would be equally hesitant to rationalize the critiques of those methods and findings by the climate change deniers. This is reminiscent of what Ortner (1995:187–188) calls "ethnographic refusal", which is a reluctance to submit to professional scrutiny the behaviors of those with whom we are in sympathy.

Gregory Bateson would fault this inattention to the lay beliefs of climate change denial. Bateson always urged us to take a broad and systemic view of environmental problems, including the way that we study problems and communicate the results of our studies. As he famously wrote, "[T]he problem of how to transmit our ecological reasoning to those whom we wish to influence in what seems to us to be an ecologically 'good' direction is itself an ecological problem" (Bateson 1972:504). The history of the development of the international climate policy regime, as recounted in Section III of this chapter, reveals little if any attention to – in Bateson's words – "those whom we wish to influence" and who, by all available evidence, are very clearly *not* being influenced by us. Part of the explanation for why this is so takes us back, again, into the early history of the development of human civilization.

3. Complications within the self

As noted previously, humans have been thinking about climate – or at least weather – and society since the dawn of civilization. Ideas about climate have been deeply imbricated in ideas about people, including ideas about the self versus the "other". There is an ancient association of self-identity and environments and climates perceived to be "temperate" and a corollary association of the opposite of the self, the alien "other", with intemperate environments and climates. Perceived environmental and climatic extremes long provided a compelling answer to the perennial question, why are human beings different? – the answer being that climes that are not "our's" produce people who are not like "us".

This argument was most famously stated in the fifth century B.C. by Hippocrates, in his *Airs, Waters, Places* (1923:109, 137): "For where the seasons experience the most violent and the most frequent changes.... So it is too with the inhabitants... ." The thread of this climate determinism can be traced onwards from Hippocrates to the medieval Islamic scholar Ibn Khaldûn (1958,1:168–169) – "The inhabitants of the zones that are far from temperate... are also farther removed from being temperate in all their conditions" – to Montesquieu (1989:234) in the eighteenth century – "As you move toward the countries of the south, you will believe you have moved away from morality itself" – and the anthropogeographer Ratzel (1896:27) writing in the nineteenth century – who argued that only the temperate latitudes could produce lasting civilization. Vestiges can even be seen in the late twentieth century popular writings of the physiologist/ecologist Jared Diamond (1997, 2005).

Since ancient times, therefore, the idea of climatic extremes has been associated with the ethnic/racial "other" – removed in both space and cultural identity. We can see a similar association of ideas in the modern discourse of climate change, which often utilizes a framing of "close" versus "far", of self versus other. This is exemplified by the public as well as academic attention to the implications of climate change for the distant and exotic – Pacific islands, Arctic regions and fauna, Alpine glaciers – as opposed to the nearby and familiar (Farbotko and Lazrus 2012). This is reminiscent of the ancient distancing of extreme climates as the abode of the "other". The parallel can prompt us to ask, why is there a compelling conceptual "welcoming niche" for an association of climate change with the distant other? Is the specter of climate change so threatening to the self, especially to self-identity, that we seize on the opportunity to distance it, or of course to deny it? One of the revelations of modern work on disasters has been to show how they impact identity and concepts of self (Erikson 1976; Carey 2008). This work has addressed how, if at all, victims try to restore their identity in the wake of disasters. But before the fact, in the event of a looming catastrophe, in the event of a perceived threat to identity, what defensive measures might people take, including denial of the reality of the threat?

There is a sedimentation to human thinking about extreme climates, society, and identity, therefore, which offers perspective on contemporary debates about climate change, and may help to explain the extreme fervor of the denialists who seem to see the assertion of modern climate change as such an existential threat.

V. Summary and conclusions

We began this chapter with the debate over "the gorilla in the room", the gorilla being climate change, or more specifically the climate scientist's view of climate change; and we asked what else is in the room, what else is going on besides the geo-physical dimensions of climate change, what is being elided, what complicates the picture? We then discussed the differentiation between the global North and South with respect to climate change, beginning with the WRI–CSE debate in the early 1990s, the geographic and historical determinants of North–South differences, and the problems with a universalist/globalist perspective that ignores them. We then attempted to trace the North–South divide through more than two decades of development of the international climate policy regime, and we found that, although this divide was prominent early on, as time went on it was over-shadowed as often as not by North–North differences. We then looked at other ways in which the North–South divide has been complicated, including differences within individual national communities, in the North as well as the South; the rise of a much discussed but little studied lay critique of climate science in the North; and the linkage of beliefs regarding climate change to an ancient association between climate and socio-cultural identity.

Our analysis has a variety of implications for theory concerning climate change and wider issues as well. First, the evidence that we presented here depicts, unexpectedly given the subject of global environmental change, a rather fractured globe. Our analysis offers further evidence of the fact that the process of globalization is not as seamless as was once supposed (Tsing 2005; Ferguson 2006). Second, our analysis suggests a variety of new dimensions of climate and climate change for study. These include not only national and international differentiation of the climate science communities, but also differences between the academic and non-academic communities, and especially the subject of climate and identity and how this may fuel denialist anxieties. Our analysis also suggests a role for the humanities, in particular the field of history, which can potentially offer missing but helpful perspectives on many aspects of the modern discourse of climate change, and which suggests that aversion to history in the climate science community, because of the way that it has been used and abused by denialists, is costly (Dove 2014, 2015). In short, our analysis suggests that a much more encompassing vision of climate change is needed, one that respects the ancient and powerful role that climate has played in the way that human society views itself and its role in the cosmos.

Our analysis offers new insight, thus, into linking geophysical change at large scales and cultural change at small ones, linking the global and the personal. It suggests a need to see climate change as not something "out there", or entirely out there, but as something also close and personal, something "in here". It suggests the need to see climate as part of human ecology, including moral ecology. It offers an avenue toward understanding the outrage when belief in the climatic foundations of one's community is challenged. The moral dimension explains the fervor of the denial; but it also points toward a powerful point of leverage, one that we did not even know existed.

Notes

1 See Hammond, Rodenburg, and Moomaw (1990, 1991).
2 The WRI report was critiqued when it came out not by the CSE alone, nor by Southern sources alone, but also – indeed, predominantly – by scientists in the North (to name but a few, see McCully 1991; Redclift 1992; Smith 1991a, 1991b; Subak 1991; Thery 1992).
3 For example, Pyne (1994) notes that the biomass of the North suffers from a "fire famine", whereas that of the South suffers from a fire glut.
4 Whereas the WRI formula permitted Northern nations to claim a greater share of the carbon sinks if their emissions increased, so too did the CSE formula permit the nations of the South to claim a greater share if their populations grew.
5 Defining "luxury" versus "survival" is of course problematic. Thus, anyone making a living by vehicular transport in the North, such as a truck or taxi driver, would disagree with the characterization of this usage as a "luxury"; conversely, there are many who draw revenue from rice fields and cattle in the South for other than "survival", including landlords, big ranchers, and private and para-statal corporations.
6 The CSE argued that geographical variables were relevant to the global warming debate, and in order to foreground them it drew a line in space (differentiating the interests of North and South). The WRI argued that historical variables were not relevant to the global warming debate, and in order to erase them it drew a line in time (between the industrial and pre-industrial eras).
7 The idea that climate variations in the atmosphere can be produced by anthropogenic causes was first proposed in 1896 by the Swedish chemist Svante Arrhenius, who hypothesized that anthropogenic carbon dioxide in the atmosphere could increase the surface temperature through a green-house effect.
8 Another possible reason that the European perspective on climate change differs from that in the U.S. is that it has more historical depth or perspective (Kempton and Craig 1993).
9 Annex II parties included all OECD members as of 1992: Australia, Austria, Belgium, Canada, Denmark, the European Economic Community (as an independent member entity), Finland, France, Germany, Greece, Iceland, Ireland, Italy, Japan, Luxembourg, Netherlands, New Zealand, Norway, Portugal, Spain, Sweden, Switzerland, the UK and the US. Annex I parties consisted of all of the Annex II parties plus the CEITs: Belarus, Bulgaria, Czechoslovakia, Estonia, Hungary, Latvia, Lithuania, Poland, Romania, the Russian Federation, and the Ukraine.

6

CONCLUSION

Reflections on the interdisciplinary project

I. Summary

We began this volume with Snow's discussion of the "two cultures" of natural science and social science. Our goal was to illustrate a way of bridging the divide by means of our own collaboration, that between a physicist and an anthropologist, on four case studies. The first concerned the "mundane science" of micro-banking in south Asia, and improved stoves and off-grid and micro-grid rural electrification in Africa, and the challenges of improving such seemingly "simple" technologies. The second case study involved peasant management of fire-climax grasslands in Southeast Asia, in the face of a "forest fundamentalism" that misunderstands and penalizes this management regime and also is responsible for a dearth of research on it. The third case compared three resources-use systems in Southeast Asia – mast fruiting in the rain forest, swidden agriculture, and the "green revolution" cultivation of high-yielding rice varieties – focusing on the extent to which environmental constraints and production limits are recognized and the extent to which the realities of periodic failure are built into the premises of the system. The fourth and final case study involved the political dynamics of the global climate change policy regimes, tracing the history of the problematic effort to apply a "one world" vision to the crisis, which initially produced a predictable schism along North–South lines but in time has produced less predictable divisions among as well as within Northern and Southern countries, involving such unforeseen issues as challenges to cultural identity and lay critiques of the scientific establishment.

II. The "boundary objects" in our collaboration

Our collaboration has not consisted of a simple application of one discipline's theory to the other, or even the simple arguing by analogy (Cohen 1994) from one discipline to the other. For example, in Chapter 2 we apply history and sociology of science insights to the way that science selects its topics; and in Chapter 3 we extend these insights to an in-depth study of the misunderstanding of an "infamous" peasant landcover or ecotype. In Chapter 4, and to some extent throughout the volume, we apply ideas of entropy to thick ethnographic description of native agricultural ecology and cosmology. Finally, in Chapter 5 we apply ideas from North–South politics and discourse analysis to the study of national and international debates about climate change, moral responsibility, and identity. In short, our path to collaboration in each case has been anything but straightforward, it has varied in each case, and elements of serendipity have been important. There was no single recipe for interdisciplinary work that we followed. The structure to our work has been much more amorphous. The constants in our collaboration, and in our analysis of our four case studies, have been the shared use of a number of different concepts or theses, which we termed "boundary objects" in the Introduction, following Star and Griesemer (1989), precisely because they facilitate conversations across disciplinary boundaries. These took the form of a number of different "heurisms" that guided our thinking, often implicitly.

Our first boundary object is a recognition of the importance of discourse, the importance not only of what conservation and development actors do, but what they say about what they do or don't do. Our analysis in Chapter 5 of the competing accounts of climate change, and its victims and villains, is one prominent example of this. Another example is in Chapter 3, in which we compare and contrast the official and folk versions of the utility of fire-climax grasslands. We see this also in Chapter 4 in our analysis of the public construction of a vision of green revolution agriculture by the scientific and policy community, as opposed to the community-level experience of its costs and benefits. There is also a discursive dimension to our analysis in Chapter 2, in our critique of the emphasis by the scientific community on esoteric topics of less importance to sustainable environmental relations at the expense of more relevant but mundane topics. Discourse analysis is, in a sense, another example of mundane science, since most scientists regard this as a part of everyday reality that lies outside the orthodox definition of the scientific object.

Our second boundary object is a belief that the view from below – in a political-economic sense – is often the most insightful one (Spivak 1988), which in the sense that the oppressed can often see reality more clearly than their oppressors. Thus, in Chapter 4 we cite the views of some of the farmers – the actual participants in and also victims of the green revolution – who were able to articulate the fault lines of this revolution much more clearly than many of its planners. In Chapter 5 we suggest that the views of climate change of even the non-scientist deniers should be taken seriously enough to study. And in Chapter 3 we represent the views of fire-climax grasslands of those local farmers who view them as one of life's boons not banes.

A third boundary object is our appreciation of taking a long historical view, as well as a comparative view, of the phenomena we are studying. In Chapters 2, 3, and 4 we examined the histories of development interventions in different fields; and in Chapter 5 we examined the evolution over time of the global climate change policy regime. In all cases, we believe that the presentist bias, and discourse of urgency that inhibits a retrospective view, is dysfunctional. For example, see Dove's (2014) effort to counter the presentist bias of the climate change discourse. Some of our comparative analyses were straightforward, such as the comparison in Chapter 5 of views of climate change both between and within nations, or the comparison in Chapter 3 of peasant and state/scientific views of the utility of fire-climax grasslands. Less obvious is our comparison in Chapter 2 of everyday and exotic subjects of study; and our comparative analysis in Chapter 4 of mast-fruiting, swidden agriculture, and green revolution agriculture represents a novel comparison and contrast of three quite disparate resource management systems. These comparative analyses demonstrate to us that unexpected or unorthodox comparisons – comparing the dissimilar, comparing the seemingly incomparable – can be the most insightful ones.

A fourth boundary object is the maxim that "there is no free lunch", no miracles or magic. Assertions of miraculous conservation and development possibilities are empirical facts, and merit our attention, study, and even respect – no less than tribal beliefs in human reciprocity with forest spirits in Borneo – but they do not describe the real world (as will be further discussed in the following section on thermodynamics and society). The real world of global industrial capitalism is, as anthropologists like Hornborg (2007:259) suggest, a zero-sum game. That is, someone can only win when someone else loses.

A fifth boundary object is our conviction that the failures of conservation and development interventions, the contradictions and "accidents", are not without meaning. The problematic histories of planned interventions that we describe in our case studies – of stoves, fire-climax grasslands, swiddens, climate change policies – all merit our attention, all provide grist for our mill. A ubiquitous and damning mistake in modern policy-making is the disinterest in studying the records of such failure. If as much effort was devoted to studying past failures as planning future successes, the track-record of global conservation and development interventions would be transformed.

A sixth boundary object is our shared belief that "engaged" science is not anti-science or non-science. The fruits of our collaboration suggest to us that the hoary distinction between pure science and applied science is, today if it has not always been, a subjective not empirical distinction, which leads to bad policy and impoverished theory. We argue that the study of real world problems and issues, like those in our four case studies, produce both the richest theory and the most insightful and successful policy.

A seventh boundary object is our shared belief in the need to be self-reflexive in scientific research. This entails not only an ongoing critical awareness and examination of our own premises and methods, but also a corresponding awareness and examination of the way that we treat the "other", our subjects. The separation between self and other in science, the objectification and resultant distancing of the "other" – like stove owners, grassland managers, swidden makers, and climate disbelievers – is the cause of much flawed science and attendant policy failures. Some compromise in the distinction between who studies, and who is studied, some respect for the perspectives and knowledge of the scientific subject, can greatly enrich both theory and practice.

Eighth and finally, returning to the initial "aha" moment that launched our collaboration many years ago – when we jointly recognized an analogy between natural processes and social processes, between the laws of physics and the beliefs of native cosmology – we believe that this analogy reflects common principles underlying both natural and human realms, which both the physics and the native cosmology were speaking to. The proposition that the human and non-human realms are ontologically distinct, is extremely difficult to defend, and rarely is defended; but in practice it continues to structure a great deal of scientific conduct, at increasingly high cost.

III. Perspectives on sustainability

Our four case studies offer a variety of insights of relevance to the current state of research and development efforts concerning sustainable conservation and development of natural resources.

1. Conservation and development policy failures as a prism and resource

The modern history of conservation and development efforts, dating roughly from the mid-twentieth century (the post-World War II era), is rife with failure. The examples presented in our own case studies – the decades of problematic efforts to "improve" simple, traditional cookstoves; the even longer span of time spent unsuccessfully trying to eradicate fire-climax grasslands, in complete ignorance of their role in peasant agro-ecology; the deleterious impacts of the green revolution on rural ecology, economy, and community; and the ongoing failure of the global community to address climate change – are more typical than anomalous. As suggested by the attention we accord them in our own case studies, such failures should not be ignored. Failures are meaningful, not simply because of the lessons they offer regarding correct versus incorrect planning, but because they offer insights into the complexities of resource-use systems that are often available from no other quarter. That is to say, failure tells us something about more fundamental dynamics of society, which may be far more important to successful development planning than a simple assessment of a failed project. Failure is "revelatory".

This is especially true of repeated mistakes. We disagree with the folk parable that "Insanity is repeating the same mistakes and expecting different results". We see repetition of mistakes – such as government efforts to reforest fire-climax grasslands, in the face of repeated evidence that such forests will be burned down by the local peasants managing and living off the grasslands – as revealing, often of something that is being achieved by the interventions notwithstanding their apparent failures (Ferguson 1990). The reflexive response to serial failure, of repeating the intervention, albeit with an "improved" variant – for example planning a state-of-the-art grassland reforestation scheme – misses the point, the systemic lesson of the failures. The systemic lesson is that there is a "higher order" problem, not with the technological goodness of an afforestation program, but with logically prior assumptions regarding the desirability of forest versus grasslands, for whom, and why.

Of most importance, we suggest that chronic difficulties and failures of implementation of conservation and development programs need to be seen systemically. By this we mean that they need to be seen as part of the problem, not simply as an obstacle to solving the problem. This is a subtle but important distinction. In the "gorilla in the room" anecdote in Chapter 5, the climate scientist recognizes that deniers of climate change are a problem, but he does not recognize them as part of *his* problem. He sees solving the problem of climate change and solving the problem of deniers of climate change as separate. But we suggest that this separation is artificial and that it contributes to the perpetuation not solution of both problems.

The challenge of achieving a systemic view, and breaking out of the pattern of serial failure, must not be underestimated. As Lohmann (1998:10) aptly puts it:

> [T]o expect development agencies to learn from the experience of the social and environmental disasters associated with their previous projects is a little like asking the actor who plays Oedipus why he never seems to catch on to the fact that the old man he meets at the crossroads in every performance is actually his father, and therefore just goes on stabbing him night after night.

In order to cease the "performance", one must step "off-stage", one must distance oneself from it. Interdisciplinary collaboration – and the confrontation of implicit norms that it provokes – is one way to achieve this distance.

2. Mundane but not simple

Throughout this volume, our subject matter has mostly been the mundane, the everyday. We have examined folk technologies, like cookstoves; folk landscapes, like fire-climax grasslands and swiddens; and folk beliefs, like disbelief in climate change and disagreement regarding its causes and effects. These are relatively neglected topics, surprisingly so given how important they are, touching the lives of literally billions of people in the world today. Also surprising, especially in light of their neglect by academia, is the complexity of these subjects. The systems of knowledge and practice for fueling and using traditional cookstoves, and managing grasslands and swiddens, for example, are embedded in age-old, intricate, and far-reaching webs of rural environmental relations, which upon close study reveal themselves to be elegant solutions to the livelihood challenges of particular socio-ecological times and places. The unanticipated and unrecognized complexity of these resource-use systems is reflected in the often problematic record of conservation and development interventions in their practice. The unseen complexities stymie development planners who fall prey to the error of seeing the rural, the local, the traditional, as regressive and simply simple.

We conclude, therefore, that the term "mundane" is itself judgmental and subjective, bearing the metropole's prejudicial assumption that to be different is to be simple, in a negative sense. Our corollary conclusion is that the term "mundane" is also political. Because stoves, grasslands, swiddens, and beliefs regarding climate are embedded in systems of natural resource use, they are also embedded in systems of power and politics. Therefore, the record of unsuccessful policy interventions in these matters has to do not only with their socio-ecological complexity, but also their political complexity. When these political dimensions are unseen, ignored, or denied, then the political character of planned interventions can also be denied, which makes them more palatable to conservation and development organizations and especially their governmental counterparts, but also makes their success all the less likely.

3. Knowledge and ignorance

Questions regarding knowledge production loomed large in our case studies. Our studies clearly demonstrate the importance of studying local systems of knowledge of natural resources and the environment, in particular in the face of the inherent prejudices of the metropole against such knowledge. The study and understanding of such local systems of knowledge and practice is only the beginning, however. In all of our analyses, we recognized the importance of the social dimensions of the construction of knowledge. There may be multiple "knowledges" of a given problem, which has implications for what is seen as a "solution" and by whom. Of most importance, we find that knowledge is, counter-intuitively, not a neutral terrain; there is a politics of knowledge. There is a politics to what is credited as knowledge – of stoves, grasslands, swiddens, climate – or not. There is also a politics to the application of knowledge. The production and amassing of knowledge of a problem does not automatically lead to its solution.

We also examined the social construction of knowledge's opposite, ignorance. We find that ignorance is not simply a function of the non-production of knowledge, but indeed is actively constructed in its own right (cf. Dove 1983). That is to say, ignorance is not simply the lack of knowledge; rather it is a "positive" thing created in its own right. As Proctor (2008:1–2,9) writes, "Ignorance is most commonly seen… as something in need of correction, a kind of natural absence or void where knowledge has yet to spread… . [But] this is an idea insufficiently explored by philosophers, that ignorance should not be viewed as a simple omission or gap, but rather as an active production." In short, energy and resources are devoted to the production of ignorance, or anti-knowledge, as well as knowledge; because ignorance can serve as many functions in society, even in state management, as does knowledge. In consequence, knowledge does not simply "flow" and erase ignorance. Its path is variously smoothed or blocked ("friction" may be created [Tsing 2005]), depending upon the vested interests and resources of the actors involved. Scientists may be unaware of this, but popular culture is not. To quote the novelist Saul Bellow, from his 1976 memoir "To Jerusalem and Back": "A great deal of intelligence can be invested in ignorance when the need for illusion is deep."[1] Examples of ignorance that we analyze include the obvious one of climate change denial, but also scientific beliefs regarding "miracle" seeds and "degraded" fire-climax grasslands, and the even less obvious example of scientific belief in "epistemic communities" with a common vision of the world.

Knowledge and ignorance are both embedded in the socio-ecological systems that they address, so the normative separation of observation from the observed is often suspect. As Bateson (1972: 504) famously said, "We are not outside the ecology for which we plan – we are always and inevitably part of it. Herein lies the charm and the terror of ecology – that the ideas of this science are irreversibly becoming a part of our own ecological system."

4. Science and the "other"

Bateson's suggestion that science is part of the ecology it studies encourages us to ask questions about matters of science that we might otherwise not, like the aforementioned lack of study of subjects like folk technologies, folk landscapes, and folk beliefs. It encourages us to ask how science constructs itself, not just through its employment of distinctive methods but through its distinctive selection of topics for study. Science's relationship to everyday reality is indeed differentiated; it selects some parts of that reality for study and not others. Some such selection is of course a necessity – the entirety of the world cannot be studied and represented.[2] But the selection that we noticed in our case studies displays a systemic bias: it is generally the knowledges and practices of the subaltern – the less wealthy, less powerful, less "developed", the marginal in short – that are neglected as subjects of study while at the same time being foremost as targets of intervention and "improvement" (Li 2007). Topic selection contributes to not just the distinction of non-scientists from scientists, but the distinction between scientific communities in the global North and South, between those with purported problems and those with the purported means of solving those problems. The selection of the scientific subject is influenced by history, politics, economics, culture.

We find not only that the gaze, the subject, of science is subjective, but so too are its premises and methods. As we showed in our analysis of the development of the global climate change policy regime in Chapter 5, universalism – viz., the belief in a single global "epistemic community" of climate science – is less an empirical description of reality than a political tactic. Scientific norms like these often provoke a backlash, but typically it is a politically impotent one. This is not so with the contemporary backlash against climate science, however, which is forcing science to begin to question the cost of some of its norms. The backlash from climate deniers raises the question: are climate science and climate denial co-producing one another? Are they co-producing one another's exaggeration of boundaries and identity, exacerbating the layman/science divide?

Our methodology is distinguished by a certain amount of reflexivity. Reaching beyond our disciplines makes it easier to identify and then problematize the scientific norms within our respective disciplines. This, in turn, helps us to see how much science itself is implicated in problems of addressing sustainability; it helps us to see how much debates about sustainability are affected by the way systems of natural resource management are studied or mis-studied, represented or mis-represented. It has been suggested that the modern natural sciences never had a "hermeneutics", a self-reflexive and critical awareness of how they do what they do (Markus 1987). Thus, the answer to Heidegger's question, "Does science think?", was "No". It has also been suggested that this has not been a problem for the modern natural sciences, that they flourished without it (ibid.). And they did flourish, up until the recent rise among political conservatives in the U.S. of skepticism of science in general, and of climate science in particular. Now the long-successful norms of the natural sciences are failing them. The failure to "think" has become a crippling handicap. It now seems as if modern science *does* need a hermeneutics, and quickly. An interdisciplinary effort like ours, with the reflexivity that this crossing and communication necessitates, may help to inform such a hermeneutics.

IV. Thermodynamics and society

From the beginning of our collaboration, the laws of thermodynamics have given a powerful intellectual stimulus to our work. Scientists generally agree that these laws govern the universe as we know it. Since human society is also part of this same universe, it follows that human society is also governed, at some level, by these laws. As the anthropologist Leslie A. White (1959:38) wrote in the mid-twentieth century, "The principles and laws of thermodynamics are applicable to cultural systems as they are to other material systems". But this question has been studied and debated ever since the laws of thermodynamics were first formulated in the mid-nineteenth century by J. R. Mayer, J. P. Joule, and Lord Kelvin, among others.[3] Even if we grant the applicability of the laws of thermodynamics to human society, some ask whether the laws exert a sufficiently fine-grained effect – relative to other determinants – to actually affect human behavior.[4]

1. The first law of thermodynamics

The first law of thermodynamics states that the total amount of energy in an isolated system remains constant; and thus energy cannot be created nor destroyed. We drew on the implications of this law – for thinking about boundaries and limits – to cast a critical eye on modern discourses of development. Our studies suggest that successful planned interventions in rural resource-use systems – that is, successful sustainable development – is hugely difficult. Accordingly, assertions to the contrary, especially assertions of "miraculous" solutions, must be viewed askance. We focused our study of this point on the premises of traditional versus high-modern agriculture in Chapter 4.

Thus, in Chapter 4 we compare conceptions of bounty and dearth, and success versus failure, in native systems of resource management on the one hand and on the other hand the agricultural science-based "green revolution" system of agriculture. We argue that acceptance of a balance between abundance and scarcity is built into the logic of the native systems but is actively – and we suggest incorrectly – denied in the logic of the green revolution system. We apply the first law of thermodynamics law heuristically to identify problematic elements in the green revolution discourse, for example the notion of so-called "miracle" seeds, which imply that something is being created from nothing. Such assertions, indeed, should be regarded as "signposts" that alert us to unrecognized, ignored, or hidden contradictions of development (Thompson, Warburton, and Hatley 1986). Miraculous claims from agricultural scientists alerted us to the likelihood that their discourse was being driven, at least in part, not by science but by politics. This insight helped to direct our search for the hidden costs to the green revolution's publicized benefits. It alerted us to the fact that benefits were being exaggerated while costs were being denied, and to the conclusion that this obfuscation was central to the science of the green revolution itself.[5]

Heuristic reference to the principles of the first law also sensitized us to claims, not just of benefits without costs, but of winners without losers. Also a signpost and also to be viewed askance, that is, are assertions of miracles where everyone wins in development interventions – the infamous "win–win solutions". As Goldman (2005) writes of an economist he interviewed in the World Bank:

> When the authors of the World Development Report '92 were drafting the report, they called me asking for examples of "win–win" strategies in my work. What could I say? *None* exists in that pure form; there are *trade-offs, not* "win–wins". But they want to see a world of win–wins, based on articles of *faith, not fact.*

In the social world as well as the physical world, when someone wins, someone else loses. This is true at macro as well as micro levels. As Hornborg (2007:270) says looking at the world system as a whole, in an essay inspired by his own efforts to apply the principles of thermodynamics to human society: when improved technology leads to saving time and space in one part of the world system, someone else in the world system must lose time and space. The ideology of win–win solutions, and the consequent assertion of neutrality in development interventions, is not an empirical but a political statement; it is a tactic.

Implied in Hornborg's statement is the idea that by drawing boundaries narrowly around a development improvement, benefits can be highlighted while costs are rendered invisible. We deal with boundary-making most explicitly in Chapter 4. We treat boundaries as social constructs, and we look at their political, economic, and environmental implications. We show how social constructions of boundaries can alter the perception of management costs, re-shuffle beneficiaries and victims, and change assessments of sustainability. Artful re-drawing of system boundaries is often what makes development "miracles" appear believable. In light of these high-stakes outcomes, we also look at the way boundaries are conceptually and strategically manipulated. For example, in Chapter 5 we apply this analysis at the national and international levels, to show the strategic, political dimensions of the way that the boundaries of the climate change problem are drawn in space, time, and topical focus. In this, as indeed in all of our analyses, we argue that the political power of boundaries comes partly from representing them not as social constructions but as natural givens. The naturally given boundaries of resource management systems tend to be rather unvarying; but their social construction permits of wide variation, which is an under-studied dimension in comparative analyses of natural resource management systems.

2. The second law of thermodynamics, entropy, and human society

The second law of thermodynamics states that the entropy of an isolated system which is not in equilibrium will tend to increase over time, approaching a maximum value at equilibrium; and although a system can undergo some processes that decrease its own entropy, the entropy of the universe as a whole irreversibly increases over time. The first expression of the second law and the concept of entropy date to publications in 1850 and 1865 by the German physicist and mathematician Rudolf Clausius. The concept of entropy has proved to be a particularly evocative one, which has led to its being "transplanted into virtually all other domains – communications, biology, economics, sociology, psychology, political science, and even art" (Rifkin 1980: 263). The reason for this may lie in the fact that the concept of entropy is itself bound up in the human condition, it is "anthropomorphic", which has led some to question the legitimacy of thermodynamics as a "legitimate" natural science (Rifkin 1980: 262). The most elaborate and persisting applications of entropy have taken place in the field of economics, commencing in the nineteenth century in the sub-field then known as "economic thermodynamics".[6] A notable early contribution to this field was from the British Nobel laureate chemist turned economist Frederick Soddy (1912:10–11, cf. 1926, 1933, 1935), writing early in the twentieth century, who argued that laws governing the relations between matter and energy "control, in the last resort, the rise and fall of political systems, the freedom or bondage of nations, the movements of commerce and industry, the origin of wealth and poverty, and the general physical welfare of the race". Soddy specifically applied the laws of thermodynamics to economics, arguing that since these laws prohibit perpetual motion, it follows that the economy cannot generate infinite wealth. Writing a half-century later, the Romanian-born economist Nicholas Georgescu-Roegen (1971) helped to develop such ideas into what eventually became the field of ecological economics.[7] Subsequent prominent contributors to this field include Herman E. Daly (1973) and Jeremy Rifkin (1980). There have been a number of different efforts to apply the principles of thermodynamics within anthropology: one school of thought has focused on using energy capture and expenditure as a measure of the evolution of human society, pioneered by Leslie White (1959; cf. Adams 1988).[8] A second body of work, influenced by Marxist theories, utilizes analyses of energy appropriation and loss, conservation and use, to illustrate "uneven development" and the production of inequality within and between societies (Ruyle 1973; Hornborg 1992, 1998, 2007; Bunker 2007).

We have also been much taken with the implications for the analysis of economic development of the concept of entropy. Arguing by analogy from the second law of thermodynamics, we can hypothesize that there will be a tendency for the material wealth of a society to disperse over time unless an effort, energy, is expended to counter this. This hypothesis offers a provocative framework for thinking about the flows of resources to rich versus poor in a country. It focuses our attention on the energy that must be expended to concentrate resources among the wealthy in the face of the entropic forces of dispersal.

We examined these forces in a paper (Dove and Kammen 2001) not included in this volume, taking Indonesia as a case study. In this paper we analyze the rhetoric versus reality of some of this country's most important rural development programs. Taking a critical view of state rhetoric regarding its generosity with its citizens, we calculate what meager resources actually flow easily from the state to its poorest citizens, such as family planning assistance, incentives to transmigrate to Indonesia's outer islands, and so on. In terms of actual practice as opposed to rhetoric, we see that most flows of resource wealth follow power, not need. For example, we find counter-intuitive resource flows *in* to the state from development programs, like those involving efforts to "help" rubber and sugarcane smallholders, which should be producing resource flows *out* from the state. Whereas the official state discourse is one of giving *to* the populace, therefore, what we call the "vernacular" structure of state governance is one of taking *from* them. The official discourse has little traction beyond officialdom: there is widespread folk recognition and mockery of the actual structures of resource appropriation and distribution.[9]

A great deal of the collective effort of Indonesian society, perhaps any society, is expended on resource concentration. That is, whereas the long-term law of the universe is entropy, the short-term law of society is often enthalpy: namely, accumulation of resources by smaller segments of society. It takes a great effort to counter these enthalpic forces, as in an anti-poverty program. Over the longer-term, however, enthalpic forces are inevitably countered in the periodic convulsions that beset human society, like the financial meltdown that struck Indonesia in the late 1990s, which is consistent with the second law. The laws of entropy and enthalpy are in opposition, therefore. Entropic dynamics are expressed in the limits to and reversals of material accumulation; whereas enthalpic dynamics are expressed in the struggle against, and even denial of (witness the green revolution) these limits and reversals.

The histories of certain objects, especially valuable ones, often illustrate these contrasting dynamics. We have elsewhere examined the social histories of Borneo's gemstones (Dove 2011). There is an age-old association of diamonds with traditional rule in the region.[10] Diamonds symbolize the ruler because he or she is located at the extreme end of this pattern of resource extraction: the ruler can take valuable gemstones from all others in the society, but no one else can take them from him or her. The value of such gemstones is based, therefore, on the fact that they are objects of desire and contest; and their value is most clearly expressed when this contest ceases – namely, when the paramount ruler holds them. The gemstones' value is expressed in their movement from one owner to another; yet their ultimate value is attained when movement is no longer possible, when they are held by the paramount ruler. In the flow of resources, thus, the point where the most valuable gemstones cease to flow is the point of greatest power; and the character of the flow up to that point is revealing of the structure of power in society.[11] In general, very valuable stones move up the hierarchy of power: thus, the *Hikayat Banjar*, the native, court-based chronicle of the Banjar kingdom of Southeast Kalimantan, written and rewritten over the period of about a century between the mid-sixteenth and mid-seventeenth centuries, tells of the historic Sambas kingdom in southwest Borneo sending a large diamond, called "Si Misim," as tribute to their overlords in the Banjar kingdom, which in turn sent the stone on to their overlords in the court of Mataram on Java (Ras 1968: 481, 483, 485).[12] Contested, sideways movement sometimes occurs, as attested to by this comment of the mid-nineteenth century observer, St. John (1862, 2:47), in a passage presciently titled in the contents page (ibid., 2:16), the "Discomfort of Possessing a Large Diamond": "I may even see the great diamond now in the possession of a Malau chief, whom [*sic*] would even give it me if I would help him to destroy a Malay noble who attacked his house in order to get possession of this famous stone: the Malay was driven off, not however before he had lodged a ball in the jaw of the Malau chief." One of the most detailed gemstone "biographies" is given by Raffles, pertaining to one of the largest diamonds to have come out of Borneo at the time of his writing early in the nineteenth century, the "Mátan Diamond" (named after the seat of the sultanate in West Kalimantan where it was originally found), which weighed 367 carats. Raffles ([1817] 1978, 1:239) recounts the movements of the Mátan Diamond up to his own day as follows:

> This celebrated diamond was discovered by a Dayak, and claimed as a droit of royalty by the Sultan of the country, Gurú-Láya [Raffles subsequently refers to this stone as an "appanage of royalty"]; which was handed over to the Pangéran of Lándak, whose brother having got possession of it, gave it as a bribe to the Sultan of Súkadána, in order that he might be placed on the throne of Lándak.

The history of the Mátan Diamond and that of the others mentioned thus afford a window into the ever-present power of enthalpy, which attracts diamonds, and the equally ever-present but opposite power of entropy – the seed of which seems indeed to be sown by enthalpy – which takes diamonds away.

As suggested by these diamond "biographies", the length of the timeframe of observation greatly affects the perception of entropy versus enthalpy. Contemporary observations of seemingly persistent wealth or poverty, even over a period of several decades or more, may suggest that entropic forces are not at work.[13] But scholars of the *longue dureé*, like Le Roy Ladurie (1974) of the French *annales* school of history, consider patterns prevailing for just a few decades to be unimportant. What matters to them is whether wealth disperses or concentrates over centuries, and at this time-scale they see an ebb and flow, cycles not stasis.[14] In general, the shift over the past generation in both the natural and social sciences from an equilibrium to a post-equilibrium paradigm has moved scholars away from a belief in stasis. For much of the twentieth century, scientific views of nature were dominated by the climax and steady-state assumptions of scholars like Clements (1916) and Odum (1953); but in the last quarter of the century a new paradigm emerged, sometimes called the "new ecology" (Scoones 1999), which disputes assumptions of equilibrium, takes adaptive disturbance to be important, and emphasizes dynamic, historical, and partly unknowable relations between society and environment (Fiedler, White, and Lediy 1997; Pickett and Ostfeld 1995). This shift upends the conventional problematizing of disorder versus order in everyday life, which is consistent with the laws of thermodynamics themselves. As Gregory Bateson (1972: 343) aptly puts it, "[W]e may say that this is the problem implicit in the Second Law of Thermodynamics: If random events lead to things getting mixed up, by what nonrandom events did things come to be sorted?" Bateson is saying that the "sorting" or ordering of society demands as much explanation as its disordering. This also applies to the concentration versus dispersal of resources, of wealth, a perspective that leads us to denaturalize the rise of human societies and naturalize their fall. As Walter Benjamin (1978/1928: 70) has also written, in another context, early in the twentieth century, "To decline is no less stable, no more surprising, than to rise. Only a view that acknowledges downfall... can advance beyond enervating amazement at what is daily repeated, and perceive the phenomena of decline as stability itself and rescue alone as extraordinary."

The further question as to what specific sets of factors determine how, when, and where societies decline, as well as rise, lies beyond our purview here; but we would briefly draw attention to the tensions that are integral to society itself,[15] the self-undermining cultural dynamics, and the extent to which they are recognized by the societies involved. There is tantalizing evidence of cultural recognition of the cycle that results from the tensions between resource concentration and resource dispersal. For example, a Chinese homily states that it takes a family just three generations to progress from muslin to silk and back to muslin. This refers to the oft-repeated scenario in which one generation struggles to rise from poverty and the wearing of muslin by amassing wealth and being able to purchase silk clothing; with the following generation squandering this wealth; and the third generation returning to the poverty and muslin clothing from whence they came. Elsewhere, across impressive historical, geographic, and cultural distances, the identical homily is repeated as "rags to rags in three generations", "clogs to clogs in three generations", "ill-gotten goods are not inherited by the third generation", and so on. Indeed, there is folk wisdom in many societies that testifies to awareness of ubiquitous tensions between resource concentration and dispersal. Scholars have long been aware of this dynamic; an example is the medieval Islamic historian Ibn Khaldûn's (1958) theorizing regarding the dynastic cycles of the Islamic states of North Africa, which he claimed characteristically runs their full course – from ascent to decline – in just three generations. Such awareness does not often extend to official discourses, however, which are frequently focused on denial and obfuscation of real versus imaginary flows. Such denial plays its own role in cycles of resource concentration and dispersal. Failure to perceive and understand the dynamics of resource concentration and dispersal is integral to the way that these same dynamics operate. That is, willful ignorance of the dynamics ensures their application. The role played by the conscious mind in these matters, and the need for scholars to recognize this, was highlighted by one of the pioneers of ecological economics, Georgescu-Roegan (1971:364), who wrote:

> Even physicists felt it necessary to remind the social scientists who have decided to ignore the essence of their object of study that "the principal problem in understanding the actions of men is to understand how they think – how their minds work". And as I have argued in many places of this book, no electrode, no microscope, indeed no physical contraption can reveal to us how men's minds work.

Social order depends upon the concentration of resources, consequently the construction of social order is all about fighting entropy and creating enthalpy. From this perspective, sustainable resource management is essentially a mitigative effort. Its goal is not to fight either entropy or enthalpy; rather, its goal is to moderate the violence of the cycles of resource accumulation and destruction. Its goal is to moderate the swings back-and-forth between entropy and enthalpy. The methodology of sustainable management must be at least in part pedagogical, therefore. Disbelief in the reality of these cycles exaggerates their influence. A prerequisite for a sustainable society, therefore, is acceptance of the inevitability of cycles of resource concentration and dispersal, which necessarily de-couples the concept of sustainability from a vision of linear growth without end.

Notes

1 Another novelist, Upton Sinclair (1935), similarly writes, "It is difficult to get a man to understand something when his [her] salary depends upon his not understanding it."
2 Cf. George Eliot's (1871–1872) famous observation: "If we could hear the squirrel's heartbeat, the sound of the grass growing, we should *die* of that *roar*."
3 Marx is thought to have pondered implications for economic theory of the then-new science of thermodynamics, but there are few if any explicit written references to it in his work.
4 As Georgescu-Roegen, who helped to develop ecological economics from the laws of thermodynamics, wrote in an afterword to Rifkin's (1980: 268) book on *Entropy*: "Jeremy Rifkin steered clear of the frequent exercises about the formal parallelism imagined to exist between entropic transformations and social phenomena: thermodynamics sets a limit to these phenomena but does not govern them."
5 Another concept from thermodynamics, the Carnot cycle, is useful for thinking about one of the resource management systems that we contrast with green revolution agriculture, namely swidden agriculture. The Carnot cycle highlights the benefits of identifying the path of minimum energy loss through a series of transactions (Cengel and Boles 2001). The cycle between the forest and the swidden ideally approximates a Carnot cycle, in that it minimizes net loss of components (e.g., soil, nutrients, biomass, or energy) so as to maximize the possibility of future repetitions, and thus the sustainability of the system.
6 See Neswald (2006) on the appeal of entropy in theological, social, and economic thought in the second half of the nineteenth century.
7 Influential applications of thermodynamics – focusing on energy flows – to the field of ecology include those by Alfred Lotka (1925) and Howard T. Odum (1971), who applied Lotka's work, and the latter's brother Eugene P. Odum (1953).
8 White's basic law of the evolution of human society is that culture evolves as the amount of energy use, and/or efficiency of energy use, increases.
9 In an analogous fashion, in the same paper (Dove and Kammen 2001), we discuss the official emphasis on gathering information and the vernacular emphasis on the very opposite, on blocking flows of information. We find that the Indonesian state's actual priority lies not in producing knowledge but in controlling the production of knowledge, which is a very different thing. Whereas the official view is that knowledge is objective and apolitical, there is a vernacular premise that knowledge is always potentially political, and that critical feedback to the state is always political. We find, partly in contrast to Scott's (1998) famous thesis, that as much as states need and produce legibility to see the world, they also need and produce illegibility so as *not* to see (parts of) it.
10 Nagtegaal (1994) entitled a paper on entrepreneurial Javanese rulers in the early modern era, "Diamonds are a regent's best friend."

11 The concept of valuable minerals "moving" has wider provenance, as in Slater's (1994) report on Amazonian miners' conception of gold as a living, feminine presence that seeks out favored men and then moves on.
12 On the impact of center-periphery relations on patterns of resource use in Indonesia, see Dove (1985b) and Dove and Kammen (2001).
13 Consider, for example, the "Dutch curse", which refers to the political-economic thesis that societies with great natural resource wealth will over-concentrate political and economic power and under-develop the distributional mechanisms and institutions of civil society. These same dynamics foster political instability, which ensures that sooner or later this entrenched enthalpy will be over-turned.
14 Ladurie (1974: 4) calls this "the immense respiration of a social structure".
15 Such tensions are an enduring subject of scholarship. Canonical contributions include Durkheim (1964/1933) on solidarity versus anomie, Marx (1887) on the inherent contradictions of capitalism, and Le Roy Ladurie (1974) on population, urbanization, and the environment.

REFERENCES

Acker, R. and D. M. Kammen. (1996) The quiet (energy) revolution: the diffusion of photovoltaic power systems in Kenya. *Energy Policy* 24: 81–111.
Adams, Richard N. (1988) *The Eighth Day: Social Evolution as the Self-Organization of Energy.* Austin (TX): University of Texas Press.
Adas, Michael. (1979) *Prophets of Rebellion: Millenarian Protest against the European Colonial Order.* Chapel Hill: University of North Carolina Press.
Adger, W. Neil. (2000) Social and ecological resilience: are they related? *Progress in Human Geography* 24(3): 347–364.
Agarwal, A. and S. Narain. (1991) *Global Warming in an Unequal World: A Case of Environmental Colonialism*, New Delhi: Centre for Science and the Environment.
Agee, James and Walker Evans. (1939) *Let Us Now Praise Famous Men: Three Tenant Families.* New York: Ballantine Books.
Agence France-Presse. (1997) International news (by-line M. Jegathesan). 15 Sept.
Agrawal, A. (1995) Dismantling the divide between indigenous and scientific knowledge. *Development and Change* 26:413–439.
Agrawal, Arun and Kent Redford. (2006) *Poverty, Development, and Biodiversity Conservation: Shooting in the Dark?* Working Paper No.26. Bronx (NY): Wildlife Conservation Society.
Ahuja, D. R. (1992) Estimating national contributions of greenhouse gas emissions. *Global Environmental Change* 2(2):83–87.
Alcorn, Janis. (1993) Indigenous peoples and conservation. *Conservation Biology* 7(2): 424–426.
Altieri, Miguel. (1987) *Agroecology: The Scientific Basis of Alternative Agriculture.* Boulder/London: Westview Press/IT Publications.
Anand, Nikhil. (2011) Pressure: the politechnics of water supply in Mumbai. *Cultural Anthropology* 26(4): S42–S64.
Anderson, E. (1971/1952) *Plants, Man and Life.* Berkeley: University of California Press,.
APHLIS (Africa Post-Harvest Loss Information System) (2014). What is APHLIS. http://aphlis.net.
Appanah, S. (1985) General flowering in the climax rain forests of southeast Asia. *Journal of Tropical Ecology* 1:25–240.

Aristotle. (1952) *Meteorologica*. Trans. H. D. P. Lee. Cambridge (MA): Harvard University Press.
Ashton, P. S., T. J. Givinish, and S. Appanah. (1988) Staggered flowering in the Dipterocarpaceae: new insights into floral induction and the evolution of mast fruiting in the aseasonal tropics. *The American Naturalist* 132(1):44–66.
Atsatt, Peter R., and Dennis J. O'Dowd. (1976) Plant defense guilds. *Science* 193:24–29.
Bagnall-Oakeley, H., C. Conroy, A. Faiz, A. Gunawan, A. Gouyon, E. Penot, S. Liangsutthissagaon, H. D. Nguyen, and C. Anwar, (1997) *Imperata* management strategies used in a smallholder rubber-based farming system. *Agroforest Syst* 36(1–3): 83–104.
Bailis, R., M. Ezzati, and D. M. Kammen. (2005) Mortality and greenhouse gas impacts of biomass and petroleum energy futures in Africa. *Science* 308: 98–103.
Balée, W. (1994) *Footprints of the Forest: Ka'apor Ethnobotany – The Historical Ecology of Plant Utilization by an Amazonian People*. Columbia University Press, New York.
Barbour, Michael G. (1996) American ecology and American culture in the 1950s: Who led whom? *Bulletin of the Ecological Society of America* 77(1): 44–51.
Barker, Randolph, Eric C. Gabler, and Donald Winkelmann. (1981) Long-term consequences of technological change on crop yield stability: the case for cereal grain. In: *Food Security of Developing Countries*. Alberto Valdes ed. pp. 53–78. Boulder: Westview Press.
Barnes, D., K. Openshaw, and R. van der Plas. (1994) What makes people cook with improved biomass stoves? Technical Paper No. 242, Energy Series. Washington DC: World Bank.
Barry, Dan. (2009) Weed heroes: the war on the invader cogongrass. *The New York Times* September 21.
Barth, Fredrik. (2008 [1956]) Ecologic relationships of ethnic groups in Swat, north Pakistan. *American Anthropologist* 58: 1079–1089.
Bartlett, H. H. (1955) *Fire in Relation to Primitive Agriculture and Grazing in the Tropics: An Annotated Bibliography*. Vol. I. University of Michigan Botanical Gardens, Ann Arbor.
Bartlett, H. H. (1956) Fire, primitive agriculture, and grazing in the tropics. In: *Southeast Asian Grasslands: Understanding a Folk Landscape*, Michael R. Dove ed., pp. 77–117. Contributions from the New York Botanical Garden, Volume 21. New York: New York Botanical Gardens Press.
Bateman, Milford. (2010) *Why Doesn't Microfinance Work?* London: Zed Books.
Bateson, Catherine Mary. (1984) *With a Daughter's Eye: A Memoir of Margaret Mead and Gregory Bateson*. New York: W. Morrow.
Bateson, Gregory. (1958/1936) *Naven*. Stanford: Stanford University Press.
Bateson, Gregory. (1972) *Steps to an Ecology of Mind*. New York: Ballantine Books.
Bawden, G. and R. Reycraft, eds. (2000) *Environmental Disaster and the Archaeology of Human Response*. University of New Mexico, Anthropological Papers 7.
Bebbington, Andrew. (1993) Modernization from below: An alternative indigenous development? *Economic Geography* 69(3): 274–292.
Beeman, Randal S. and James A. Pritchard. (2001) *A Green and Permanent Land: Ecology and Agriculture in the Twentieth Century*. Lawrence (KS): University Press of Kansas.
Bellow, Saul. (1976) *To Jerusalem and Back: A Personal Account*. New York: Viking Press.
Benjamin, Walter. (1978 [1928]) *Reflections: Essays, Aphorisms, Autobiographical Writings*. Trans. Edmund Jephcott. New York: Schocken Books.
Bennett, John. (1976) *The Ecological Transition*. New York: Pergamon Press.
Bennett, John W. (1977) Ecosystem analogies in cultural ecology. In: *The Concept and Dynamics of Culture*, Bernardo Bernardi ed., pp. 177–207. The Hague: Mouton.

Bentley, Jeffery W. (1992) Alternatives to pesticides in Central America: Applied studies of local knowledge. *Culture and Agriculture* 44:10–13.
Berkes, Fikret and Carl Folke, eds. (2000) *Linking Social and Ecological Systems: Management Practices and Social Mechanisms for Building Resilience.* Cambridge (UK): Cambridge University Press.
Berkes, Fikret, Johan Colding, and Carl Folke. (2003) *Navigating Social-ecological Systems*, Cambridge (UK): Cambridge University Press.
Berlin, Brent, Dennis Breedlove, and Peter Raven. (1974) *Principles of Tzeltal Plant Classification: An Introduction to the Botanical Ethnography of a Mayan-Speaking People of Highland Chiapas.* New York: Academic Press.
Bilger, Burkhard. (2009) Annals of invention – hearth surgery: the quest for a stove that can save the world. *New Yorker* December 21.
Birks, J. B., ed. (1962) *Rutherford at Manchester.* London: Heywood.
Biswas, Soutik. (2010) BBC News, Medak, Andhra Pradesh. India's micro-finance suicide epidemic. Updated 16 Dec. 2010. Web. http://www.bbc.com/news/world-south-asia-11997571. Accessed 22 August 2014.
Blaikie, Piers. (1985) *The Political Economy of Soil Erosion in Developing Countries.* New York: Longman.
Blewitt, John, ed. (2013) *Sustainable Development.* 4 vols. Abingdon (UK): Routledge.
Bloch, Maurice. (1974) Symbols, song, dance and features of articulation: Is religion an extreme form of traditional authority? *European Journal of Sociology* 15:55–81.
Bodansky, D. (2010) The Copenhagen Climate Change Conference: A post-mortem. University of Georgia School of Law. http://www.indiaenvironmentportal.org.in/files/The%20 Copenhagen%20Climate%20Change%20Conference.pdf (accessed 20 April 2010).
Bond, W. J. and J. E. Keeley. (2005) Fire as a global "herbivore": the ecology and evolution of flammable ecosystems. *Trends in Ecology and Evolution* 20: 387–394.
Bongaarts, J. (1992) Population growth and global warming. *Population and Development Review* 18(2):299–319.
Bouquet, M. (1995) Exhibiting knowledge: The trees of Dubois, Haeckel, Jesse and Rivers at the Pithecanthropus centennial exhibition. In: *Shifting Contexts: Transformations in Anthropological Knowledge*, M. Strathern ed., pp. 31–55. London: Routledge.
Bourdieu, Pierre. (1977) *Outline of a Theory of Practice.* Trans. Richard Nice. (Original 1972, Librairie Droz, Switzerland.) Cambridge: Cambridge University Press.
Brandon, K., K. Redford and S. Saunderson. (1998) *Parks in Peril: People, Politics, and Protected Areas.* Washington DC: Nature Conservancy.
Braun, B. (2002) *The Intemperate Rainforest: Nature, Culture, and Power on Canada's West Coast.* Minneapolis: University of Minnesota Press.
Brechin, Steven R., Peter R. Wilshusen, Crystal L. Fortwangler, Patrick C. West, eds. (2003) *Contested Nature: Promoting International Biodiversity and Social Justice in the Twenty-First Century.* Albany: SUNY Press.
Brookfield, H. (1992) "Environmental colonialism", tropical deforestation, and concerns other than global warming. *Global Environmental Change* 2(2):93–96.
Brosius, J. Peter. (1997) Endangered forest, endangered people: environmentalist representations of indigenous knowledge. *Human Ecology* 25(1):47–69.
Brush, Steven and Boris Stabinsky, eds. (1996) *Valuing Local Knowledge: Indigenous People and Intellectual Property Rights.* Washington DC: Island Press.
Bryant, Bunyan. (1995) *Environmental Justice: Issues, Policies, and Solutions.* Washington DC: Island Press.

Bunker, Stephen G. (2007) Natural values and the physical inevitability of uneven development under capitalism. In: *Rethinking Environmental History: World-System History and Global Environmental Change*, Alf Hornborg, J. R. McNeil, and Joan Martinez-Alier eds., pp. 239–258. Lanham (MD): Altamira Press.

Bush, Vannevar. (1945/1990) *Science The Endless Frontier – A Report to the President by the Director of the Office of Scientific Research and Development*. Washington, DC: United States Government Printing Office.

Buttel, F. H. (1992) Environmentalization: Origins, processes, and implications for rural social change. *Rural Sociol.* 57(1): 1–27.

Byerlee, Derek, and Akmal Siddiq. (1994) Has the green revolution been sustained? The quantitative impact of the seed-fertilizer revolution in Pakistan revisited. *World Development* 22(9):1345–1361.

Cairns, Malcolm, ed. (2007) *Voices from the Forest: Integrating Indigenous Knowledge into Sustainable Upland Farming*. Washington (DC): Resources for the Future.

Caldecott, Julian. (1990) Eruptions and migrations of bearded pig populations. *Bongo* 18:2–12.

Carey, M. (2008) The politics of place: inhabiting and defending glacier hazard zones in Peru's Cordillera Blanca. In: *Darkening Peaks: Glacier Retreat, Science, and Society*. B. Orlove, E. Wiegandt, and B. H. Luckman eds., pp. 229–240. Berkeley, Los Angeles, and London: University of California Press.

Carpenter, C. (1987) Brides and Bride-Dressers in Contemporary Java. Ph.D. dissertation, Cornell University.

Carse, Ashley. (2014) *Beyond the Big Ditch: Politics, Ecology, and Infrastructure at the Panama Canal*. Cambridge (MA): MIT Press.

Carson, Rachel. (1962) *Silent Spring*. New York: Fawcett World Library.

Casillas, C. and D. M. Kammen. (2010) The energy–poverty–climate nexus. *Science* 330:1182. DOI: 10.1126/science.1197412.

Cassman, Kenneth G., and P. L. Pingali. (1995) Intensification of irrigated rice systems: learning from the past to meet future challenges. *GeoJournal* 35(3):299–305.

Cassman, Kenneth G., Surajit K. De Datta, D. C. Olk, J. Alcantara, M. Samson, J. Descalsota, and M. Dizon. (1995) Yield decline and the nitrogen economy of long-term experiments on continuous, irrigated rice systems in the tropics. In: *Soil Management: Experimental Basis for Sustainability and Environmental Quality*. R. Lal and B. A. Stewart, eds., pp. 181–222. Boca Raton (FL): CRC Lewis.

Cengel, Y. A. and M. A. Boles. (2001) *Thermodynamics: An Engineering Approach*. New York: McGraw Hill.

Chambers, Robert. (1983) *Rural Development: Putting the Last First*. London (UK): Longman Scientific and Technical.

Chokkalingam, U., W. De Jong, J. Smith and C. Sabogal, eds. (2001) *Journal of Tropical Forest Science* 13(4). Special Issue. Secondary Forests in Asia: Their Diversity, Importance, and Role in Future Environmental Management.

Clark, Brett and Richard York. (2005) Dialectical nature: reflections in honor of the twentieth anniversary of Levins and Lewontin's *The Dialectical Biologist*. *Monthly Review: An Independent Socialist Magazine* 57(1): 13–22.

Clark, S. G., M. M. Steen-Adams, S. Pfirman, and R. L. Wallace. (2011). Professional development of interdisciplinary environmental scholars. *Journal of Environmental Studies and Sciences* 1(2): 99–113.

Clarke, W. C. (1966) From extensive to intensive shifting cultivation: A succession from New Guinea. *Ethnology* 5(4): 347–359.

Clausius, Rudolf. (1850) Über die bewegende Kraft der Wärme, Part I, Part II. *Annalen der Physik* 79: 368–397, 500–524.
Clausius, Rudolf. (1865) *The Mechanical Theory of Heat – with its Applications to the Steam Engine and to Physical Properties of Bodies*. London: John van Voorst.
Clay, Jason. (1991) Cultural survival and conservation: lessons from the past twenty years. In: *Biodiversity: Culture, Conservation, and Ecodevelopment*. M. L. Oldfield and J. B. Alcorn, eds., pp. 248–273. Boulder (CO): Westview Press.
Clements, F. E. (1916) *Plant Succession: An Analysis of the Development of Vegetation*. Washington (DC): Carnegie Institution.
Cohen, I. Bernard. (1994) *Interactions: Some Contacts between the Natural Sciences and the Social Sciences*. Cambridge (MA): MIT Press.
Conklin, Harold C. (1954) The Relation of Hanuno'o Culture to the Plant World. Yale University Ph.D. dissertation. Ann Arbor: University Microfilms.
Conklin, Harold C. (1955) *Hanuno'o Agriculture: A Report on an Integral System of Shifting Cultivation in the Philippines*. Forestry Development Paper No. 12. Rome: Food and Agriculture Organization.
Conklin, H. C. (1959) Shifting cultivation and succession to grassland climax. *Proceedings of the Ninth Pacific Science Congress* 7: 60–62.
Conklin, Harold C. (1980) *Ethnographic Atlas of Ifugao: A Study of Environment, Culture, and Society in Northern Luzon*. New Haven: Yale University Press.
Coomes, O. T., F. Grimard, and G. J. Burt. (2000) Tropical forests and shifting cultivation: Secondary forest fallow dynamics among traditional farmers of the Peruvian Amazon. *Ecological Economics* 32: 109–124.
Cosgel, Martin. (2009) Conversations between anthropologists and economists. In: *Economic Persuasions*, S. Gudeman ed., pp. 81–96. New York, Oxford: Berghahn Books.
Crate, Susan A. and Mark Nuttall, eds. (2009) *Anthropology and Climate Change: From Encounters to Actions*. Walnut Creek (CA): Left Coast Press.
Cronon, W. (1992) A place for stories: nature, history and narrative. *Journal of American History* 78(4) March: 347–1376.
Cronon, W. (1995) The trouble with wilderness, or getting back to the wrong nature. In: *Uncommon Ground: Rethinking the Human Place in Nature*, William Cronon ed., pp. 69–90. New York: W. W. Norton.
Curran, L. M., I. Caniago, G. D. Paoli, D. Astianti, M. Kusneti, M. Leighton, C. E. Nirarita, and H. Haeruman. (1999) Impact of El Niño and logging on canopy tree recruitment in Borneo. *Science* 286(5447): 2184–2188.
Daly, Herman E., ed. (1973) *Toward a Steady-State Economy*. San Francisco: W. H. Freeman.
Daly, Herman E. and Alvaro Umana, eds. (1982) *Energy, Economics, and the Environment: Conflicting Views of an Essential Interrelationship*. Westview Press.
D'Antonio, C. M. and P. M. Vitousek. (1992) Biological invasions by exotic grasses, the grass/fire cycle, and global change. *Annual Review of Ecological Systems* 23:63–87.
Davies, D. (1988) The evocative symbolism of trees. In: *The Iconography of Landscape*, D. Cosgrove and S. Daniels eds., pp. 32–42. Cambridge: Cambridge University Press.
De Foresta, H. and G. Michon. (1997) The agroforest alternative to *Imperata* grasslands: When smallholder agriculture and forestry reach sustainability. Special issue: Agroforestry innovations for *Imperata* grassland rehabilitation, D. P. Garrity, ed. *Agroforestry Systems* 36(1-3): 105-120.
Deleuze, G. and F. Guattari. (1987) *A Thousand Plateaus: Capitalism and Schizophrenia*. Trans. Brian Massumi. (Orig. *Mille Plateaux*, vol. 2 of *Capitalisme et Schizophrénie*, 1980, Les Editions de Minuit, Paris). University of Minnesota Press, Minneapolis.

Demeritt, David. (2001) The construction of global warming and the politics of science. *Annals of the Association of American Geographers* 91(2): 307–337.
Denevan, W. M. (1992) The pristine myth: The landscape of the Americas in 1492. *The American Geographer* 82(3): 369–385.
Derrida, J. (1978) *Writing and Difference*, A. Bass, trans. Chicago: University of Chicago Press.
Diamond, J. (1990) Bach, God and the jungle. *Natural History* 12(90): 22–27.
Diamond, Jared M. (1997) *Guns, Germs, and Steel: The Fates of Human Societies*. New York: W. W. Norton.
Diamond, Jared M. (2005) *Collapse: How Societies Choose to Fail or Succeed*. New York: Viking.
Dove, Michael R. (1983) Theories of swidden agriculture and the political economy of ignorance. *Agroforestry Systems* 1:85–99.
Dove, Michael R. (1985a) The agroecological mythology of the Javanese, and the political economy of Indonesia. *Indonesia* 39: 1–36.
Dove, Michael R. (1985b) *Swidden Agriculture in Indonesia: The Subsistence Strategies of the Kalimantan Kantu'*. Berlin: Mouton.
Dove Michael R. (1986) The practical reason of weeds in Indonesia: Peasant versus state views of *Imperata* and *Chromolaena*. *Human Ecology* 14(2): 163–190.
Dove, Michael R. (1993) The responses of Dayak and bearded pig to mast-fruiting in Kalimantan: An analysis of nature–culture analogies. In: *Tropical Forests, People, and Food: Biocultural Interactions and Applications to Development*, C. M. Hladik, A. Hladik, O. F. Linares, H. Pagezy, A. Semple, and M. Hadley eds., pp. 113–123. Man and the Biosphere Series, Vol. 13. Paris/Carnforth: UNESCO/Parthenon Publishing.
Dove, Michael R. (1994) The existential status of the Pakistani farmer: a study of institutional factors in development. *Ethnology* 33(4):331–351.
Dove, Michael R. (2000) The life-cycle of indigenous knowledge, and the case of natural rubber production. In: *Indigenous Environmental Knowledge and its Transformations*, R. F. Ellen, A. Bicker, and P. Parkes eds., pp. 213–251. Amsterdam: Harwood.
Dove, Michael R. (2001) Inter-disciplinary borrowing in environmental anthropology and the critique of modern science. In: *New Directions in Anthropology and Environment: Intersections*, C. L. Crumley ed., pp. 90–110. Walnut Creek (CA): AltaMira Press.
Dove, Michael R. (2006) Equilibrium theory and inter-disciplinary borrowing: a comparison of old and new ecological anthropologies. In: *Reimagining Political Ecology*, A. Biersack and J. B. Greenberg eds., pp. 43–69. Durham (NC): Duke University Press.
Dove, Michael R. (2007a) Kinds of fields. In: *Fine Description: Ethnographic and Linguistic Essays by Harold C. Conklin*, J. Kuipers and R. McDermott eds., pp. 410–427. Southeast Asia Monograph Series, Volume 56, Yale University.
Dove, Michael R. (2007b) Perceptions of local knowledge and adaptation on Mt. Merapi, Central Java. In: *Modern Crises and Traditional Strategies: Local Ecological Knowledge in Island Southeast Asia*, R. F. Ellen ed., pp. 238–262. New York/Oxford: Berghahn Books.
Dove, Michael R. (2008) Symbiotic relationships between human populations and *Imperata cylindrica*: The question of ecosystemic succession and preservation in South Kalimantan. In: *Southeast Asian Grasslands: Understanding a Folk Landscape*, Michael R. Dove ed., pp. 326–344. Contributions from the New York Botanical Garden, Volume 21. New York: New York Botanical Gardens Press.
Dove, Michael R. (2011)*The Banana Tree at the Gate: The History of Marginal Peoples and Global Markets in Borneo*. Yale Agrarian Studies Series, James C. Scott ed. New Haven: Yale University Press.

Dove, Michael R., ed. (2014) *The Anthropology of Climate Change: A Historical Reader*. Malden (MA): Wiley/Blackwell.

Dove, Michael R. (2015) Historic decentering of the modern discourse of climate change: the long view from the Vedic sages to Montesquieu. In: *Climate Cultures: Anthropological Perspectives on Climate Change*, Jessica Barnes and Michael R. Dove eds. Yale Agrarian Studies Series. New Haven (CT): Yale University Press.

Dove, Michael R. and Daniel M. Kammen. (2001) Vernacular models of development: an analysis of Indonesia under the "New Order". *World Development* 29(4): 619–639.

Dove, Michael R., Percy E. Sajise, and Amity A. Doolittle, eds. (2011) Beyond the sacred forest: complicating conservation in southeast Asia. In: *New Ecologies for the Twenty-First Century*, Arturo Escobar and Dianne Rocheleau eds. Durham (NC): Duke University Press.

Dunham, S. Anne. (2009) *Surviving Against the Odds: Village Industry in Indonesia*. Durham (NC): Duke University Press.

Durkheim, Emile. (1964/1933) *The Division of Labor in Society*. George Simpson trans. (Original *De la division du travail social*, Paris, Félix Alcan, Éditeur.) New York: Free Press.

Earth Negotiation Bulletin (ENB). Vol.12, No.176 (2001), No. 189 (2001), No. 260 (2004), No. 291 (2005), No. 318 (2006), No. 354 (2007), No. 295 (2008), No. 447 (2009), No. 459 (2009), No. 472 (2010), No. 478 (2010).

Edelman, M. (1974) The political language of the helping professions. *Politics and Society* 4(3): 295–310.

Eliot, George. (1871–1872) *Middlemarch: A Study of Provincial Life*. Edinburgh and London: William Blackwood.

Ellen, Roy F., ed. (2007) *Modern Crises and Traditional Strategies: Local Ecological Knowledge in Island Southeast Asia*. New York/Oxford: Berghahn Books.

Ellen, Roy F. (2008 [1999]) Forest knowledge, forest transformation: political contingency, historical ecology and the renegotiation of nature in central Seram. In: *Environmental Anthropology: A Historical Reader*, Michael R. Dove and Carol Carpenter eds., pp. 321–338. Malden (MA): Blackwell.

Ellen, Roy F., Peter Parkes, and Alan Bicker, eds. (2000) *Indigenous Environmental Knowledge and its Transformations*. Amsterdam: Harwood.

Emerson, Ralph Waldo. (1849) Nature. In: *Nature; Addresses and Lectures*. Boston: J. Munroe.

Endersby, Jim. (2003) Escaping Darwin's shadow. *Journal of the History of Biology* 36:385–403.

Erikson, Kai T. (1976) *Everything in its Path: Destruction of Community in the Buffalo Creek Flood*. New York: Touchstone/Simon and Schuster.

Escobar, Arturo. (1995) *Encountering Development. The Making and Unmaking of the Third World*. Princeton (NJ): Princeton University Press.

Ezzati, M. and D. Kammen. (2001) Indoor air pollution from biomass combustion and acute respiratory infections in Kenya: An exposure-response study. *The Lancet* 358: 619–624.

Ezzati, M., R. Bailis, D. M. Kammen, T. Holloway, L. Price, L. A. Cifuentes et al. (2004) Energy management and global health. *Annual Review of Environment and Resources* 29: 383–419.

Fairhead, J. and M. Leach. (1996) *Misreading the African Landscape: Society and Ecology in Forest–Savanna Mosaic*. Cambridge: Cambridge University Press.

Farbotko, C., and H. Lazrus. (2012) The first climate refugees? Contesting global narratives of climate change in Tuvalu. *Global Environmental Change* 22(2):382–390.

Ferguson James. (1990) *The Anti-Politics Machine: "Development," Depoliticization and Bureaucratic Power in Lesotho*. Cambridge: Cambridge University Press.

Ferguson, James. (2006) *Global Shadows: Africa in the Neoliberal World Order*. Durham (NC): Duke University Press.

Fiedler, Peggy L., Peter S. White, and Robert A. Lediy. (1997) The paradigm shift in ecology and its implications for conservation. In: *The Ecological Basis of Conservation: Heterogeneity, Ecosystems, and Biodiversity*, Steward T. A. Pickett, Richard S. Ostfield, Moshe Sshachak, and Gene E. Likens eds., pp. 83–92. New York: Chapman and Hall.

Field, Erica, Rohini Pande, John Papp, and Natalia Rigol. (2013) Does the classic microfinance model discourage entrepreneurship among the poor? Experimental evidence from India. *American Economic Review* 103 (6): 2196–2226.

Florman, Samuel C. (1976) *The Existential Pleasure of Engineering*. New York: St Martin's Press.

Fosberg, F. R. (1962) Tropical Pacific grasslands and savannas. *Proceedings of the Ninth Pacific Science Congress*. pp. 118–123.

Fox, James J. (1991) Managing the ecology of rice production in Indonesia. In: *Indonesia: Resources, Ecology, and Environment*, Joan Hardjono ed., pp. 61–84. Singapore: Oxford University Press.

Franklin, Sarah. (1995) Science as culture, cultures of science. *Annual Review of Anthropology* 24:163–184.

Frazer, J. G. (1951) *The Golden Bough: A Study in Magic and Religion*, abr. edn. MacMillan, New York.

Freebairn, Donald K. (1995) Did the green revolution concentrate incomes? A quantitative study of research reports. *World Development* 23(2): 265–279.

Friedman, Jonathan. (1975) Tribes, states, and transformations. In: *Marxist Analyses and Social Anthropology*, M. Bloch ed., pp. 161–202. London (UK): Malaby.

Friedman, Thomas L. (1999) *The Lexus and the Olive Tree*. New York: Anchor/Random House.

Frossard, David. (2005) In field or freezer? Some thoughts on genetic diversity maintenance in rice. In: *Conserving Nature in Culture: Case Studies from Southeast Asia*, M. R. Dove, P. E. Sajise. and A. A. Doolittle eds., pp. 144–166. Southeast Asia Monograph Series, Volume 54, Yale University.

Fujimura, Joan. (1992) Crafting science: standardized packages, boundary objects, and "translation". In: *Science as Practice and Culture*, Andrew Pickering ed., pp. 168–211. Chicago: University of Chicago Press.

Gagnon, Alexandre S., Andrew B. G. Bush, and Karen E. Smoyer-Tomic. (2001) Dengue epidemics and the El Niño Southern Oscillation. *Climate Research* 19: 35–43.

Gallagher, K. S. (2009) *Acting in Time on Energy Policy*, Washington, DC: Brookings Institution Press.

Gardner, Martin. (1960) *The Annotated Alice: Alice's Adventures in Wonderland and Through the Looking Glass by Lewis Carroll*. New York: Bramwall House.

Garrity, D. P. (1997a) Agroforestry innovations for *Imperata* grassland rehabilitation: Workshop recommendations. *Agroforest Syst* 36 (1–3): 263–274.

Garrity, D P. ed. (1997b) Special issue: Agroforestry innovations for *Imperata* grassland rehabilitation. *Agroforestry Systems* 36(1–3).

Geertz, Clifford. (1971) *Agricultural Involution: The Processes of Ecological Change in Indonesia*. Berkeley (CA): University of California Press.

Georgescu-Roegen, N. (1971) *The Entropy Law and the Economic Process*. Cambridge (MA): Harvard University Press.

Goldman, Michael. (2005) *Imperial Nature: The World Bank and Struggles for Social Justice in the Age of Globalization*. New Haven (CT): Yale University Press.

Goldman, Stanford. (1960) Further consideration of cybernetic aspects of homeostasis. In: *Self-Organizing Systems*, M. C. Yovits and Scott Cameron eds., pp. 108–121. New York: Pergamon Press.

Gottlieb, Anthony. (2014) Let's have a dialogue. "Plato at the Googleplex," by Rebecca Newberger Goldstein. Sunday Book Review, *New York Times*, April 18.

Gouyon, A., H. de Foresta, and P. Levang. (1993) Does "jungle rubber" deserve its name? an analysis of rubber agroforestry systems in southeast Sumatra. *Agroforestry Systems* 22:181–206.

Gross, Daniel R. (1975) Protein capture and cultural development in the Amazon Basin. *American Anthropologist* 77:526–549.

Gross, Paul R. and Norman Levitt. (1994) *Higher Superstition: The Academic Left and Its Quarrels with Science*. Baltimore/London: Johns Hopkins University Press.

Grove, Richard H. and John Chappell, eds. (2000) *El Niño: History and Crisis: Studies from the Asia-Pacific Region*. Knapwell: White Horse.

Grubb, Michael, David G. Victor, and Chris Hope. (1991) Pragmatics in the greenhouse. *Nature* 354: 348–350.

Grubler, A., N. Nakicenovic, and D. G. Victor. (1999) Dynamics of energy technologies and global change. *Energy Policy* 27: 247–280.

Gudeman, Stephen and Alberto Rivera. (1990) *Conversations in Colombia: The Domestic Economy in Life and Text*. New York: Cambridge University Press.

Gupta, Akhil. (1998) *Postcolonial Developments: Agriculture in the Making of Modern India*. Durham (NC): Duke University Press.

Haas, Peter M. (1992) Introduction: Epistemic communities and international policy coordination. *International Organization* 46(1): 1–35.

Hadiwidjojo G. P. H. (1956) Alang-Alang Kumitir. Paper read at the Radyapustaka (Court library). Solo (Central Java, Indonesia), December 28.

Hamilton, I. (2009) Lessons from Copenhagen: Has the UN played its last card? *Carbon Positive*. http://www.carbonpositive.net/ viewarticle.aspx?articleID=1789

Hammond, A. L., E. Rodenburg, and W. R. Moomaw. (1990) Accountability in the greenhouse. *Nature* 347:705.

Hammond, A. L., E. Rodenburg, and W. R. Moomaw. (1991) Calculating national accountability for climate change. *Environment* 33(1):11–35.

Hamzah, Z. (1993) Pembinaan HTI di Tanah Kosong dan Tanah Alang-Alang (I) (Regulation of tree plantations in empty lands and *Imperata* Lands (I)). *Mangala Wanabakti* 9(3): 1–6.

Haraway, Donna. (1991) *Simians, Cyborgs, and Women: The Reinvention of Nature*. London: Free Association Books.

Haraway, Donna. (1992) The promises of monsters: a regenerative politics for inappropriate/d others. In: *Cultural Studies*, Lawrence Grossberg, Cary Nelson, and Paula A. Treichler eds., pp. 295–337. New York: Routledge.

Hardin, Rebecca and Melissa J. Remis. (2006) Biological and cultural anthropology of a changing tropical forest: a fruitful collaboration across subfields. *American Anthropologist* 108(2): 273–285.

Harlan, J. R. (1982) Human interference with grass systematics. In: *Grasses and Grasslands: Systematics and Ecology*, J. R. Estes, R. J. Tryl and J. N. Brunken eds., pp. 37–50. Norman (OK): University of Oklahoma Press.

Harrison, Robert P. (1992) *Forests: The Shadow of Civilization*. Chicago: University of Chicago Press.

Hass, J. and M. O'Dillon eds. (2003) El Niño in Peru: Biology and culture over 10,000 years. *Fieldiana Botany* 43.
Hayes, P. and K. R. Smith. (1993) Introduction. In: *The Global Greenhouse Regime: Who Pays?*, Peter Hayes and Kirk R. Smith eds., pp. 3–19. London: Earthscan; Tokyo: UN University Press.
Headland, Thomas N., and Robert C. Bailey. (1991) Introduction: Have hunter-gatherers ever lived in tropical rain forest independently of agriculture? Theme issue. *Human Ecology* 19(2):115–122.
Hecht, S. (2010) The new rurality: Globalization, peasants and the paradoxes of landscapes. *Land Use Policy* 27(2): 161–169.
Hecht, Susanna and Alexander Cockburn. (1989) *The Fate of the Forest: Developers, Destroyers and Defenders of the Amazon.* London: Verso.
von Heland, Jacob and Carl Folke. (2013) A social contract with the ancestors – culture and ecosystem services in southern Madagascar. *Global Environmental Change.* http://dx.doi.org/10.1016/j.gloenvcha.2013.11.003.
Herschbach, D. R. (1995) Ben Franklin's "Scientific Achievements". *Harvard Magazine*, November–December.
Hesiod. (1914) *Works and Days*. Trans. G. Evelyn-White. Gloucester (UK): Dodo Press.
Hewitt, K. (1995) Sustainable disasters: Perspectives and powers in the discourse of calamity. In: *Power of Development*, J. Crush ed., pp. 115–128. New York: Routledge.
Hippocrates. (1923) *Airs Waters Places*. Trans. W. H. S. Jones. Cambridge (MA): Harvard University Press.
Hodgkinson, K. C., G. N. Harrington, G. F. Griffin, J. C. Noble and M. D. Young. (1984) Management of vegetation with fire. In: *Management of Australia's Rangelands.* G. N. Harrington, A. D. Wilson & M. D. Young eds., pp. 141–156. Clayton (Aust.): Commonwealth Scientific and Industrial Research Organization.
Holling, Crawford S., Paul Taylor, and Michael Thompson. (1991) From Newton's Sleep to Blake's Fourfold Vision: Why the climax community and the rational bureaucracy are not the ends of the ecological and social-cultural roads. *Annals of Earth* 9(3):19–21.
Hornborg, Alf. (1992) Machine fetishism, value, and the image of unlimited good: toward a thermodynamics of imperialism. *Man* (n.s.) 27: 1–18.
Hornborg, A. (1998) Towards an ecological theory of unequal exchange: articulating world system theory and ecological economics. *Ecological Economics* 25(1): 127–136.
Hornborg, Alf. (2007) Footprints in the cotton fields: the industrial revolution as time-space appropriation and environmental load displacement. In: *Rethinking Environmental History: World-System History and Global Environmental Change*, Alf Hornborg, J. R. McNeil, and Joan Martinez-Alier eds., pp. 259–272. Lanham (MD): Altamira Press.
Horne, E. C. (1974) *Javanese–English Dictionary*. Yale University Press, New Haven.
Hulme, Mike. (2011) Reducing the future to climate: a story of climate determinism and reductionism. *Osiris* 26: 245–266.
Ibn Khaldûn. (1958) *The Muqaddimah: An Introduction to History*. Trans. Franz Rosenthal. 3 vols. New York: Bollingen Foundation.
Ingold, Tim. (1990) An anthropologist looks at biology. *Man.* 25(2): 208–229.
Ingold, Tim. (2008/1993) Globes and spheres: The topology of environmentalism. In: *Environmental Anthropology: A Historical Reader*, Michael R. Dove and Carol Carpenter eds., pp. 462–469. Malden (MA): Wiley-Blackwell.
International Energy Agency (IEA). (2012) *World Energy Outlook 2012.* Paris: Organization for Economic Cooperation and Development.
IPCC. (2007) *Climate Change 2007. Mitigation of Climate Change*. Contribution of Working Group III to the Fourth Assessment Report of the Intergovernmental Panel on

Climate Change, B. Metz, O. Davidson, P. Bosch, R. Dave, and L. Meyer, eds. New York: Cambridge University Press.

Jackson, J. B. (1984) *Discovering the Vernacular Landscape*. New Haven (CT): Yale University Press.

Jacobson, A. and D. M. Kammen. (2007) Engineering, institutions, and the public interest: evaluating product quality in the Kenyan solar photovoltaics industry. *Energy Policy* 35: 2960–2968.

Janković, Vladimir. (2000) *Reading the Skies: A Cultural History of English Weather, 1650–1820*. Chicago: University of Chicago Press.

Janković, Vladimir. (2007) Gruff Boreas, deadly calms: a medical perspective on winds and the Victorians. *Journal of the Royal Anthropological Institute* (N.S.)13(S1): S147–S164.

Janzen, Daniel H. (1974) Tropical blackwater rivers, animals, and mast-fruiting of the Dipterocarpaceae. *Biotropica* 6(2):69–103.

Janzen, Daniel H. (1976) Why bamboos wait so long to flower. *Annual Review of Systematics* 7:347–391.

Jasanoff, Sheila. (2004a) Heaven and Earth: The politics of environmental images. In: *Earthly Politics: Local and Global in Environmental Governance*, Sheila Jasanoff and Marybeth Long Martello eds., pp. 31–52. Cambridge (MA): MIT Press.

Jasanoff, Sheila. (2004b) *States of Knowledge: The Co-Production of Knowledge and Social Order*. London: Routledge.

Jorgenson, A. B. (1989) A natural view: Pwo Karen notions of plants, landscapes, and people. *Folk* 31:21–51.

Kagan, Jerome. (2009) *The Three Cultures: Natural Sciences, Social Sciences, and the Humanities in the Twenty-First Century*. New York: Cambridge University Press.

Kahan, Dan. (2012) Why we are poles apart on climate change. *Nature* 488(7411): 255.

Kammen, D. M. (1995) Cookstoves for the developing world. *Scientific American* 273: 72–75.

Kammen, D. M. and W. F. Lankford. (1990) Comparative study of box-type solar cookers in Nicaragua. *Solar & Wind Technology* 7: 463–472.

Kammen, D. M. and W. F. Lankford. (1991) Designing better solar cookers. *Nature* 351:21.

Kandlikar, M., and A. Sagar. (1999) Climate change research and analysis in India: an integrated assessment of a South–North divide. *Global Environmental Change* 9(2): 119–138.

Kato, Tsuyoshi. (1994) The emergence of abandoned paddy fields in Negeri Sembilan, Malaysia. *Southeast Asian Studies* 32(2):145–172.

Kellert, Stephen R. (2008) *Borrowed Knowledge and the Challenge of Learning Across Disciplines: The Case of Chaos Theory*. Chicago: University of Chicago Press.

Kempton, W. and P. P. Craig. (1993), European perspectives on global climate change. *Environment* 35(3):16–45.

Komarek, E. V. (1967) Fire – and the ecology of man. *Annual Proceedings of the Tall Timbers Fire Ecology Conference* 6:143–170. Tallahassee (FL.): Tall Timbers Research Station.

Kotchen, M. J., and O. R. Young. (2007). Meeting the challenges of the anthropocene: Towards a science of coupled human–biophysical systems. *Global Environmental Change* 17(2), 149–151.

Kroeber, Alfred L. (1963) *Cultural and Natural Areas of Native North America*. Berkeley (CA): University of California Press.

Krugman, Paul. (2014) Interests, ideology and Climate. Op-Ed, *The New York Times*, June 8.

Lahsen, Myanna. (2004) Transnational locals: Brazilian experience of the climate regime. In: *Earthly Politics: Local and Global in Environmental Governance*, Sheila Jasanoff and Marybeth L. Martello eds., pp. 151–172. Cambridge (MA): MIT Press.

Lahsen, Myanna. (2007) Trust through participation? Problems of knowledge in climate decision making. In: *The Social Construction of Climate Change: Power, Knowledge, Norms, Discourses*, M. E. Pettenger ed., pp. 173–196. London: Ashgate.

Lahsen, Myanna. (2008) Experiences of modernity in the greenhouse: A cultural analysis of a physicist "trio" supporting the backlash against global warming. *Global Environmental Change* 18:204–219.

Lahsen, Myanna. (2009) A science–policy interface in the global south: the politics of carbon sinks and science in Brazil. *Climatic Change* 97(3): 339–372.

Lahsen, Myanna. (2010) The social status of climate change knowledge: An editorial essay. *Wiley Interdisciplinary Reviews: Climate Change* 1(2): 162–171.

Lahsen, Myanna et al. (2010) Impacts, adaptation and vulnerability to global environmental change: challenges and pathways for an action-oriented research agenda for middle-income and low-income countries. *Current Opinion in Environmental Sustainability* 2(5): 364–374.

Lansing, J. Stephen. (1991) *Priests and Programmers: The Technologies of Power in the Landscape of Bali*. Princeton (NJ): Princeton University Press.

Lansing, J. Stephen. (2006) *Perfect Order: Recognizing Complexity in Bali*. Princeton (NJ): Princeton University Press.

Laris, Paul. (2008) An anthropogenic escape route from the 'Gulliver syndrome' in the west African savanna. *Human Ecology* 36: 789–805.

Latour, Bruno. (1988) *Science in Action: How to Follow Scientists and Engineers Through Society*. Cambridge (MA): Harvard University Press.

Latour, Bruno. (1990) *Representation in Scientific Practice*. Cambridge (MA): MIT Press.

Latour, Bruno. (1993) *We Have Never Been Modern*. Trans. Catherine Porter. Cambridge (MA): Harvard University Press.

Latour, B. (2004) Why has critique run out of steam? From matters of fact to matters of concern. *Critical Inquiry* 30:225–248.

Le Roy Ladurie, Emmanuel. (1974) *The Peasants of Languedoc*, trans. John Day. Urbana: University of Illinois Press.

Leiserowitz, A. (2005) American risk perceptions: Is climate change dangerous? *Risk Analysis*, 25(6): 1433–1442.

Leiserowitz, A. (2006) Climate change risk perception and policy preferences: The role of affect, imagery, and values. *Climatic Change* 77: 45–72.

Leiserowitz, A. (2010) Climate change risk perceptions and behavior in the United States. In: *Climate Change Science and Policy*, S. Schneider, A. Rosencranz, and M. Mastrandrea, eds. Washington (DC):Island Press.

Lenoir, Timothy. (1997) *Instituting Science: The Cultural Production of Scientific Disciplines*. Stanford: Stanford University Press.

Lévi-Strauss, C. (1966) *The Savage Mind*. Chicago: University of Chicago Press.

Levins, Richard and Richard Lewontin. (1985) *The Dialectical Biologist*. Cambridge/London: Harvard University Press.

Lewis, H. T. (1989) Ecological and technological knowledge of fire: Aborigines versus park rangers in northern Australia. *American Anthropologist* 91(4): 940–961.

Li, Peng et al. (2014) A review of swidden agriculture in southeast Asia. *Remote Sensing* 6: 1654–1683.

Li, Tania Murray. (2000) Articulating indigenous identity in Indonesia: Resource politics and the tribal slot. *Comparative Studies in Society and History* 42(1):149–179.

Li, Tania Murray. (2007) *The Will to Improve: Governmentality, Development, and the Practice of Politics*. Durham (NC): Duke University Press.
Liu, Jianguo. (2007) Complexity of coupled human and natural systems. *Science* 317(5844): 1513–1516.
Lohmann, Larry. (1998) *Missing the Point of Development Talk: Reflections for Activists*. The Cornerhouse Briefing No.9. Dorset (UK).
Lotka, Alfred J. (1925) *Elements of Physical Biology*. Baltimore (MD): Williams and Wilkins.
Machlis, G. E., J. E. Force and W. R. Burch Jr, (1997). The human ecosystem part I: the human ecosystem as an organizing concept in ecosystem management. *Society & Natural Resources* 10(4): 347–367.
Maffi, Luisa. (2001) *On Biocultural Diversity: Linking Language, Knowledge, and the Environment*. Washington DC/London: Smithsonian Institution Press.
Malinowski, Bronislaw. (1935) *Coral Gardens and Their Magic: A Study of the Methods of Tilling the Soil and of Agricultural Rites in the Trobriand islands*. New York: American Book Company.
Margalef, Ramon. (1968) *Perspectives in Ecological Theory*. Chicago: University of Chicago Press.
Marks, Jonathan. (2009) *Why I Am not a Scientist: Anthropology and Modern Knowledge*. Berkeley: University of California Press.
Markus, G. (1987) Why is there no hermeneutics of natural sciences? Some preliminary theses. *Science in Context* 1(1): 5–51.
Marx, Karl. (1887) *Capital: A Critical Analysis of Capitalist Production*. Trans. Samuel Moore and Edward Aveling, ed. Frederick Engels. London: Swan Sonnenschein, Lowrey, & Co.
McCully, P. (1991) Discord in the Greenhouse: How WRI is Attempting To Shift The Blame For Global Warming. *Ecologist* 21(4):157–165.
McIntosh, Roderick J. et al. ed. (2000) *The Way the Wind Blows: Climate, History and Human Action*. New York: Columbia University Press.
McWilliams, J. E. (2011) Worshipping weeds: The parable of the tares, the rhetoric of ecology, and the origins of agrarian exceptionalism in early America. *Environmental History* 16(2): 290–311.
Meggers, Betty J. (1971) *Amazonia: Man and Culture in a Counterfeit Paradise*. Chicago (IL): Aldine, Atherton.
Meine, Curt and Richard L. Knight, eds. (1999/1935) *The Essential Aldo Leopold: Quotations and Commentaries*. Madison: University of Wisconsin Press.
Mertz, Ole, Christine Padoch, Jefferson Fox, R. A. Cramb, Stephen J. Leisz, Nguyen Thanh Lam, and Tran Duc Vien. (2009) Swidden change in Southeast Asia: Understanding causes and consequences. *Human Ecology* 37(3): 259–264.
Microfinance Information Exchange. (2009) *MicroBanking Bulletin* Issue #19, December.
Mitchell, J. K. (1992) Editor's Note. *Global Environmental Change* 2(2):82.
Montesquieu, Charles de Secondat, baron de. (1989) *The Spirit of the Laws*. Trans./ed. Anne M. Cohler, Basia Carolyn Miller, Harold Samuel Stone. (Orig: *Esprit des loix*, trans. Thomas Nugent, 2nd edn. London: J. Nourse and P. Vaillant.) Cambridge: Cambridge University Press.
Moore, Amelia. (2010) Climate changing small islands: considering social science and the production of island vulnerability and opportunity. *Environment and Society: Advances in Research* 1: 116–131.
Moran, Emilio F., ed. (1984) *The Ecosystem Concept in Anthropology*. Boulder (CO): Westview Press for the American Association for the Advancement of Science.
Mosko, Mark S. (2009) The Fractal Yam: Botanical Imagery and Human Agency in the Trobriands. *Journal of the Royal Anthropological Institute* (N.S.) 15: 679–700.

Muller, B. (2010) Copenhagen 2010, Failure or final wake-up call for our leaders. Oxford Institute for Energy Studies. http://www.oxfordenergy.org/pdfs/EV49.pdf

Mulyoutami, Elok, Laxman Joshi, Ilahang, Gede Wibawa, and Eric Penot. (n.d.) *Establishing Rubber Agroforests on Degraded Imperata Grassland in West Kalimantan*. Bogor: ICRAF.

Mwandosya, Mark J. (1999) *Survival Emissions: A Perspective from the South on Global Climate Change Negotiations*. Dar es Salaam: Centre for Energy, Environment, Science, and Technology.

Nagtegaal, L. W. (1994) Diamonds are a regent's best friend: Javanese Bupati as political entrepreneurs. In: *State and Trade in the Indonesian Archipelago*, G J. Schutte, ed., pp. 77–97. Working Papers 13. Leiden: Koninklijk Instituut voor Taal-, Land- en Volkenkunde.

Najam, A. (2004) The view from the South: Developing countries in global environmental politics. In: *The Global Environment: Institutions, Law and Policy*, R. Axelrod and D. Downie et al. eds., pp. 225–243. Washington, DC: Congressional Quarterly Press.

Nazarea, Virginia, ed. (1999) *Ethnoecology: Situated Knowledge/Located Lives*. Tucson: University of Arizona Press.

Neidel, David. (2006) The Garden of Forking Paths: History, Its Erasure and Remembrance in Sumatra's Kerinci Seblat National Park. Ph.D. dissertation, Yale University School of Forestry and Environmental Studies and Department of Anthropology.

Nemet, G. F. and D. M. Kammen. (2007) U.S. energy research and development: Declining investment, increasing need, and the feasibility of expansion. *Energy Policy* 35(1): 746–755.

Neswald, Elizabeth R. (2006) *Thermodynamik als kultureller Kampfplatz: Zur Faszinationsgeschicte der Entropie, 1850–1915*. Freiburg: Rombach Verlag.

Netting, R. McC. (1990) Links and boundaries: Reconsidering the Alpine village as ecosystem. In: *The Ecosystem Approach in Anthropology*, E. F. Moran ed., pp. 229–245. Ann Arbor: University of Michigan Press.

Newell, B., C. L. Crumley, N. Hassan, E. F. Lambin, C. Pahl-Wostl, A. Underdal, and R. Wasson. (2005) A conceptual template for integrative human–environment research. *Global Environmental Change* 15(4): 299–307.

Oakeshott, Michael Joseph. (1962) *Rationalism in Politics, and Other Essays*. London: Methuen.

Odum, Eugene P. (1953) *Fundamentals of Ecology*. Philadelphia: Saunders College.

Odum, Howard T. (1971) *Environment, Power and Society*. New York: Wiley.

Oreskes, Naomi. (2010) *Merchants of Doubt: How a Handful of Scientists Obscured the Truth on Issues from Tobacco Smoke to Global Warming*. New York: Bloomsbury Press.

Orlove, Benjamin S. et al. (2002) Ethnoclimatology in the Andes. *American Scientist* 90: 428–435.

Orlove, B., E. Wiegandt, and B. H. Luckman, eds. (2008) *Darkening Peaks: Glacier Retreat, Science, and Society*. Berkeley (CA): University of California Press.

Orlove, Ben, Heather Lazrus, Grete K. Hovelsrud, and Alessandra Giannini. (2015) How longstanding debates have shaped recent climate change discourses. In: *Climate Cultures: Anthropological Perspectives on Climate Change*, Jessica Barnes and Michael R. Dove eds. Yale Agrarian Studies Series. New Haven (CT): Yale University Press.

Ortner, S. B. (1973) On key symbols. *American Anthropologist* 75(5): 1338–1346.

Ortner, Sherry. (1995) Resistance and the problem of ethnographic refusal. *Comparative Studies in Society and History* 37(1):173–193.

Ortolano, Guy. (2009) *The Two Cultures Controversy: Science, Literature, and Cultural Politics in Postwar Britain*. Cambridge: Cambridge University Press.

Otto, J. S. and N. E. Anderson. (1982) Slash-and-burn cultivation in the Highlands South: A problem in comparative agricultural history. *Comparative Study of Society and History* 24:131–147.

Oxford English Dictionary. (1999) CD-rom version. New York: Oxford University Press.

Padoch, Christine, Kevin Coffey, Ole Mertz, Stephen J. Leisz, Jefferson Fox, and Reed L. Wadley. (2010) The demise of swidden in Southeast Asia? Local realities and regional ambiguities. *Geografisk Tidsskrift, Danish Journal of Geography* 107(1): 29–41.

Parr, Catherine L. et al. (2014) Tropical grassy biomes: Misunderstood, neglected, and under threat. *Trends in Ecology and Evolution* 29(4): 13–22.

Pellow, David N. (2004) *Garbage Wars: The Struggle for Environmental Justice in Chicago*. Cambridge (MA): MIT Press.

Pelzer, K. J. (1978a) *Planter and Peasant: Colonial Policy and the Agrarian Struggle in East Sumatra, 1863–1947*. Verhandelingen 84. The Hague: Martinus Nijhoff.

Pelzer, Karl J. (1978b) Swidden cultivation in southeast Asia: Historical, ecological, and economic perspectives. In: *Farmers in the Forest: Economic Development and Marginal Agriculture in Northern Thailand*, Peter Kunstadter, E. C. Chapman, and Sanga Sabhasri eds., pp. 271–286. Honolulu (HI): East-West Center.

Peres, C. and John Terborgh. (1995) Amazonian nature reserves: An analysis of the defensible status of existing conservation units and design criteria for the future. *Conservation Biology* 9: 34–46.

Perkins, John H. (1997) *Geopolitics and the Green Revolution: Wheat, Genes, and the Cold War*. New York: Oxford University Press.

Peters, C. M., A. H. Gentry, and R. O. Mendelsohn. (1989) Valuation of an Amazonian rainforest. *Nature* 339:655–656.

Peterson, Richard B., Diane Russell, Paige West, and J. Peter Brosius. (2008) Seeing (and doing) conservation through cultural lenses. *Environmental Management* DOI 10.1007/s00267-008-9135-1.

Pettenger, M. E., ed. (2007) *The Social Construction of Climate Change: Power, Knowledge, Norms, Discourses*. London: Ashgate.

Pickering, Andrew, ed. (1992) *Science as Practice and Culture*. Chicago: University of Chicago Press.

Pickering, Andrew. (1995) *The Mangle of Practice: Time, Agency, and Science*. Chicago: University of Chicago Press

Pickett, S. T., and M. L. Cadenasso. (2002). The ecosystem as a multidimensional concept: meaning, model, and metaphor. *Ecosystems* 5(1): 1–10.

Pickett, Stuart T. A. and R. S. Ostfeld. (1995) The shifting paradigm in ecology. In: *A New Century for Natural Resource Management*, R. L. Knight and S. F. Bates eds., pp. 261–278. Washington (DC): Island Press.

Pimentel, David. (1991) Pesticides and world food supply. *Chemistry in Britain* July:646–647.

Pœrregaard, Karsten. (1989) Exchanging with nature: *T'inka* in an Andean village. *Folk* 31: 53–73.

Pollan, Michael. (2001) *The Botany of Desire: A Plant's-Eye View of the World*. New York: Random House.

Pollan, Michael. (2006) *The Omnivore's Dilemma: A Natural History of Four Meals*. London: Penguin Books.

Posey, Darell, ed. (1999) *Cultural and Spiritual Values of Biodiversity*. London: Intermediate Technology Publications, for UNEP.

Potter, L. (1997) The dynamics of *Imperata*: Historical overview and current farmer perspectives, with special reference to South Kalimantan, Indonesia. *Agroforestry Systems* 36(1–3): 31–51.

Potter, L. (1988) Indigenes and colonisers: Dutch forest policy in south and east Borneo (Kalimantan) 1900 to 1950. In: *Changing Tropical Forests: Historical Perspectives on Today's Challenges in Asia, Australaia and Oceania*, John Dargavel, Kay Dixon, and Noel Semple, eds. pp.127–149. Canberra : Centre for Resource and Environmental Studies.

Proctor, Robert N. (2008) Agnotology: A missing term to describe the cultural production of ignorance (and its study). In: *Agnotology: The Making and Unmaking of Ignorance*, Robert N. Proctor and Londa Schiebinger eds., pp. 1–33. Stanford (CA): Stanford University Press.

Prum, V. (2007) Climate change and North–South divide: Between and within. *Forum of International Development Studies* 34: 223–244.

Puri, R. (2005) Postabandonment ecology of Penan forest camps: Anthropological and ethnobiological approaches to the history of a rain forested valley in East Kalimantan In: *Conserving Nature in Culture: Case Studies from Southeast Asia*, Michael R. Dove, Percy E. Sajise, and Amity A. Doolittle eds., pp. 1–82. Southeast Asia Monograph Series, Volume 54, Yale University.

Pyne, S. J. (1982) *Fire in America: A Cultural History of Wildland And Rural Fire*. Princeton (NJ): Princeton University Press.

Pyne, S.J. (1993) Keeper of the flame: A survey of anthropogenic fire. In: *Fire in the Environment: Its Ecological, Climatic, and Atmospheric Chemical Importance*, P.J. Crutzen and J.G. Goldammer, eds. Pp. 245–255. Chichester (UK): John Wiley.

Pyne, S.J. (1994) Maintaining focus: An introduction to anthropogenic fire. *Chemosphere* 29(5): 889–991.

Radcliffe-Brown, A. R. (1952) *Structure and Function in Primitive Society: Essays and Addresses*. New York: Free Press.

Raffles, Thomas Stafford. (1978 [1817]) *The History of Java*. 2 vols, reprint. Kuala Lumpur: Oxford University Press.

Raffles, Hugh. (2002) *In Amazonia: A Natural History*. Princeton: Princeton University Press.

Rappaport, Roy A. (1979) *Ecology, Meaning, and Religion*. Richmond (CA): North Atlantic Books.

Rappaport, Roy A. (1984/1968) *Pigs for the Ancestors: Ritual in the Ecology of a New Guinea People*. 2nd edn. New Haven: Yale University Press.

Rappaport, Roy A. (1994) Humanity's evolution and anthropology's future. In: *Assessing Cultural Anthropology*, Robert Borofsky ed., pp. 153–167. New York: McGraw-Hill.

Ras, J.J. (1968) *Hikajat Bandjar: A Study in Malay Historiography*. Koninklijk Instituut voor Taal-, Land- en Volkenkunde: Bibliotheca Indonesica 1. The Hague: Martinus Nijhoff.

Ratzel, Friedrich. (1896–1898) *The History of Mankind*. Trans. A. J. Butler. London/New York: Macmillan.

Redclift, M. (1992) Throwing stones in the greenhouse. *Global Environmental Change* 2(2):90–92.

Redford, Kent H., Bert Klein, and Carolina Murcia. (1992) Incorporation of game animals into small-scale agroforestry systems in the neotropics. In: *Conservation of Neotropical Forests: Working from Traditional Resource Use*, Kent H. Redford and Christine Padoch eds., pp. 333–358. New York: Columbia University Press.

Rhee, Suk Bae. (2006) Brokering Authority: Translating Knowledge, Policy and Practice in Forestry Institutions in Indonesia. Ph.D. dissertation, Yale University School of Forestry and Environmental Studies.

Ribot, Jesse C., Antonio Rocha Magalhães, and Stahis S. Panagides, eds. (1995) *Climate Variability, Climate Change, and Social Vulnerability in the Semi-Arid Tropics*. Cambridge/New York: Cambridge University Press.

Rich, Bruce. (1994) *Mortgaging the Earth: The World Bank, Environmental Impoverishment, and the Crisis of Development*. Boston (MA): Beacon Press.

Rifkin, J. (1980) *Entropy: A New World View*. New York: Viking Press.

Rival, L., ed. (1998) *The Social Life of Trees: Anthropological Perspectives on Tree Symbolism*. Oxford: Berg.

Roberts, J. Timmons, and Bradley C. Parks, eds. (2007) *A Climate of Injustice: Global Inequality, North–South Politics, and Climate Policy*. Cambridge (MA)/London: MIT Press.

Rosaldo, Renato. (1993/1989) *Culture and Truth: The Remaking of Social Analysis*. Boston: Beacon Press.

Ross, Andrew, ed. (1996) *Science Wars*. Durham/London: Duke University Press.

Roué, Marie. (2006) Cultural Diversity and Biodiversity. Special issue of *International Social Science Journal* 187.

Runk, Julie Velásquez. (2009) Social and river networks for the trees: Wounaan's riverine rhizomic cosmos and arboreal conservation. *American Anthropologist* 111(4): 456–467.

Ruttan, V. (1996) What happened to technology adoption-diffusion research? *Sociologia Ruralis* 36(1): 51–73.

Ruyle, E. E. (1973) Slavery, surplus, and stratification on the Northwest Coast: The ethnoenergetics of an incipient stratification system. *Current Anthropology* 14(5): 603–631.

Sagar, A., and M. Kandlikar. (1997) Knowledge, rhetoric and power: International politics of climate change. *Economic and Political Weekly* 32(46): 3139–3148.

Sahlins, Marshall. (1972) *Stone Age Economics*. Chicago (IL): Aldine.

Sahlins, Marshall. (1976a) *Culture and Practical Reason*. Chicago: University of Chicago Press.

Sahlins, Marshall. (1976b) *The Use and Abuse of Biology: An Anthropological Critique of Sociobiology*. Ann Arbor: University of Michigan Press.

Sandweiss, Daniel H. and Jeffrey Quilter, eds. (2008) *El Niño, Catastrophism, and Culture Change in Ancient America*. Cambridge (MA): Harvard University Press for Dumbarton Oaks Research Library and Collection.

Schärer, H. (1963) *Ngaju Religion: The Conception of God Among a South Borneo People*, R. Needham (trans.). Koninklijk Instituut voor Taal-, Land- en Volkenkunde, Translation Series 6. The Hague: Martinus Nijhoff.

Scheper-Hughes, Nancy. (1995) The primacy of the ethical: Propositions for a militant anthropology. *Current Anthropology* 36(3):409–440.

Schnitzer, Daniel, Deepa Shinde Lounsbury, Juan Pablo Carvallo, Ranjit Deshmukh, Jay Apt, and Daniel M. Kammen. (2014) Microgrids for rural electrification: A critical review of best practices based on seven case studies (United National Foundation). http://energyaccess.org/images/content/files/MicrogridsReportFINAL_high.pdf

Schumacher, E. F. (1973) *Small is Beautiful: Economics as if People Mattered*. New York: Harper and Row.

Schwaner, C. A. L. M.(1853–1854) *Borneo, Beschrijving van het stroomgebied van den Barito en reizen langs eenige voorname rivieren van het zuid-oostelijk gedeelte van dat eiland*. 2 vols. Amsterdam: P. N. van Kampen

Scoones, I. (1999) New ecology and the social sciences: What prospects for a fruitful engagement? *Annual Review of Anthropology* 28: 479–507.

Scott, James C. (1976) *The Moral Economy of the Peasant: Rebellion and Subsistence in Southeast Asia*. New Haven: Yale University Press.

Scott, James C. (1998) *Seeing Like A State: How Certain Schemes to Improve the Human Condition Have Failed*. New Haven: Yale University Press.

Scott, James C. (2009) *The Art of Not Being Governed: An Anarchist History of Upland Southeast Asia*. New Haven (CT): Yale University Press.

Selin, Helaine, ed. (2003) *Nature Across Culture: Views of Nature and the Environment in Non-Western Cultures*. Dordrecht: Kluwer.

Sen, Amartya. (1981) *Poverty and Famines: An Essay on Entitlement and Deprivation*. Oxford: Oxford University Press.

Shea, John P. (1940) Our pappies burned the woods. *American Forests*, April:159–162, 174.

Sherman, D. G. (1980) What "green desert"? The ecology of Batak grassland farming. *Indonesia* 29: 113–148.

Shipton, Parker. (1994) Land and culture in tropical Africa: Soils, symbols, and the metaphysics of the mundane. *Annual Review of Anthropology* 23:347–377.

Shiva, Vandana (1991*)* *The Violence of the Green Revolution: Third World Agriculture, Ecology, and Politics*. London/Atlantic Highlands (NJ): Zed Books.

Sigaut, F. (1979) Swidden cultivation in Europe: A question for tropical anthropologists. *Social Science Information* 18(4/5):679–694.

Sillitoe, Paul, ed. (2007) *Local Science vs Global Science: Approaches to Indigenous Knowledge in International Development*. New York/Oxford: Berghahn Books.

Sinclair, Upton. (1935) *I, Candidate for Governor: And How I Got Licked*. New York, Farrar & Rinehart.

Slater, Candace (1994) 'All that glitters': Contemporary Amazonian miners' tales. *Comparative Studies in Society and History* 36(4): 720–742.

Smith, Kirk R. (1991a) Commentary/overview: The Greenhouse Index. *Environment* 33(2):5,42–43.

Smith, Kirk. (1991b) Allocating responsibility for global warming: The Natural Debt Index. *Ambio* 20(2):95–96.

Smith, K. R. (2014) Cookstoves clean up health on two fronts. *Nature* 511: 31.

Smith, K. R., J. M. Samet, I. Romieu, and N. Bruce. (2000) Indoor air pollution in developing countries and acute lower respiratory infections in children. *Thorax* 55: 518–532.

Snow, C. P. (1959/1998) *The Two Cultures*. Cambridge (UK): Cambridge University Press.

Soddy, Frederick. (1912) *Matter and Energy*. New York: H. Holt and Co.

Soddy, Frederick. (1926) *Wealth, Virtual Wealth and Debt. The Solution of the Economic Paradox*. New York: Dutton.

Soddy, Frederick. (1933) *Money Versus Man; A Statement of the World Problem from the Standpoint of the New Economics*. New York: E. P. Dutton.

Soddy, Frederick. (1935) *The Role of Money; What It Should Be, contrasted With What it Has Become*. New York: Harcourt, Brace and Co.

Sofoulis, Zoë. (2005) Big water, everyday water: A sociotechnical perspective. *Continuum: Journal of Media & Technical Studies* 19(4): 445–463.

Sokal, Alan. (1996) Transgressing the boundaries: Toward a transformative hermeneutics of quantum gravity. *Social Text* 14 (1/2): 217–252.

Sokal, Alan and Jean Bricmont. (1998) *Fashionable Nonsense: Postmodern Intellectuals' Abuse of Science*. New York: Picador.

Solbrig, O. T. (1993) Ecological constraints to savanna use. In: *The World's Savannas: Economic Driving Forces, Ecological Constraints and Policy Options for Sustainable Land Use*, M. D. Young and O. T. Solbrig eds., pp. 21–47. Paris, Carnforth (UK): UNESCO, Parthenon.

Songqiao, Z. (1992) Comments on global warming in an unequal world. *Global Environmental Change* 2(2): 93–96.
Soulé, Michael E. and Gary Lease, eds. (1995) *Reinventing Nature? Responses to Postmodern Deconstruction*. Washington DC: Island Press.
Spivak, Gayatri Chakravorty. (1988) Can the subaltern speak? In: *Marxism and the Interpretation of Culture*, Cary Nelson and Lawrence Grossberg eds., pp. 271–313. Urbana (IL): University of Illinois Press.
St. John, Spenser. (1974 [1862]) *Life in the Forests of the Far East*. 2 vols. Kuala Lumpur: Oxford University Press.
Star, S. L. (1999) The ethnography of infrastructure. *American Behavioral Scientist* 43(3): 377–391.
Star, Susan L. and James R. Griesemer. (1989) Institutional ecology, "translations" and boundary objects: Amateurs and professionals in Berkeley's Museum of Vertebrate Zoology, 1907–39. *Social Studies of Science* 19(3): 387–420.
Steward, Julian H. (1955) *Theory of Culture Change: The Methodology of Multilinear Evolution*. Urbana (IL): University of Illinois Press.
Stewart, Mart A. (2005) If John Muir had been an agrarian: American Environmental history west and south. *Environment and History* 11: 139–162.
Stewart, Pamela J. and Andrew Strathern, eds. (2008) *Exchange and Sacrifice*. Durham (NC): Carolina Academic Press.
Stokes, Donald E. (1997) *Pasteur's Quadrant: Basic Science and Technological Innovation*. Washington, DC: Brookings Institution Press.
Stone, Glenn D. (1994) Agricultural intensification and perimetrics: Ethnoarchaeological evidence from Niger. *Current Anthropology* 35: 317–324.
Stott, P. (1991) Recent trends in the ecology and management of the world's savanna formations. *Progress in Physical Geography* 15(1): 18–28.
Strathern, Marilyn. (2006) A community of critics? Thoughts on new knowledge. *Journal of the Royal Anthropological Institute* (N.S.) 12: 191–209.
Strauss, Sarah and Benjamin S. Orlove, eds. (2003) *Weather, Climate, Culture*. Oxford/New York: Berg.
Subak, S. (1991) Commentary/overview: The Greenhouse Index. *Environment* 33(2):2–3.
Sustainable Energy for All. (2012) *Report of Task Force Two: Energy Access*. New York: United Nations
Swyngedouw, E. (2006) Circulations and metabolisms: (hybrid) natures and (cyborg) cities. *Science as Culture* 15(2): 105–121.
Taussig, Michael T. (1980) *The Devil and Commodity Fetishism in South America*. Chapel Hill: University of North Carolina Press.
Terborgh, John. (1999) *Requiem for Nature*. Washington DC: Island Press.
Thaker, J., and A. Leiserowitz. (2014) Shifting discourses of climate change in India. *Climatic Change* 123(2): 107–119.
Theophrastus. (1926) Concerning weather signs. Trans. Sir Arthur Hort. In: *Enquiry Into Plants, and Minor Works on Odours and Weather Signs*, Volume II, pp. 390–433. Cambridge (MA): Harvard University Press.
Thery, D. (1992) Should we drop or replace the WRI Global Index? *Global Environmental Change* 2(2):88–89.
Thompson, E. P. (1963) *The Making of the English Working Class*. London (UK): V. Gollancz.
Thompson, E. P. (1971) The moral economy of the English crowd in the 18th century. *Past & Present* 50: 76–136.

Thompson, M., M. Warburton and T. Hatley. (1986) *Uncertainty on a Himalayan Scale: An Institutional Theory of Environmental Perception and a Strategic Framework for the Sustainable Development of the Himalaya*. London: Ethnographica.

Thoreau, Henry David. (1964/1854). *Walden; or, Life in the Woods. On the Duty of Civil Disobedience*. New York: Holt, Rinehart and Winston.

Thrupp, L. A., S. Hecht & J. Browder. (1997) *The Diversity and Dynamics of Shifting Cultivation: Myths, Realities, and Policy Implications*. Washington (DC): World Resources Institute.

Tomich, T. P., J. Kuusipalo, K. Menz and N. Byron. (1997) Imperata economics and policy. *Agroforestry Systems* 36(1–3): 233–261.

Traweek, Sharon. (1988) *Beamtimes and Lifetimes: The World of High Energy Physicists*. Cambridge (MA): Harvard University Press.

Truett, Joe C. (2010) *Grass: In Search of Human Habitat*. Berkeley (CA): University of California Press.

Tsing, Anna L. (1999) Becoming a tribal elder and other green development fantasies. In: *Transforming the Indonesian Uplands: Marginality, Power and Production*, Tania M. Li ed., pp. 159–202. London: Berg.

Tsing, Anna Lowenhaupt. (2005) *Friction: An Ethnography of Global Connection*. Princeton (NJ): Princeton University Press.

Tuck-Po, L. (2004) *Changing Pathways: Forest Degradation and the Batek of Pahang, Malaysia*. Lanham (MD): Lexington Books.

Vandenbeldt, R. J. (1993) Imperata grasslands in Southeast Asia: Executive summary. In: *Imperata Grasslands in Southeast Asia: Summary Reports from the Philippines, Malaysia, and Indonesia*, R. J. Vandenbeldt ed., pp. 1–5. The Forestry/Fuelwood Research and Development Project, Report #18. Washington (DC): Winrock International.

Vetter, Jeremy. (2006) Wallace's other line: Human biogeography and field practice in the eastern colonial tropics. *Journal of the History of Biology* 39:89–123.

Virgil. (2004) *Georgics*. Trans. Peter Fallon. Oxford: Oxford University Press.

Wallerstein, Immanuel. (1974) *The Modern World System. Vol. 1, Capitalist Agriculture and the Origins of the European World Economy in the Sixteenth Century*. New York: Academic Press.

Wallerstein, Immanuel. (1980) *The Modern World System. Vol. 2, Mercantilism and the Consolidation of the European World Economy, 1600–1750*. New York: Academic Press.

Watts, Michael. (1983) *Silent Violence: Food, Famine and Peasantry in Northern Nigeria*. Berkeley (CA): University of California Press.

Wessing, R. (1992) A tiger in the heart: The Javanese rampok macan. *Bijdragen tot de Taal-, Land-en Volkenkunde* 148(2): 287–308.

Weber, Max. (1946) *From Max Weber: Essays in Sociology*. H.H. Gerth and C. Wright Mills, trans. and eds. New York: Oxford University Press.

White, Gilbert. (1937/1789). *The Natural History of Selborne, in the Country of Southampton*. Oxford: Oxford University Press.

White, Leslie A. (1959) *The Evolution of Culture: The Development of Civilization to the Fall of Rome*. New York: McGraw-Hill.

White, Leslie A. (1969/1949) *The Science of Culture: A Study of Man and Civilization*. New York: Farrar, Straus and Giroux.

Whyte, R. O. (1962) The myth of tropical grasslands. *Tropical Agriculture* 39(1): 1–11.

Wilkinson, R. J. (1959) *A Malay–English Dictionary (Romanised)*. 2 vols. London (UK): Macmillan.

Williams, Raymond. (1980) *Problems in Materialism and Culture: Selected Essays*. London: NLB.

Winarto, Yunita T. (2004) *Seeds of Knowledge: The Beginning of Integrated Pest Management in Java*. Southeast Asia Monograph Series, Volume 53, Yale University.

Winarto, Yunita T. (2011) The ecological implications of central vs local governance: The contest over integrated pest management in Indonesia. In: *Beyond the Sacred Forest: Complicating Conservation in Southeast Asia*, Michael R. Dove, Percy E. Sajise, and Amity A. Doolittle eds., pp. 276–301. Durham (NC): Duke University Press.

Wissler, Clark. (1922) *The American Indian*. New York/London (UK): Oxford University Press.

Wolf, Eric R. (1982) *Europe and the People Without History*. Berkeley (CA): University of California Press.

Woodruff, Rosalie and Charles Guest. (2000) Teleconnections of the El Niño phenomenon: Public health and epidemiological prospects. In: *El Niño: History and Crisis*, Richard H. Grove and John Chappell eds., pp.,89–108. Cambridge (UK): White Horse Press.

Woodward, A., K. R. Smith, D. Campbell-Lendrum, D. D. Chadee, Y. Honda, Q. Liu, J. Olwach, B. Revich, R. Sauerborn, Z. Chafe, U. Confalonieri, and A. Haines. (2014) Climate change and health: On the latest IPCC report. *The Lancet*. Available online 2 April (2014) ISSN 0140-6736, http://dx.doi.org/10.1016/S0140-6736(14)60576-6.

World Health Organization (WHO). (2014) Seven million premature deaths annually linked to air pollution. http://www.who.int/entity/mediacentre/factsheets/fs292/en/index.html

World Resources Institute (WRI). (1990) *World Resources 1990–1991* New York: Oxford University Press.

Worster, D. (1990) The ecology of order and chaos. *Environmental History Review* 14(1/2): 1–18.

Wright, Angus. (2005) *The Death of Ramón González: The Modern Agricultural Dilemma*. Rev. edn. Austin (TX): University of Texas Press.

Wynne-Edwards, V. C. (1965) Self-regulating systems in populations of animals. *Science* 147: 1543–1547.

Yapa, Lakshman. (1993) What are improved seeds? An epistemology of the green revolution. *Economic Geography* 69(3):254–273.

Yunus, Muhammad. (1991) *Banker to the Poor: Micro-Lending and the Battle Against World Poverty*. New York: Public Affairs/Perseus Book.

Zheng, Cheng and Daniel Kammen. (2014) An innovation-focused roadmap for a sustainable global photovoltaic industry. *Energy Policy* 67: 159–169.

Zimmermann, Francis. (1987) *The Jungle and the Aroma of Meats: An Ecological Theme in Hindu Medicine*. Berkeley: University of California Press.

INDEX

Page references in *italic* indicate figures and tables

abundance and scarcity: literature on external perceptions and misperceptions of 73; and moral ecology 68–91; resource exploitation and views of abundance 76; and world hunger 91; *see also* green revolution, mast-fruiting, swidden agriculture
Adaptation Fund 109
Adas, M. 9
Adger, W. N. 9
Africa: Guinea 58–9; North, Islamic states 131; off-grid/micro-grid rural electrification 25, 30–9; *see also* Kenya, Lesotho, sub-Saharan Africa
Agarwal, A. and Narain, S. 97–8, 101
Agee, J. and Evans, W. 7
Agence France-Presse (news service) 55
agriculture: agricultural sciences/ scientists 13, 22, 126; boundaries of 88, 89–90; costs and benefits dichotomy 88, 93n26; crop hybridization 36, 38, 90; imperialist 79; industrialized 82; "miraculous" 82–3, 92n19, 124, 126; pests 84–6; production/consumption relationship and boundary 89, 91; rice farming 36, 38, 69; swidden 71–2, 74–5, 75, 76, 87, 91n7; *see also* green revolution, high-yielding variety (HYV) agriculture, "miracle" crops, moral ecology
Agroforestry Systems (journal) 45
Ahuja, D. R. 101
air pollution, indoor 13, 22, 27, 27, 30
Alabama 60–1
Anderson, E. 49
AOSIS (Association of Small Island States) 105
appropriate technology (AT) movement 35–6, 42n17
Aprovecho Research Center 21
Aristotle 23
Ashton, P. S. et al. 71
Asia *see* South Asia, Southeast Asia
Association of Small Island States (AOSIS) 105
Atsatt, P. R. and O'Dowd, D. J. 85
Australia 108

Bagnall-Oakeley, H. et al. 63
Bali Action Plan (BAP) 109–10; *see also* climate change
Bangladesh 25–6, 30
Banjarese people: gemstones 129; hunting wild cattle on grasslands 62; land use in south Kalimantan 51, 52, 53; livestock grazing on *Imperata cylindrica* 53; oxen and plough 53
Ban Ki-moon 111

banking, mundane 25–6; *see also* micro-credit
Barbour, M. G. 10–11
Barth, F. 69
Bartlett, H. H. 58
Batek people 48–9
Bateson, G. 7, 8, 114–15, 124, 130; epigraph 94
Beckmann, David 91
Beeman, R. S. and Pritchard, J. A. 79, 92n19
Beijing Declaration 105, 106; *see also* climate change
Bellow, S. 124
Benjamin, W. 130–1
Bennett, J. 9, 11
Berlin, B. et al. 8
biomass fuels 13, 22, *24*, 27, 98, *98*
Blaikie, P. 79
Borlaug, Norman 70, 91; *see also* green revolution
Borneo: gemstones 129–30; mast-fruiting 70–1, 73–4, *74*, *76*; swidden agriculture 71–2, 74–5, *75*, *76*, *87*; *see also* Banjarese people, Dayak people, Kantu' people
borrowing, interdisciplinary 8–10, 11
boundaries: of agriculture 88, 89–90; boundary definition 16; and climate change 16, 96–116; and morality 69; narrow drawing of 16; normative misstatements of system boundaries 16; permeability of 15–16; of resource management systems 15–16, 69, 86, 127 *see also* resource management, natural; as social constructs 69, 86, 89–90, 127; *see also* boundary objects
boundary objects ix, 8, 17, 118–21
Bourdieu, P. 10, 24
Braun, B. 62
Brazil *97*, 111, 112
bricolage 23; see also Lévi-Strauss, C.
Bush, V. 37, 42nn18–19
Buttel, F. H. 50
Byerlee, D. and Siddiq, A. 77
Byrd–Hagel Resolution 108; *see also* climate change

camphor (*Dryobalanops aromatica*) 47
Canada *97*, *104*, 108
Canadian Agency for International Development 59
capitalism 82, 102, 120; epigraph (Marx) 68

carbon/greenhouse gas emissions *see* climate change, greenhouse gas emissions
carbon sinks 98, *98*, 99, 108; *see also* climate change
Carnot cycle 132n5; *see also* physics
Carroll, Lewis 91–2n12; epigraph 68
Center for Science and Environment (CSE), India: report 98, 99; WRI debate x, 16, 96–100, *97*, *98*, 101, 117n6; *see also* climate change
Centro Internacional de Mejoramiento de Maiz y Trigo (CIMMYT), Mexico 77
CFCs 100; *see also* climate change
Chambers, R. 88
'Changing Atmosphere: Implications for Global Security', Toronto conference 106; *see also* climate change
China 29, *97*, 105, *105*, 106, 107, 108, 109, 110, 111
Clausius, R. 127; *see also* entropy
Clean Development Mechanism 108; *see also* climate change
Clements, F. E. 10, 52, 130
Climate Action Network (CAN) 103; *see also* climate change
climate change 94–117; Bali Action Plan 109–10; Beijing Declaration *105*, 106; and CFCs 100; complications in the North–South divide at the global level 103–12; complications within Northern nations 113–15; complications within Southern nations 112–13; CSE report 98, 99; First World Climate Conference, Geneva 103, *104*; and the folk tradition of climate knowledge 113; global warming xi, 16, 97–8, *98*, 100–1, 103–6, 114; as "the gorilla in the room" 95–6, 122; and historical synchronicity/asynchronicity 100–1; initial North–South fault line 96–102; Intergovernmental Negotiating Committee for a Framework Convention on 106; Intergovernmental Panel on Climate Change (IPCC) 103,105; Kyoto Protocol 103–5, *104–5*, 107–9, 110, 111, 112; lay critique 113–14; major events in development of international climate policy regime, 1979-2010 *104*; North–South

dimension during evolution of international climate policy regime *105*; and "one world" versus many 101–2; overview of study 16–17; Rio Summit *105*, 106, 108; scientist skeptics 113; and self-identity 115–16; and social scientists 114; Special Climate Change Fund 109; UN Framework Convention on *see* UNFCCC; universalist framing of 101–2, 116; WRI–CSE debate x, 16, 96–100, *97*, *98*, 101, 117n6; WRI report 97, 98–9, 100, 101, 117n2; *see also* greenhouse gas emissions
climate science 113
Cohen, I. B. xi-n2, 1, 8, 19n14
collaboration, interdisciplinary 3, 6–10; boundary objects ix, 8, 17, 118–21; case studies *see* climate change; grasslands; mundane science; resource management, natural; models of 7; theorization of 10–11
Conklin, H. C. 8, 20n17; *see also* swidden agriculture
conservation: and development policy failures as a prism and resource 120, 121–2; ecology 50; global conservation movement and forests 50; in human-modified landscapes 50; Integrated Conservation and Development Projects (ICDPs) 3; *see also* resource management, natural
Consultative Group on International Agricultural Research (CGIAR) 70
cooking, mundane 27–30, *27–9*
cookstoves 27–30, *28–9*; *see also* mundance science
credit *see* micro-credit
Cronon, W. 14, 45, 50
crop hybridization 36, 38, 90
crop pests 84–6
CSE *see* Center for Science and Environment (CSE), India; *see also* climate change

Daly, H. E. 128; and Umana, A. 7
D'Antonio, C. M. and Vitousek, P. M. 55
Darwin, Charles 2; and Rutherford, Ernest, 1st Baron 19n4
Davies, D. 46
Dayak people 69–70, 73–5, 77–8, 79–81, 82, 84, 86, 87–8, *87*, 93n24; *see also* Kantu' people

dearth *see* abundance and scarcity
declensionist discourses 43–66; *see also* deforestation
De Foresta, H. and Michon, G. 54
deforestation 47; Reducing Emissions from Deforestation and Degradation (REDD) 51, 109
Deleuze, G. and Guattari, F. 47; epigraph 43
Deli tobacco 58, 59; *see also* swidden agriculture
Demeritt, D. 102
Denmark 106
Derrida, J. 5–6
development logic 59–61
Diamond, J. M. 9, 115
diamonds 129–30; *see also* Banjarese people
disciplinarity 4–6, *5*; *see also* interdisciplinarity
discourse analysis 119; *see also* fire, forests, grasslands
Dove, M. R. ix–x, 4, 10, 52, 67n5, 72, 120; and Kammen, D. M. 128, 132n9
Dunham, S. A. 25
Durkheim, E. 8, 133n15

Earth Summit, Rio de Janeiro *105*, 106, 108; *see also* climate change
ecology: 1950s shift in 10; and Barbour 10–11; and the bias against the mundane 22–3; borrowing from 8, 10, 11; climate as part of 117; conservation ecology 50; division within 2; embeddedness of knowledge and ignorance in socio-ecological systems 124; and Rappaport 8, 11; *see also* climate change, grasslands, moral ecology
economic thermodynamics 127–8; *see also* entropy
electrification, off-grid/micro-grid 25, 30–9
Eliot, G. 132n2
El Niño Southern Oscillation (ENSO) 71, 77
Emissions Trading System 108; *see also* Reducing Emissions from Deforestation and Degradation (REDD)
enthalpy 18, 129, 130, 131–2; *see also* physics

entropy 18, 127, 128; and enthalpy 18, 129, 130, 131–2; *see also* Clausius, R., Georgescu-Roegen, N., physics
environment: declensionist discourses 43–66; degradation of global 3; and development logic 59–61; environmental relations 51–4, 69, 84–6, 123; equilibrium-based model 50; exchange between society and 79–86; morality of vegetative trajectories 51–4; UN Environment Program 103; *see also* climate change, ecology, forests, grasslands, moral ecology, sustainability
Environmental Integrity Group 108; *see also* climate change
equilibrium *see* Clements, F. E.
Ethnological Society of London 2
European Union (EU) 107, 108, 109, 110, 111, 112; *see also* climate change

Fairhead, J. and Leach, M. 52, 58–9, 61–2
fallow dynamics 50
FCCC *see* UNFCCC (United Nations Framework Convention on Climate Change)
Ferguson, J. 59
fire 54–6
First World Climate Conference, Geneva 103, *104*; *see also* climate change
Fish, Stanley 90
forests: belief in spirits of the forest 68–9, 79–81, 91n2; bias 46–54; and fire 54–6; as focus of Western environmentalism 49–51; fundamentalism 14, 50, 51, 118; natural afforestation 52, *81*; secondary 50; tropical forest masting 70–1, 73–4, *74*, *76*, 92nn16–17; *see also* deforestation, grasslands, rain forest
Fosberg, F. R. 55
Framework Convention on Climate Change, UN *see* UNFCCC; *see also* climate change
frankincense (*Boswellia* spp.) 47
Franklin, Benjamin 35, 40n1; epigraph 21
Frazer, J. G. 46, 47

G-77 nations 105, *105*, 107, 108, 109, 110, 111, 112; *see also* climate change

Gates Foundation 13
GCC (Global Climate Coalition) 103; *see also* climate change
Geertz, C. 56
gemstones 129–30
gender 26, 27, 30, 37, 41n11
Georgescu-Roegen, N. 128, 131, 132n4; *see also* entropy
Germany 106
Giles, E. 55
Global Alliance for Clean Cookstoves 41n11
Global Climate Coalition (GCC) 103; *see also* climate change
Global Lighting and Energy Access Partnership (Global LEAP) 42n14; *see also* mundane science
global warming xi, 16, 97–8, *98*, 100–1, 103–6, 114 *see also* climate change
Goldman, M. 126
Goldman, S. 8
Google Ngram 5, *5*, 19n8
Grameen Bank, Bangladesh 13, 25–6, 41n7; *see also* micro-credit
grasslands: anthropogenic 43–66; and cultural myth 48–9; and development logic 59–61; and fire 54–6; and the forest bias 46–54; interventions and failures 57–9; and the morality of vegetative trajectories 51–4; myths 54–6, 63; overview of study 14–15; rehabilitation efforts 56, 57–8; research studies 63–4; review implications for future studies 65; savannization 47; seen as wastelands 15, 45, 57, 64; "unmanaged" 54–6; *see also Imperata cylindrica*
greenhouse gas emissions 95, 97–100, *98*, 102, *104*–5, 105–12; Clean Development Mechanism 108; Emissions Trading System 108; Joint Implementation of emissions-reduction projects 108; Kyoto Protocol 103–5, *104*–*5*, 107–9, 110, 111, 112; Reducing Emissions from Deforestation and Degradation (REDD) 51, 109; WRI versus CES figures for countries with highest 97; *see also* climate change
green revolution 13, 15; dichotomizations of costs and benefits 88, 91, 93n26; and pests

85–6; and the Red Queen syndrome 91–2n12; resource management 69–70, 72–3, 75–7, 76, 78–9, 81–6, 82, 87–91, 87; *see also* high-yielding variety (HYV) agriculture, "miracle" crops
Guinea 58–9
gum benjamin (*Styrax* spp.) 47

habitus 24
Hadiwidjojo, G. P. H. 48
Haraway, D. 45
Hayes, P. and Smith, K. R. 101
Hecht, S. and Cockburn, A. 7, 58
Heidegger, Martin 125
Hesiod 23, 49
Hewitt, K. 23
high-yielding variety (HYV) agriculture 72–3, 75–7, 76, 81, 82, 83, 85, 87 *see also* green revolution; alternative names 84; "miracle" crops/seeds 82–3, 92n19, 124, 126; and pests 85–6
Hikayat Banjar 129
Hippocrates 23, 115
Hodgson, Peter 108
Hornborg, A. 93n25, 120, 126–7
Hulme, M. 113
hunger 13, 91, 102
hybridity *see also* interdisciplinarity; of mundane science 40
HYV agriculture *see* high-yielding variety (HYV) agriculture

Ibn Khaldûn 115, 131; epigraph 94
ICDPs (Integrated Conservation and Development Projects) 3
ignorance 123–4
illnesses, in poor communities 13, 22
Imperata cylindrica 15, 44, 48, 52, 53, 55, 59, 60–1, 64; in Alabama 60–1; and rubber 63, 65; *see also* grasslands
INC (Intergovernmental Negotiating Committee for a Framework Convention on Climate Change) 106; *see also* climate change
India 16, 30, 106, 111, 113
indigenous knowledge ix, 7, 14, 24
Indonesia: grasslands 55, 57, 59, 60–1; resource concentration 129; *see also* Banjarese people, Borneo, Dayak people, Java, Kalimantan, Kantu' people, Sumatra
Integrated Conservation and Development Projects (ICDPs) 3

Integrative Graduate Education and Research Traineeship Program (IGERT), National Science Foundation 2–3
interdisciplinarity: and borrowing 8–10, 11; case studies *see* climate change; grasslands; mundane science; resource management, natural; and Derridean logic 5–6; and directionality 9–10; and disciplinarity 4–6, 5; and Integrated Conservation and Development Projects 3; interdisciplinary institutions 2–3; *see also* boundaries, collaboration
Intergovernmental Negotiating Committee for a Framework Convention on Climate Change (INC) 106; *see also* climate change
Intergovernmental Panel on Climate Change (IPCC) 103, 105; *see also* climate change
International Rice Research Institute (IRRI) 36, 76–7
Isaiah 46–7

Jackson, J. B. 57
Janzen, D. H. 72, 92n17
Japan 106, 108–9
Jasanoff, S. 103
Java 90, 129; *Imperata cylindrica* 48, 60–1; rice farming 36, 38, 69 *see also* green revolution; wedding ritual objects 48
jiko stoves 28–9, 28–9
Joule, J. P. 125

Kahan, D. 113–14
Kalimantan: South 51, 52, 67n5; Southeast 51, 129; West 70, 130 *see also* Banjarese people, Borneo, Dayak people, Kantu' people;
Kammen, D. M. ix–x, 4
Kantu' people 66n1, 68–9, 71–2, 73–4, 74–5, 75, 77–8, 78, 79–81, 80, 84, 85, 86, 91n9
Kellert, S. R. 8
Kelvin, William Thomson, 1st Baron 125
Kenya 22, 28
knowledge: contests over 23; folk/lay 23–4, 113; and ignorance 123–4; indigenous ix, 7, 14, 24; politics of 23, 124–5; practical

23–4; production 43, 123; situated 24
Komarek, E. V. 55
Kroeber, A. L. 69
Kyoto Protocol 103–5, *104–5*, 107–9, 110, 111, 112; *see also* climate change

Lahsen, M. 101–2, 112, 113
Laris, P. 52
Latour, B. 4, 8, 51, 114; epigraph 94
Least Developed Country Fund 109; *see also* climate change
Leavis, F. R. 1
Leiserowitz, A. 114
Lenoir, T. 9–10, 20n16
Leopold, Aldo 2, 7
Le Roy Ladurie, E. 130
Lesotho 59
Lévi-Strauss, C. 5, 23; *see also* bricolage
lighting, mundane 30–2, *31, 33–5*
logic: Derridean 5–6; development logic 59–61; systemic 73–9

malaria 13, 22
Malinowski, B. 24
Marx, K. 19n11, 82, 132n3; epigraph 68
Marxist theories 82, 90, 128; neo-Marxist 69
MASIPAG (peasant science movement) 36
mast-fruiting 70–1, 73–4, *74, 76*, 92nn16–17
Mátan Diamond 129–30
Mayer, J. R. 125
McWilliams, J. E. 51
micro-credit 13, 14, 25–6; Microcredit Summit 26; *see also* Grameen Bank, Bangladesh
micro-grids 25, 30–9
"miracle" crops 82–3, 92n19, 124, 126 *see also* high-yielding variety (HYV) agriculture
Montesquieu, C. de Secondat, baron de 115
Montreal Protocol on Substances that Deplete the Ozone Layer 103
moral ecology: and climate 94, *98*, 100, 117 *see also* climate change; environmental relations 51–4, 69, 84–6, 123; and natural resource management 68–91; time, space and 69; and vegetative trajectories 51–4
morality: and boundaries 69; and climate change 94, *98*, 100, 117;
environmental relations 51–4, 69, 84–6, 123; moral economy 15, 69; of vegetative trajectories 51–4; *see also* moral ecology
Muir, John 50–1
multi-disciplinary research *see* interdisciplinarity
mundane science 21–40, 122–3; fallacy of anti-science 38; fallacy of etic versus emic driven 38; fallacy of rejection of scientific and technological progress 35–6; fallacy of competition between basic and applied research 37; fallacy of science as a zero-sum game 36; fallacy of technological determinants 37; hybridity of 40; micro-grids 25, 30–9; mundane banking case study 25–6; mundane cooking case study 27–30, *27–9*; mundane lighting case study 30–2, *31, 33–5*; overview of study 12–14; policy recommendations 39; scientific bias against studying the mundane 22–4, 40–1n5; wider theoretical implications 40; *see also* ovens, solar
myrrh (*Commiphora* spp.) 47
myth: of distinction between savage and civilized minds 5; grassland myths 54–6, 63; grasslands and cultural myth 48–9

National Adaptation Programs of Action 109; *see also* climate change
Nationally Appropriate Mitigation Actions (NAMAs) 109, 110; *see also* climate change
National Science Foundation 37
neo-Marxism 69; see also Marx, K., Marxist theories
Netherlands 13, 106
New Yorker 21
New York Times 60
New Zealand 108
NGOs (non-governmental organizations) 21, 26, 66–7n4, 103, 106

Oakeshott, M. J. 23–4
Odum, E. P. 52, 130, 132n7
Odum, H. T. 19n12, 132n7
OPEC (Organization of Petroleum Exporting Countries) 105
Ortner, S. B. 46, 70, 114

ovens, solar 32, *35*; *see also* mundane science

Pakistan *24*, 77, 83, 88–9
Parr, C. L. et al. 50, 51
peasant science movement (MASIPAG) 36
pedagogy 132
Pelzer, K. J. 58
pesticides 36, 85–6; *see also* green revolution
pests 84–6
Philippines 36
physics *see* Carnot cycle, enthalpy, entropy, thermodynamics
pine resins 47
political capital 10, 11, 12
Pollan, M. 47, 83
post-structuralism 3, 5
Potter, L. 51
Proctor, R. N. 123–4
Pulau Bangka 55; *see also* Indonesia
Pwo people 80
Pyne, S. J. 55, 117n3

Radcliffe-Brown, A. R. 8
Raffles, T. S. 129–30
rain forest 50, 68–9; *see also* mast-fruiting, swidden agriculture
Rappaport, R. A. 8, 10, 11, 69, 73
Ratzel, F. 115
Redclift, M. 98
Reducing Emissions from Deforestation and Degradation (REDD) 51, 109; *see also* climate change
reflexivity 17, 18, 120–1, 125
resource concentration 128, 129, 130–1, 132
resource dispersal 18, 128, 130–1, 132
resource management, natural 68–91, 131–2; boundaries 15–16, 69, 86, 127; character of relations with nature 79–82; and cycles of resource concentration 131, 132; Dayak model 69–70, 73–5, 77–8, 79–81, 82, 84, 86, 87–8, *87*; exchange between society and environment 79–86; green revolution 69–70, 72–3, 75–7, *76*, 78–9, 81–6, *82*, 87–91, *87*; HYV agriculture 72–3, 75–7, *76*, 81, *82*, 85, *87* see also green revolution; local versus extra-local exchange 86–7; mast-fruiting 70–1, 73–4, *74*, *76*; "miraculous" agriculture 82–3, 92n19, 126 *see also* high-yielding variety (HYV) agriculture; overview of study 15–16; pedagogy and sustainable management 132; and pest relations 84–6; and social order's dependence on concentration of resources 131–2; swidden cultivation 71–2, 74–5, *75*, *76*, *87*; and systemic logic 73–9; system scope 77–9; understanding success and failure 73–7
rhizomatic thinking 48
rice farming 36, 38, 69; *see also* green revolution, swidden agriculture
Rifkin, J. 127, 128, 132n4
Rio de Janeiro, Earth Summit *105*, 106, 108
Roberts, J. et al. 103
Roosevelt, Franklin D. 42n18
Rosaldo, R. 20n17
rubber (*Hevea brasiliensis*) 51, 71, 74, 75, 78, 84, 128; and *Imperata cylindrica* 63, 65
Russia 107–9
Rutherford, Ernest, 1st Baron 19n4

Sahlins, M. 8, 11, 73
Sambas kingdom 129
savannization 47
scarcity *see* abundance and scarcity
Schumacher, E. F. 20n19, 35
science: agricultural sciences/scientists 13, 22, 126 *see also* green revolution; bias against studying the mundane 22–4, 40–1n5; climate 113; *cordon sanitaire* 12, 22, 49; division between arts, humanities and 1–2; engaged 17, 120; and the "other" 89, 120–1, 124–5; peasant science movement (MASIPAG) 36; and reflexivity 17, 18, 120–1, 125; Science and Technology Studies 3; "science of suffering" 13; scientific belief/disbelief and group identity 114; "two cultures" of natural and social science 1–4; "wars" 3–4, 114; *see* also mundane science;
Scott, J. C. 15, 24, 56, 69
self-identity, and climate change 115–16
Sen, A. 89, 91
Shea, J. P. 56

162 Index

Shiva, V. 82, 83
Sinclair, U. 132n1
Snow, C. P. 1–2, 6–7, 12, 18–19n1
social science: and interdisciplinarity 7, 9 *see also* interdisciplinarity; post-modern critique 89; "science of suffering" 13; "two cultures" of natural and social science 1–4; see also climate change
Social Text 3
society: and enthalpy 18, 129, 130, 131–2; exchange between environment and 79–86; social order's dependence on concentration of resources 131–2; and thermodynamics 18, 125–32; *see also* entropy
Socolow, Robert H. 40–1n5
Soddy, F. 128
Sokal, A. 3, 11
solar cells 30
solar lights *31*, *35*, 42nn15–16
solar ovens 32, *35*
solar power *34*, 41n7, 100
Songqiao, Z. 101
South Asia: micro-credit 13, 14, 25–6; *see also* Bangladesh, India, Pakistan, Sri Lanka
Southeast Asia 6, 85; grasslands 51–65; *see also* Indonesia, Philippines, Thailand
South, global *see* Brazil, Center for Science and Environment (CSE), India, China, India, South Asia, Southeast Asia
Soviet Union 106
Special Climate Change Fund 109; *see also* climate change
Sri Lanka 30
Star, S. L. and Griesemer, J. R. ix, 119
Steward, J. H. 69
Stewart, M. A. 50–1
St. John, S. 129
Stott, P. 50
stoves 27–30, 28–9; *see also* mundane science
Strathern, M. 7, 11
sub-Saharan Africa 27
Sumatra *60*
sustainability: anthropology and physics of sustainable environmental systems 1–18; and conservation and development policy failures as a prism 120, 121–2; pedagogy and sustainable management

132; perspectives 121–32; and resource management *see* resource management, natural
swidden agriculture 71–2, 74–5, *75*, *76*, *87*, 91n7; *see also* Conklin, H. C.
symbolic capital 10
systemic logic 73–9

Thailand 80
Theophrastus 23
thermodynamics: Carnot cycle 132n5; economic 127–8; first law of 18, 126–7; second law of 18, 127–32; and society 18, 125–32
Thompson, E. P. 15, 69
Thompson, M. M. et al. 64, 126
Thoreau, H. D. 49
tobacco, Deli 58, 59
Tomich, T. P. et al. 63, 64
torches, solar *31*, *35*, 42n16; *see also* mundane science
Toronto conference, "Changing Atmosphere: Implications for Global Security" 106; *see also* climate change
trans-disciplinary research *see* interdisciplinarity
trees: versus grasses in Western and non-Western thought 46–9; longevity of 66n1; naturalization of tree symbols 46–7; *see also* forests, rain forest
Truett, J. C. 51

Ukraine 108
UNFCCC (United Nations Framework Convention on Climate Change) 106–7; COP-6 Bonn *105*, 108; COP-7 Marrakesh *105*, 109; COP-15 Copenhagen *105*, 111; COP/MOP-3 Bali *105*, 107, 109; COP/MOP-4 Poznan *105*, 110; *see also* climate change
United Nations: Environment Program (UNEP) 103, 110; Framework Convention on Climate Change *see* UNFCCC; General Assembly 103
United States of America: agriculture 82; and the Bali Conference 110; Byrd–Hagel Resolution 108; and COP/MOP-4 Poznan 110; federal research budget 37; fire use debate in grassland and forest management 56; greenhouse gas emission figures, WRI and CES *97*; and the

Kyoto Protocol *104*, 106, 108, 111; lay critique of climate change 113–14

Vandenbeldt, R. J. 52, 64
vegetative trajectories, morality 51–4
vicious and virtuous cycle theory 32, *33*
Virgil 23, 49

Wallace, Alfred Russel 2
Weber, M. 64
White, G. 49
White, L. A. 8, 125, 128, 132n8
Williams, R. 14, 56
Wissler, C. 69
WMO (World Meteorological Organization) 103; *see also* climate change
World Bank 20n20, 26, 30, 59
World Climate Conference, Geneva 103, *104*; *see also* climate change
World Meteorological Organization (WMO) 103; *see also* climate change
World Resource Institute (WRI): CSE debate x, 16, 96–100, *97*, *98*, 101, 117n6; report 97, 98–9, 100, 101, 117n2; *see also* climate change
World Resources 97
world systems perspectives 69
Worster, D. 50, 52
WRI *see* World Resource Institute

Yapa, L. 79, 88

Yunus, Muhammad 25, 26; *see also* Grameen Bank, Bangladesh, microcredit

eBooks
from Taylor & Francis
Helping you to choose the right eBooks for your Library

Add to your library's digital collection today with Taylor & Francis eBooks. We have over 50,000 eBooks in the Humanities, Social Sciences, Behavioural Sciences, Built Environment and Law, from leading imprints, including Routledge, Focal Press and Psychology Press.

Choose from a range of subject packages or create your own!

Benefits for you
- Free MARC records
- COUNTER-compliant usage statistics
- Flexible purchase and pricing options
- 70% approx of our eBooks are now DRM-free.

Benefits for your user
- Off-site, anytime access via Athens or referring URL
- Print or copy pages or chapters
- Full content search
- Bookmark, highlight and annotate text
- Access to thousands of pages of quality research at the click of a button.

ORDER YOUR FREE INSTITUTIONAL TRIAL TODAY

Free Trials Available

We offer free trials to qualifying academic, corporate and government customers.

eCollections
Choose from 20 different subject eCollections, including:

- Asian Studies
- Economics
- Health Studies
- Law
- Middle East Studies

eFocus
We have 16 cutting-edge interdisciplinary collections, including:

- Development Studies
- The Environment
- Islam
- Korea
- Urban Studies

For more information, pricing enquiries or to order a free trial, please contact your local sales team:
UK/Rest of World: **online.sales@tandf.co.uk**
USA/Canada/Latin America: **e-reference@taylorandfrancis.com**
East/Southeast Asia: **martin.jack@tandf.com.sg**
India: **journalsales@tandfindia.com**

www.tandfebooks.com